James Hamlyn Hill

A Dissertation on the Gospel Commentary of S. Ephraem the Syrian

with a scriptural index to his works

James Hamlyn Hill

A Dissertation on the Gospel Commentary of S. Ephraem the Syrian
with a scriptural index to his works

ISBN/EAN: 9783337238643

Printed in Europe, USA, Canada, Australia, Japan

Cover: Foto ©Lupo / pixelio.de

More available books at **www.hansebooks.com**

A DISSERTATION

ON THE

GOSPEL COMMENTARY

OF

S. EPHRAEM THE SYRIAN

WITH A

Scriptural Index to his Works

BY

The Rev. J. HAMLYN HILL, D.D.

FORMERLY SENIOR SCHOLAR OF S. CATHARINE'S COLLEGE, CAMBRIDGE
AUTHOR OF AN ENGLISH VERSION OF "MARCION'S GOSPEL"
AND OF "TATIAN'S DIATESSARON"

EDINBURGH
T. & T. CLARK, 38 GEORGE STREET
1896

[All rights reserved]

REVERENDISSIMO IN DEO PATRI

WILLELMO DALRYMPLE MACLAGAN, S.T.P.

ARCHIEPISCOPO EBORACENSI

VITÆ SPIRITUALIS CULTORI, SACRORUM STUDIORUM FAUTORI

EVANGELISTÆ STRENUO, FIDEI DEFENSORI

ARGUMENTUM HOC, QUALECUMQUE SIT

DE SACROSANCTORUM EVANGELIORUM ANTIQUITATE

ET VERITATE

GRATI ET MIRANTIS ANIMI

INDICIUM

EO QUO DECET OBSEQUIO

D. D. D.

JACOBUS HAMLYN HILL

CONTENTS

	PAGE
INTRODUCTION,	1
PARALLELISMS,	39
THE EPHRAEM FRAGMENTS,	75
SCRIPTURAL INDEX,	121
APPENDIX,	171

DISSERTATION ON S. EPHRAEM SYRUS.

INTRODUCTION.

Of the life of S. Ephraem the Syrian little is known with certainty; and this is not because there is any lack of details regarding it, but because the various accounts that have come down to us differ materially from each other and from statements contained in his works; and because these accounts partake of a legendary character, and relate not only wonderful visions, but also many miracles alleged either to have been wrought by him or to have happened to him or those connected with him. These supernatural incidents are not unfrequently connected with statements of fact which it is impossible to reconcile with the chronology of known events in his life. It will be sufficient to mention here such particulars as seem to be trustworthy. The chief sources of information, besides occasional statements in the Fathers, are —(1) the history of his life given in the *Acta S. Ephraemi*, contained in the third Syriac-Latin volume of the Roman edition of his works; (2) another version of the same, contained in a codex at Paris, and lately published by Dr. Lamy in his second volume of supplementary works; and (3) his own statements, particularly in his Testament contained in the second Greek-Latin volume, pp. 230–247 and 395–410.

He was born in Mesopotamia, probably at Nisibis on the Masius, a tributary of the Euphrates, where his father is said to have been a heathen priest, early in the reign of Constantine, most likely in A.D. 306, as Dr. Lamy contends (vol. B, 4, 16, 91). Being expelled from home because he was friendly with Christians, he placed himself under the care of S. James, Bishop of Nisibis, by whom he was trained in the faith, and whom he accompanied to Nicaea on the occasion of the Council. He is said to have been baptized during this journey, at the age of eighteen. Shortly after the death of Constantine, Nisibis was besieged by the Persian king Sapor (A.D. 337–338); and Ephraem is said to have rendered valuable help to its bishop in the defence of the town. When the Emperor Jovian ceded Nisibis to the Persians (A.D. 363), Ephraem left the place, and resided for about a year at Amida, after which he went on to Edessa on the river Daisan, which at that time and for some centuries was the chief seat of learning and of Christianity in Mesopotamia. Here the most active and important part of his life was spent. As he had not been brought up to any trade, he supported himself by acting as assistant to a keeper of baths, until the preaching of a monk from the neighbouring mountains convinced him that it was his duty to give up all worldly employments, and lead a life of retirement and self-mortification. He thereupon became a kind of hermit-monk, and lived in a cavern of the mountains close to Edessa. In this seclusion he gave himself up to study, and soon began to write his Commentaries on the books of the Old Testament.

There seems no doubt that he visited Caesarea in Cappadocia, where S. Basil was the bishop. Setting aside what is fabulous in the accounts of this visit, we may conclude that S. Ephraem acquired great influence over this bishop, and that a strong friendship continued between them afterwards. Basil is said to have ordained him a deacon; but at that time Ephraem would not accept the priesthood. Whether he ever accepted it afterwards is doubtful; certainly not for a long time, for he came to be generally known as the Deacon of Edessa. He is said to have spent eight years in Egypt, visiting Alexandria and the monastic institutions in the desert, and opposing Arianism; but it is difficult to find room for so long a visit in the events of his life, and much doubt exists whether he really went there.

Whilst staying at Caesarea, he was suddenly recalled to Edessa by the news that the heretical doctrines of Bardesanes, a Gnostic, were becoming popular there, and leading many astray. Bardesanes, in the second century, had embodied the doctrine of aeons, in its various forms, in 150 psalms compiled in imitation of the Psalms of David; and these psalms had been set to music by his son Harmonius. In Ephraem's absence, these had been introduced into Edessa, and were being sung even by boys and girls, who learnt the words by heart, and then sang them to the accompaniment of a guitar. The heresies of Arius, Manes, and Marcion were also spreading there. To counteract these, Ephraem himself composed a large number of hymns on a variety of subjects, but chiefly in connection with the life of Jesus—His nativity, His baptism, His fasting, many incidents of His ministry, His passion, resurrection, and ascension. These were all in verse, the lines in many cases being uniformly of five or seven syllables; but in others the metre was more varied, and often complicated; the number of lines in a verse also varied considerably. Sozomen asserted that Ephraem copied the metres and tunes of Harmonius; and at III. 128 A, we find: "The end of seventeen discourses to the measures of Bardesanes' odes." It seems probable, however, that S. Ephraem, after beginning with existing metres and tunes, proceeded to compose others of his own. This is a natural inference from the variety and complexity of his metres, as shown by Dr. Lamy, and his frequent reference to another of his own hymns for the tune to be employed. Although there was little rhythm and no rhyme in these compositions, the tunes and the regular lengths of the lines assisted the memory, and gave interest to the words. But the chief charms of these sacred songs consisted in the noble sentiments and lofty aspirations which they embodied, and the beautiful words and metaphors in which these were clothed by this eloquent and imaginative writer. Their author took upon himself the office of musical director; and, in order that they might be worthily rendered in the public services of the Church, he organised a choir of young women to sing them, selecting them from those whom he was training to become nuns, and who had already taken the vow of virginity. This action of S. Ephraem is represented as having succeeded. His compositions became more popular than those of Bardesanes, and the number of heretics in Edessa decreased.

Near the close of his life he is said to have saved the city of Edessa from famine. The crops had failed through drought; but some of the wealthier inhabitants had secret stores of grain, which they were afraid to produce, lest they should be robbed of the whole by the starving people. But, when S. Ephraem was called in from his cave, such was their confidence in him that they entrusted him with the whole; and his influence over the people was so great, that they were content to accept such rations as he doled out to them; and thus the supplies were made to last until the more fruitful season that followed put an end to the distress.

S. Ephraem died A.D. 373. By his own desire, he was buried in a plain garment in the burial-ground for strangers; but shortly after his body was exhumed and buried in the tomb of the bishops of Edessa.

Of the writings of S. Ephraem, Sozomen asserted that they contained more than three million lines. Their general character is fairly described by Cardinal Bellarmine as "pious rather than learned." In interpreting Scripture, he takes a position between the allegorical school of Alexandria and the literal school of Antioch. Unfortunately, many copies of works of his were lost or rendered illegible through the foundering in the Nile of a ship that was bringing them to Rome for Pope Clement XI. early in the eighteenth century.

The principal printed edition of his writings is that made by the Maronite, Peter Mobarek, and completed after his death by J. S. E. Assemani. It was published in six folio volumes at Rome, A.D. 1732-1743. Previous to this, there existed an edition in Greek, with a Latin translation, in three folio volumes, published by Voss at Rome, A.D. 1589; and a later edition in Greek, containing the text of 156 discourses obtained from eighteen MSS. in the Bodleian Library, and published in folio by Thwaites at Oxford, A.D. 1709.

As Edessa was near Armenia, many of his works were translated into Armenian at an early date, probably in the fifth century; and in 1836 the Mechitarist Fathers at the Armenian monastery of S. Lazzaro, near Venice, published an

Armenian edition in four octavo volumes, compiled by Father J. B. Aucher from the MSS. in their possession. This edition contained a Commentary on the Gospel narrative, which was translated into Latin by Dr. Moesinger of Salzburg, A.D. 1876, and of which more will be said hereafter; a Commentary on S. Paul's Epistles, of which a Latin translation was published by the Mechitarist Fathers in 1893; and a variety of other compositions, metrical, didactic, and controversial.

Portions of his works have also been published by Overbeck at Oxford in 1865, by Bickell at Leipsic in 1866, and others; and by Morris and Burgess in English translations. In addition to these, a very valuable collection of Syriac works, *not included in the Roman edition*, has been published at Mechlin by Dr. Lamy in three quarto volumes, with a Latin rendering, A.D. 1882–1889.

In the present essay, for convenience of reference the principal volumes will be designated as follows:—The three Syriac-Latin volumes of the Roman edition will be called I., II., III.; the three Greek-Latin volumes of the same will be called a, β, γ; the three volumes of Dr. Lamy, A, B, C; the Commentary on S. Paul's Epistles, P; and Dr. Moesinger's translation of the Gospel Commentary, M. Thus β, p. 17, or more fully, Eph. β, p. 17, will denote the seventeenth page of the second Greek-Latin volume of the Roman edition of S. Ephraem's works.

Volumes I., II., and III. contain—(1) Syriac Commentaries on the majority of the canonical books of the Old Testament; so that, with those added in B, the only missing ones are Ruth, the Books of the Chronicles, the historical parts of which are treated of with the Books of Kings, and all from Ezra to the Song of Solomon in the order of our Authorised Version; (2) Discourses, often metrical, on special texts, on the Nativity, against heresies, against disputers, for funerals, for exhortation, on Paradise, and on various topics.

Volumes a, β, γ contain sermons and hortatory and other discourses in Greek, with a Latin translation, a small portion at the end of γ being in Latin only. Most of these are genuine; but the authorship of some is doubtful. It may be taken as certain that Ephraem did not write them in Greek;

but there are evidences that some at least of his works were translated into Greek almost immediately after they were written. It is not, therefore, surprising to find them appearing in that language. Unfortunately, the quotations from the Old Testament in these three volumes have not been literally translated from the Syriac, but the corresponding passages have been inserted in the words of the Septuagint.

We now come to the main question which we propose to consider in this volume, namely, whether the Gospel Commentary published in the Armenian edition of S. Ephraem's works, and more recently in a Latin version by Dr. Moesinger, is really the work of this Father, and based upon the *Diatessaron* of Tatian.

From the testimony of early writers, it may be taken as certain that Ephraem did write a Commentary on the Gospel narrative, and that he used the order of Tatian as the basis of his remarks. His contemporary, Gregory of Nyssa, says[1] that Ephraem interpreted accurately and verbally all the Old and New Testament. Dionysius Bar-Salibi, Bishop of Amida in Mesopotamia, who died A.D. 1207, in his preface to the Gospel of S. Mark, wrote: "Tatian, a disciple of Justin the philosopher and martyr, selected from the four Gospels and wove together and compiled a Gospel, which he called *Diatessaron*, *i.e.* miscellany. This writing Mar Ephraem interpreted: its commencement was, 'In the beginning was the Word.'" The value of this testimony is greatly increased by the discovery of Dr. Rendel Harris (published in the *Contemporary Review* for August 1895, pp. 273–277), that Bar-Salibi was quoting from a Commentary of Isho'dad made about A.D. 850; and that Bar-Hebraeus, who seemed to differ from Bar-Salibi, was in fact quoting him with the addition of words from Eusebius. This statement of Isho'dad bears within it an inherent probability, from what we know concerning the large circulation and general use of the *Diatessaron* in Syria about this time. The *Doctrine of Addai*, speaking of Edessa, where Ephraem afterwards lived, says: "Moreover, much people day by day assembled, and came together for prayer, and for the reading of the Old Testament and the New, the

[1] Assemani, *Bibl. Or.* i. 56.

Diatessaron." Nearer to his own date, Aphraates, the Persian sage, and his own bishop, James of Nisibis, made free use of the *Diatessaron* in their writings. And in the following century, Theodoret, Bishop of Cyrrhus, near the Euphrates, about A.D. 420, in his book on Heresies, says of the *Diatessaron*: " I myself found more than two hundred such books held in respect in the Churches of our parts." Thus, whilst it is extremely unlikely that S. Ephraem would write Commentaries on so many parts of Holy Scripture and yet leave out the Gospels, it seems natural that he should write one upon the " combined Gospel," which he found in common use in Edessa, rather than write four separate Commentaries on the " distinct Gospels."

When, therefore, we find in the Armenian version of Ephraem's works (vol. II. pp. 5–260) a work bearing the title, " Exposition of the Concordant Gospel, made by S. Ephraem, a Syrian Teacher," we see no *à priori* reason for supposing that it is not what it professes to be; and we are free to consider, without any antecedent objection, whether its contents are such as to agree with its title.

After publishing it in Armenian, Father Aucher proceeded to make a Latin version of this Commentary, and this version he seems to have completed in A.D. 1841; but though he lived thirteen years longer, his translation was not published. Whilst his Armenian edition was in the press, the Mechitarist Fathers had another Armenian MS. of the Commentary presented to them. This is in the handwriting of the great scholar Nerses Lamprouensis himself, and written, strange to say, in the very same year as that in which their other MS. of the Commentary was written. This is shown by a note which Nerses added at the end: " Glory and giving of thanks be unto Him who is the beginning and the end, from the humble Nerses, who wrought out this work in the year 644." This date, according to the Armenian reckoning, corresponds to A.D. 1195, and agrees with the date given in the MS. previously possessed by these Fathers. The MS. of Nerses is now known as Codex B, the other being called Codex A.

The Mechitarist Fathers subsequently decided to publish a Latin version of the Commentary; and for this purpose they placed in the hands of Dr. Moesinger, Professor of Theology at Salzburg, the MS. translation already made by Father Aucher, the Codex of Nerses, and the printed text of Codex A. With these he was enabled to publish at Venice, in 1876, the Latin version, which forms the subject of the present work, and from which the accompanying collection of the Fragments of the *Diatessaron* contained in the Commentary was in the first instance obtained. It is the publication of Moesinger's version which has drawn so much attention to this Commentary as a means of ascertaining the nature of the *Diatessaron*, and has enabled persons unacquainted with the Armenian language to examine its contents for themselves.

An examination of the work thus placed within our reach results in evidence favourable to both views—(1) that it was written by Ephraem, and (2) that it is based upon the *Diatessaron*. In the first place, it resembles in its style the Commentaries of Ephraem on the Old Testament. There is the same method of taking a few words and remarking upon them, sometimes briefly and sometimes at great length on particular points. Then there is the absence of Greek scholarship, and the presence of remarks, often mistaken, or assuming what is fabulous, but showing great ingenuity and much piety. The description [1] which the writer gives of the state of the Church where he lived, applies very well to the Church of Edessa after the banishment of its bishop, Barses, by the Emperor Valens. The attacks which the writer makes against the Marcionites in several passages, point also to Ephraem, who was in the habit of putting into his works controversial and other remarks against heretics, and especially against these. The frequent warnings to monks, and praises of an ascetic life, point to the same author.

For the purpose of the present work, a careful comparison has been made between the contents of this Commentary and the acknowledged works of S. Ephraem, resulting in the discovery of a large number of resemblances and parallelisms of opinion, metaphor, etc., which tend to show a common authorship. Some of these are of a very striking character, whilst others are less conclusive. As similarities of thought and argument generally occur at the repetitions of some text with which they are connected, it was found advisable to

[1] Cf. Moes. p. 281.

tabulate the whole of the texts quoted *or alluded to* by S. Ephraem in any of his works, including this Commentary, and to seek for parallelisms wherever a text was noticed in the Commentary and also in any of the other works. After this Table of References had been arranged, it was compared with the MS. references to the New Testament, which the late Dean Burgon compiled from a portion of S. Ephraem's works. The references given by Mr. Morris in his translation of the Homilies of S. Ephraem have also been included. The parallelisms are given at the close of this Introduction, and the Table of References at a later part of the work.

These indications of authorship receive confirmation from the fact that Syriac forms of expression abound in the Armenian version, showing that it is really a translation from that language, and that the translator, in his anxiety to preserve the meaning of his author, has been too literal in his rendering. There is evidence also that some of the passages cited from the Old Testament have been taken according to the peculiar readings of the Syriac version. Dr. Rendel Harris has called attention[1] to some of these, and has also shown that some Syriac writers of an early date quoted as the words of S. Ephraem passages that are found identically, or nearly so, in this Commentary alone of all his works.

And further, the internal evidence also points to the *Diatessaron* as being the work upon which Ephraem's remarks in this Commentary are based. This Armenian document is a Commentary on a Gospel narrative which commenced with the words, "In the beginning was the Word," as the *Diatessaron* is said by Bar-Salibi to have begun. There is no allusion to the genealogies; and this agrees with the statement of Theodoret, that they were absent from Tatian's Harmony. Its various readings follow the Curetonian Syriac rather than the Peschito, suggesting that it deals with a work of earlier date than the latter; and, above all, its contents pass from one Gospel to another in some such way as those of the *Diatessaron* must have done. The writer takes a few words of the Gospel narrative sometimes from one of our Gospels and sometimes from another, whilst not unfrequently the passage he selects for his remarks is of a composite nature, evidently

[1] Cf. *The Contemporary*, August 1895, pp. 271-287.

derived from the blending together of parallel passages from
different Gospels. No other work of such a character and of
so early a date is known, except Tatian's, on which such a
Commentary could have been based; for the Harmony of
Ammonius consisted of the Gospel of S. Matthew in its entirety,
with parallel passages from the other Gospels placed at the
side of it, but not interwoven with it. In a word, the evidence
is overwhelming and conclusive that in Dr. Moesinger's work
we have a translation of the actual Commentary which
Ephraem the Syrian wrote, and which he based upon the
Diatessaron of Tatian in the form which that work had
assumed in his day.

Having thus decided that the *Diatessaron* is the ground-
work of the Commentary, we have next to consider how far
it is possible to reconstruct that Harmony by selecting from
the Commentary the quotations contained in it, and placing
these, whenever possible, in their original order. Now, it
would be a simple matter to pick out all the quotations made
from the Gospel narrative, and place them exactly in the
order in which we find them in the Commentary. But this
would not give us a true picture, *pro tanto*, of the *Diatessaron*,
because Ephraem often quoted texts from distant parts of
the Harmony by way of argument or of passing illustrations;
and to place these in the order of the Commentary would not
be to place them in the order of the *Diatessaron*. If, then, we
begin by taking out *all* the Gospel quotations in order, we
must next proceed to remove from them all texts which
appear to have been cited out of their true order for any
object discoverable in the settings in which they appear, and
then we may conclude that the remainder are in the same
relative order as they occupied in Ephraem's copy of the
Diatessaron. For there is no reason to doubt that Ephraem
went gradually and consecutively through the Harmony in
order in choosing the subjects for his remarks.

In doing this, the reader will find himself assisted by the
fact that certain passages are printed in spaced type in Dr.
Moesinger's work, and some also within inverted commas, corresponding generally, but not always, to the two classes of texts
above mentioned, namely, those given by Ephraem *in* and *out
of* their true order respectively. Something of the same kind

had been attempted in both the Armenian MSS., the plan adopted by the scribes being to write certain passages in red ink. This, however, was not done thoroughly, the red ink passages being very irregular in both cases, often skipping several pages, especially in Codex A; and the red ink passages of Codex A are not always identical with those of Codex B. The red ink is also used sometimes to give prominence to certain words, which indicate in most instances that a new subject of comment has begun, though the words thus marked are words of Ephraem and not of the Gospel. One red ink passage is worthy of special notice from its peculiarity. It is as follows: "The Order and Solemnity of the Apostles of the Lord" (Moes. p. 51). This is placed immediately after Ephraem's remarks upon the calling of S. Nathanael, and is followed by remarks upon the apostolic office, and the class of men selected for it by our Lord. This and other shorter remarks of the kind suggest that Ephraem's copy of the *Diatessaron* was divided into sections with suitable headings, or more probably that he himself had drawn up a course of lectures with such headings for the use of his disciples, and subsequently incorporated these lectures into his Gospel Commentary.

Passing from the MSS., we find in the printed Armenian text of Codex A a more complete set of texts marked out from the rest by inverted commas. These may be taken as embodying the views of Father Aucher, after considering the passages marked in one of the codices. Finally, the spaced type and inverted commas of Dr. Moesinger's work may be regarded as giving the result of his examination of these earlier documents; and any passages marked by him and not by any of them, or *vice versâ*, may be taken as receiving such variation on account of the personal opinion of Dr. Moesinger himself. There is nothing authoritative in the red ink or inverted commas or spaced type. From the fact that these two latter represent the ideas of competent men, well versed in the Armenian dialect, who have devoted much time and study to this Commentary, they are entitled to great weight, and should not be disregarded except upon very clear evidence. In general, there is no cause to set aside their judgment; but in a few instances it seems advisable to do so, as may be seen from the consideration of the following lists:—

Passages that are spaced, but should be either (A) *plain, or* (B) *in inverted commas.*

Moesinger.
Page   Line

6 18 Lucem ... tenebrae ... non vicerunt (A).
50 35 Hic est Christus (A).
52 2 Et cum Dominus eo veniret (A).
74 4 Ut non dedignaretur venire et salvare servum suum. Et quum annuisset, ut iret (A).
95 1 Si me persequuti sunt, persequentur et vos (B).
122 10 Occidit sol (B), cf. Jer. xv. 9, Syriac version; A.V. "her sun is gone down."
125 28 Si vis perfectus esse, vade, vende omnia quae habes (B).
129 9 In Bethsaida (A).
130 12 Susceperunt eum Galilaei (B).
„   32 In domo Israel (A).
163 5 Gaudere, ait, oportebat, quia frater tuus mortuus erat, et vivit, et ad vitam revocatus est (B).
211 3 Si dixerint vobis: Ecce hic est, nolite credere. Sicut fulgur quod resplendet (B).
223 20 Viri justi . judicabunt eos (B).

Spaced passages which are not quotations.

51 5 Ordo et solemnitas Apostolorum Domini.
162 33 Decem drachmae et centum oves.
163 20 De villico.
174 32 Divitis et Lazari.
181 30 Pharisaei qui orabat.
190 7 In judice hoc peccatore.
205 9 Simon leprosus.
218 27 Talenta sua.
226 1–7 Dominum and Domine, twice each.
232–3 Aut (several times).
256–7   „   „
267   „   „
268   Primo; secundo.
269   Porro (twice); rursus.

Passages in plain type, which should be either (A) *spaced,
or* (B) *in inverted commas.*

Moesinger.
Page Line

8 26 Quomodo fiet istud (A).
15 17 Dixit Maria (A).
22 31 Cogitavit ut tacite eam dimitteret (A).
27 8 Qui Christus Domini . est (A).
„ 31 Spes bonis filiis hominum (A).
37 23 Virtute et spiritu Eliae (B).
40 18 Patrem multarum gentium feci te (B).
42 4 Lex et prophetae usque ad Ioannem (B).
53 6 Dixit ea servis (A).
„ 13 Dicit ad eum : Fili, vinum non habent hic. Et dicit
       ei Jesus : Quid est mihi et tibi, mulier ? (B).
57 31 Regnum coelorum evangelizabitur (B).
58 4 Qui baptizati sunt, non deest eis quidquam (B).
„ 17 Ad Duodecim dixit (B).
74 15 Ibunt in tenebras exteriores (A).
80 8 Cum vidisset . . . hoc quoque ei absconditum non
       esse (A).
87 9 Infirma Dei . fortiora sunt hominibus (B).
91 24 Non (B).
94 15 Qui veniunt ad vos in vestibus ovinis, intus autem
       sunt lupi rapaces (A).
95 23 Ad urbes quo ipse erat venturus (A).
100 31 Postquam discipuli Ioannis abierant (A).
105 17 Melius fuisset, si natus non esset (B).
111 25 Autem (A).
112 28 Melius erat, si natus non fuisset (B).
116 9 Supra stellas coelorum ponam thronum meum (B).
117 29 Et qui habetis . afflictiones (A). There is no
       Armenian for " graves."
119 7 In ruinam et in resurrectionem (B).
121 26 Ille . immundus . . . transivit per loca arida . . .
       ut inveniret requiem, sed non invenit (A).
            Note that " Ille " is a mistake for " Spiritus,"
         as in many other passages of this work,
         these words being expressed by the same
         Armenian word.

Moesinger.
Page Line

122 8   Inflatus est venter ejus (B)—a continuation of the quotation according to the Syriac version.
123 17   Cur me bonum vocas ? (B).
124 13   After "seminaret" insert in spaced type, "aliud cecidit prope viam et." This is implied by the context.
126 2   Relictis omnibus sequuti sunt cum (B).
127 1   Et respondit eis, hoc opus esse inimici (A).
128 8   Iterum comparavit regnum coelorum . quod immiscetur farinae (A).
129 11   Et assumpserunt eum et foras duxerunt ad praecipitium montis (A).
130 3   Ira impleti sunt (A).
134 9   Ne quid ex eis pereat (A).
137 30   Et qui blasphemat Deum, crucifigatur (A as part of the *Diatessaron*).
138 10   Postea non studet honorare patrem et matrem (A).
141 10   Dicit ei: Mea aqua e coelo descendit (A).
 „ 32   Dicit mulier (A).
142 25   Mulieri dixerunt (A).
144 13   Sicut Moyses te edocuit (A).
145 13   Sicut praecepit vobis Moyses (A).
146 10   Ei dixit (A).
147 18   Dixit eis (A).
 „ 19   Judaei itaque propterea persequebantur . quia non solum die sabbati sanabat (A).
148 2   Ideo (B)—include with the rest.
154 29   Quum descenderent de monte, eis mandavit (B).
156 1   Species faciei ejus immutata est (A).
159 2   Post sex dies eos assumpsit et in montem duxit (A).
160 23   Dixit illi viro (A).
161 6   Praeveniens Simoni dixit (A).
 „ 14   Dominus haereditas eorum erat (B).
 „ 30   Vade ergo, et tu quoque da quasi unus ex alienis (A).
162 18   Respondit eis et dixit: . . . Dicunt ei (A).
165 18   Et factum est, ut venientes ei narrarent de Galilaeis, quorum sanguinem Pilatus miscuit cum sacrificiis eorum (A).

Moesinger.
Page Line

171 29 Amans cum intuitus est (A).
172 15 Amans . cum intuitus est (A).
173   4 In amore cum intuitus est (A).
  „   6 Induebatur purpura (B).
175 19 Abrahamum . . . vidit, et Lazarum in sinu ejus (A).
  „ 36 Primi existimarunt, quod plus essent accepturi (A).
180   9 Festina . et descende . . . quia ad te diversurus sum (A).
  „ 36 Coepit clamare et dicere (A).
181 13 Quis est hic? . Jesus Nazarenus (A).
182   3 Hic descendit justior (A).
183   4 Maledixit ficulneae et arefacta est (A).
  „ 14 Esurivit et festinanter venit ad ficum (A).
184 14 Vidit Dominus eam, et flevit super eam, et dixit ei: Utinam cognosceres tu hanc diem tuam (B).
186   7 Omnia bene fecit (B).
191   5 Donec populum doceret eique praedicaret (A).
192   4 Se non dignum esse ut portet corrigias calceamentorum ejus (B).
  „ 10 Et sepe munivit eam . . . et torcular praeparavit in ea . et aedificavit in ea turrim (A).
  „ 14 Post haec misit filium suum (A).
  „ 23 Sed cum vidissent, filium venisse, dixerunt (A).
193 12 Lapis . qui percussit simulacrum, factus est mons magnus, et impleta est ex eo universa terra (B).
194 15 Respondit ei (A).
195   4 Dixit ad eum (A).
196 25 Qui ab initio homicida erat (A).
197   3 Nos sumus filii Abrahae (A).
198   1 Veniet nox (A).
  „ 28 Luto . oblinivit oculos ejus (A).
200 22 Dixitque ad discipulos (A).
  „ 23 Respondent ei (A).
203 26 Caeco ab utero matris se ipse obvium fecit (B).
206 18 Fur erat (B).
207   8 Videns eam coepit flere super eam (A).

Moesinger.
Page Line
207 13 Abraham pater tuus . diem meum vidit et gavisus est (B).
„   19 Vidit Abraham diem meum et gavisus est (B).
„   26 Clamabant pueri et dicebant (A).
210 10 Ecce, intus in corde vestro est (A).
„   26 Forsitan seniores nostri cognoverunt, quod hic verus sit Christus (B).
211   7 Nolite ergo exire (B).
215 18 Propter electos (A).
218 33 Qui quinque talenta acceperat (A).
219   2 Qui unum talentum acceperat (A).
223   4 Et majora faciet (A). Accidentally omitted by Moesinger after "faciet."
224   8 Quum dies . . . consummati essent, vertit faciem suam, ut irent Ierosolymam, et . . . a se rejecit (B).
235 18 Deinceps (A).
239 11 Purpura eum induerunt (A).
242 18 Quis . ex vobis arguet me de peccato (B)?
„   27 Quum cum in crucem egerunt, crucifixerunt cum eo et duos malefactores (A).
245 33 Sol (A).
„   34 Obtenebratus est (A).
246 11 Venerunt . judicia dirutionis Ierosolymorum (A).
257   5 Obscuratus est sol (B).
266   2 Petiit corpus Jesu (A).
„   5 Justus erat . . . in consilio et operibus[1] eorum non consenserat (A).
269 28 Tuam ipsius animam pertransibit gladius (B).
286 19 A principio erat verbum (B).

Passages in inverted commas, that should be spaced.

69 14 Qui percutit maxillam tuam, porrige ei et alteram partem.
122   2 Revertar . in domum meam priorem cum septem sociis meis.

[1] Arm. "opere."

Moesinger.
Page   Line

162   19   Non licet ... Moyses permisit nobis, cur ergo non licet?
191   32   Ego vado.
  „   33   Quis fecit voluntatem patris sui?

When Moesinger's Latin edition came into the hands of Dr. Zahn, Professor of Theology at Erlangen, he saw in it the means of reproducing (with the occasional assistance of the Homilies of Aphraates and other Syriac works) a fragmentary outline of the original work of Tatian, from which a valuable idea of its arrangement could be formed. Accordingly, he submitted to a careful examination all the citations from the Gospels that he found in it, and removed from them all that seemed to be quoted out of their true order for some special purpose of argument or illustration. On the hypothesis that S. Ephraem quoted the remainder in the order which they occupied in his copy of the *Diatessaron*, there would thus remain a series of fragments, very broken and disconnected and with serious breaches of continuity, but yet in their original order. Some of these gaps he filled up by inference, and some more conjecturally; and in this way he was enabled to publish an approximate Table of Contents of the Harmony, which underlay the Commentary, and which he saw no reason to doubt was some form of Tatian's work.

Zahn's valuable and scholarly work appeared in 1881; and the interest it aroused on the subject of the *Diatessaron* caused attention to be drawn to an Arabic manuscript, No. XIV. in the Vatican Library, which purported to be a copy of the *Diatessaron* itself; and this again led, by an interesting chain of circumstances, to the discovery of a similar Arabic manuscript in Egypt. For the history of these MSS., and the evidence by which it has been established that they really are copies of Tatian's Harmony in two of the forms which it assumed after centuries of use, the reader is referred to the Introduction to my English version of the Arabic *Diatessaron*, published by Messrs. T. & T. Clark of Edinburgh, under the title, *The Earliest Life of Christ*, etc., where he will also find particulars relating to another version, a Latin one considerably modified from the original order, which is now known as the *Codex Fuldensis*.

An Arabic version of the *Diatessaron*, based upon a comparison of the two Arabic MSS. above mentioned, and accompanied by a Latin translation, was published by Father Agostino Ciasca at Rome in 1888, seven years after the appearance of Zahn's book. A comparison shows that the Table of Contents implied in the Armenian Commentary, as approximately reconstructed by Zahn, agrees[1] almost entirely with the order of Ciasca's Arabic Harmony. Now this order is in many cases very different from what we should have expected, and contains several very singular arrangements and displacements, such as no two independent harmonisers could possibly have concurred in making, so that no one could personally make a detailed comparison between them without arriving at the conclusion that the Armenian Commentary was based upon a Harmony which originally came from the same author as these Arabic Harmonies were primarily derived from. And as we have seen that S. Ephraem made use of a form of Tatian's *Diatessaron* for compiling the former, we may safely conclude that these Arabic MSS. are translations of copies of that work also, as in fact they are represented as being by their respective scribes. By comparing the text of the Arabic with the fragments of texts preserved in the Commentary, we find that the wording is in many places altered, so that the *text* of the Arabic cannot be taken as the text which S. Ephraem had in his copy of the *Diatessaron*; but it is the text only that has been materially altered between the times of Ephraem and the translation into Arabic; the *order* has not been materially changed in that period, though, of course, it may have been changed between Tatian and Ephraem. It is important, however, to bear in mind that the text of Ephraem's copy is not always to be ascertained with precision, on account of the freedom with which he uses it. His quotations are so interwoven with his own remarks, that they are often partially paraphrased, and it is impossible to decide how much is exact quotation, and how much not. We can see how real this difficulty is, by considering those cases in which he quotes the same passage

[1] Cf. Appendix.

more than once, with different readings in it, all of which cannot have been in his copy. Whilst some of these inconsistencies arise from intentional modifications to suit his own remarks, others, no doubt, are due to his quoting from memory, and being in some cases led astray by the resemblance of two similar texts. To the same causes we may attribute the fact that he sometimes omits a few words in making a quotation. We must not too hastily conclude that the words were not in his *Diatessaron*; for in several instances where such omissions occur, the passage is found to be quoted in full in another part of the Commentary, showing that S. Ephraem only quoted so much, whether continuous or not, as suited his present purpose, as the following table shows:—

Instances of variation in the quotation of the same passage in the Armenian Commentary.

Moesinger.
Page

28 Nunc dimittis servum tuum in pace.
226 Nunc dimittis, Domine, servum tuum secundum verbum in pacem.

28–9 Pertransibit gladius. Cf. Moes. p. 28, note 7, "Pertransibis gladium."
269 Tuam ipsius animam pertransibit gladius.

7 Gratia et veritas per Jesum facta est.
36 Per Moysen est lex; veritas ejus per Jesum Dominum nostrum.
55 Lex per Moysen data est, gratia et veritas per Jesum facta est.

41 Ecce, hic est agnus Dei, hic est, qui venit tollere peccata mundi.
43 Ecce, venit agnus Dei, et is est, qui tollit peccata mundi.
99 Ecce, agnus Dei [et] hic est, qui tollit peccata mundi.
101, 103 Ecce, agnus Dei.
208 Ecce [ait] agnus Dei, qui tollit peccata mundi.
238 Hic est agnus Dei, hic est, qui sua inmolatione tollit peccata mundi.

Moesinger.
Page

6 Populus, qui sedebat in tenebris. . . .
51 Populus, qui ambulabat in tenebris. . . .
66 Qui dicit fratri suo, fatue.
68 Qui dicit fratri suo, vilis aut stulte. *N.B.*—" Fatue" and "stulte" are for the same Armenian word.
65, 69, 70 Qui percutit maxillam tuam, porrige ei et alteram partem.
133 Si quis te percusserit in maxillam, praebe ei et alteram [maxillam].
223 Qui percutit maxillam tuam.
72 Ubi thesauri vestri sunt, ibi erunt et corda vestra.
170 Ubi thesaurus tuus est, ibi est et cor tuum.
72 Qui habet, dabitur ei, et qui non habet, etiam quod putat se habere, auferent ab eo.
73 Qui habet, dabitur ei, et qui non habet, etiam hoc auferent ab eo.
192 Qui habet, dabitur ei, et abundabit, et qui non habet, et id quod rapuit, auferent ab eo. Cf. note to Fragments, xliii. 37.
235 Id quod habebat, ablatum est ab eo.
81 Quis me tetigit? virtus magna exiit a me.
83 Quis tetigit me? Ego scio, virtutem magnam a me exiisse.
„ Quis me tetigit? quia virtus magna exiit a me.
88 Virtus exivit a me.
63 In quamcunque domum intraveritis, primum dicite: Pax huic domui.
92 In quamcunque domum intraveritis, primum salutate domum.
94 Si ab hac persequentur vos, fugite denuo in aliam civitatem.
„ Si ex ista regione vos ejicient, fugite in aliam.
95 Si ejicerint vos ex illa civitate, fugite in aliam.
„ Si vos ejicerint ex una civitate, fugite in aliam.
N.B.—" Persequi" and "ejicere" are used for the same Armenian verb.

Moesinger.
Page

111 Neque hic, neque illic dimittetur illi.
112 Non remittetur ei, neque hic, neque illic.
  „ Non ei remittetur neque in hoc mundo, neque in illo.

117 Venite ad me, qui laboratis et onerati estis, [et qui habetis graves afflictiones] et ego reficiam vos.
127 Venite ad me, omnes defatigati. *N.B.*—" Defatigati " = " onerati " in the Armenian.

118 Sicut Jonas fuit in ventre piscis tres dies et tres noctes, ita oportet Filium hominis intrare in cor terrae tres dies et tres noctes.
119 Ita erit Filius hominis in corde terrae.
230 Sicut Jonas erat in ventre piscis, ita erit Filius hominis in corde terrae.

58 Nisi manducaveritis carnem ejus, et biberitis sanguinem, non est vobis vita.
245 Si quis carnem meam non sumpserit, vitam non habet.

59 Et canes satiantur.
138 Et canes de micis mensae domini sui edunt.

141 Sed veri adoratores in spiritu et veritate adorabunt.
143 Sed veri adoratores adorabunt Patrem per Spiritum Sanctum in veritate.

143 Si vis, Domine, potes me sanare.
144 Si vis, potes me mundare. [Several times, once with " Domine " prefixed.]
145 Si vis, potes me mundare. [At p. 145 it should be " sanare," as on 143, but not on 144.]

143 Vade, ostende te ipsum.
144 Vade ad eos . . . et offer munus.
  „ Vade ostende te ipsum sacerdotibus.
145 Vade ad sacerdotes propter testimonium eorum.

146 Surge, tolle grabbatum tuum, et vade.
  „ Sta in pedibus, sume grabbatum tuum, et vade in domum tuam.
148 Surge, tolle lectum tuum.

146 Quis dixit tibi: Tolle lectum tuum.
 „ Quis praecepit tibi tollere lectum tuum super te die sabbati?
147 Quis praecepit tibi tollere lectum tuum super te?
199 Quis jussit te portare lectum. [Armenian, " to take up thy bed."]

151 Pater neminem judicat, sed omne judicium in manus Filii sui dedit.
213 Pater neminem judicat, sed omne judicium Filio tradidit.

153 Quid de me dicunt homines, quod sit Filius hominis? Respondent ei: Nonnulli dicunt, quod sit Elias, alii quod sit Jeremias.
156 Quid dicunt de me homines, quod sim? ei dixerunt: Alii dicunt, quod Elias sis,[1] alii Jeremias, alii unus ex prophetis.

65 Ecce ascendimus Hierosolymam, et implebuntur, quaecunque scripta sunt de me.
154 Ecce ascendimus Hierosolymam et implentur omnia, quae scripta sunt de me, quia oportet Filium hominis in crucem agi et mori.
178 Ecce, imus nos Hierosolymam et tenebunt et in crucem agent eum.

154 Absit, Domine.
155 Absit a te, Domine, ut hoc facias.
156 Absit hoc a te.
229 Absit hoc a te, Domine.

154 Vade retro, Satana, quia scandalum es mihi.
155 Vade retro, Satana . . . quia non cogitas, quae Dei sunt, sed quae hominis.
229 Vade retro a me, Satana, quia non cogitas, quae Dei, sed quae hominum sunt.

166 Homo quidam plantaverat in vinea sua ficum.
184 Viro cuidam erat ficulnea in vinea sua.

[1] Armenian, "sit."

Page	
169–173	Several variations and partial quotations of *Diat.* xxviii. 43: Nemo bonus nisi tantum unus, etc.
176	Nemo venit et nos conduxit.
177	Nemo [ajunt] nos conduxit mercede. [*N.B.*—" Mercede" is not in the Armenian.]
174	Oculus tuus malus est, sed ego liberalis sum.
176	Si ego liberalis sum, oculus vester[1] cur malus est.
177	[Si] oculus tuus malus est. [The Armenian omits "si."]
177	Da nobis potestatem ut sedeat unus a dextris tuis et alter a sinistris.
178	Da nobis ut sedeamus ad dextram tuam et ad sinistram tuam.
187	Itaque si terrena dixi vobis et non credidistis, quomodo, si coelestia dixero vobis, credetis?
188	Si terrena dixi vobis et non creditis, si de coelo dicam vobis, quomodo credetis?
168	Nemo est [ait] qui ascendit in coelum, nisi qui et descendit de coelo, Filius hominis.
187	Et nemo ascendit in coelum . . . nisi qui descendit de coelo.
188	Qui descendit de coelo.
189	Et nemo est qui ascendit in coelum, nisi qui descendit de eo, Filius hominis.
189	Et sicut Moyses exaltavit serpentem in deserto, ita exaltari oportet Filium hominis.
230	Sicut Moyses exaltavit serpentem in deserto, ita exaltabitur[2] Filius hominis.
184	Et vos, si habueritis fidem et non dubitaveritis in corde vestro, dicetis huic monti, et transferetur.
185	Si dixeritis huic monti, fiet. . . . Mittere in mare.
„	Si dixeritis huic monti, vade, mittere in mare.
„	Si credideritis nec dubitaveritis.
189	Si habueritis fidem [ait] ut granum sinapis, dixeritis huic monti: Transfertor, et transferetur.

[1] Armenian, "tuus." [2] Armenian, "exaltatur."

Moesinger.
Page

204 Si habetis fidem, ut granum sinapis, dicetis monti huic: Transferre, et transferetur a facie vestra.

110 Diliges Dominum Deum tuum, hoc est magnum mandatum.

194 Ut diligas Dominum Deum tuum et proximum tuum sicut te ipsum.

„ Diliges proximum tuum sicut te ipsum.

121 Si mihi non creditis, operibus meis credatis.
191 Si mihi non creditis, saltem operibus credatis.

202 Nonne hic aperuit oculos caeci?
203 Nonne poterat iste ita facere, ut hic non moreretur?
249 Is [ajunt] qui oculos caeci aperuit, nonne potuit[1] facere, ut iste non moreretur?[1]

„ Hic qui aperuit oculos caeci.

99 Propter populum dico hoc, ut credant.
234 Propter turbas istas[2] facio, ut credant.

204 Et venient postmodum Romani et tollent gentem nostram, legem et locum istum.

205 Cavete,[3] ne Romani veniant et destruant urbem nostram et populum nostrum.

184 Utinam cognosceres tu hanc diem tuam!
207 Si cognovisses tu saltem hunc diem pacis tuae. . . .

109 Hanc horam nemo scit.
179 Illam horam nemo scit. [" Illam " = the same Armenian as hanc above.]
215 Illud momentum nemo scit. [" Illud momentum " should be " hanc horam."]
216 Diem illum nemo scit.

75 Discedite in ignem aeternum, quod paratum est Satanae et angelis ejus.
216 Discedite a me maledicti Patris mei in ignem aeternum, quia non novi vos.

---

[1] Armenian, "poterat . . . moriatur."
[2] Armenian, "turbam istam," cf. note to Fragments, xxxviii. 26.
[3] A mistake! The Armenian means " kill him."

Moesinger.
Page

159 Unus ex vobis me traditurus est.
219 Unus ex vobis, qui panem mecum edit, iste est, qui me tradet.

233 Non mea, Pater, sed voluntas tua fiat.
234 Non sicut mea voluntas, sed sicut tua.
 „ Non mea voluntas fiat, sed tua.
 „ Non mea voluntas fiat, sed tua voluntas.

158 Manete, donec accipietis virtutem.
274 Sed vos permanebitis in Ierusalem donec accipietis promissionem Patris mei.

In the present work we give a translation of all the quotations from the Gospel narrative that are to be found in Ephraem's Commentary, including some that Dr. Moesinger has overlooked. This is the only complete English version of these Fragments. It was made at the suggestion of the Rev. J. Armitage Robinson, Norrisian Professor of Divinity in the University of Cambridge, who himself thoroughly revised it by means of the Armenian printed text and MSS., thereby eliminating many inaccuracies that he found in Moesinger's Latin version. The majority of the notes which accompany this translation are also due to Professor Robinson's investigations. In this translation we possess a much closer approximation to the text of the *Diatessaron* as it existed in S. Ephraem's day than is given in the Latin version; so that it represents a distinct advance upon anything we before possessed, for wherever its readings differ from those of Dr. Moesinger, they may be taken to be nearer to the actual words of Ephraem. There are two circumstances which greatly add to its trustworthiness: first, that Professor Robinson visited the monastery of S. Lazzaro for the purpose of examining Codex A and Codex B, and comparing them with one another and with the printed Armenian text; and secondly, that the Armenian words of these citations have for the most part been compared with the corresponding passages of the Armenian Vulgate, to see whether the various readings could be due to the translator of the Commentary from Syriac to Armenian, who might have inserted the readings of his own Armenian Gospels. Professor Robinson's researches throw light upon many passages which presented difficulties to the student of Moesinger's work, and his frequent references to the readings of the two codices, as given in the notes, will be found very helpful and interesting to scholars.

Now a difficulty occurred as to the form in which these Fragments should be arranged for publication. To have separated them into four parts according to our four Gospels would have been to destroy the harmony, besides presenting difficulties where the same words occur in more than one Gospel, and where the words are of a composite nature. To have published them in the order in which they came, regardless of the fact that very many of them are manifestly introduced out of their true place for special reasons, would have been to convey a false impression of the order of the *Diatessaron*. To have left out these illustrative texts and only published in their existing order those texts which could be relied upon as having the order of the Harmony, would have been to waste a large part of the material at our disposal. The plan actually adopted has been to put them all in the order of the Arabic *Diatessaron*; for, as we have already shown, this cannot differ to any considerable extent from the *order* of Ephraem's *Diatessaron*. In this way a place is found for every citation, including the many to whose position in the *Diatessaron* the Commentary affords no clue; and, as a rule, the rest fall into their true places naturally by this process. In the very rare exceptions the marginal references or footnotes call attention to the fact. In the left margin are shown the chapters and verse divisions of the Arabic *Diatessaron* as given in our English version[1] thereof, so that it is easy to compare the reading of the Arabic at any point with that of Ephraem. In the right margin is shown the page or pages of Moesinger's work at which each extract occurs, so that a similar comparison with that work can easily be made.

In his Commentaries on the books of the Old Testament, S. Ephraem occasionally calls attention to various readings in the passages under discussion, comparing his own Syriac reading with that of the Hebrew or the Septuagint. It is therefore not surprising to find him doing the same in our

[1] *The Earliest Life of Christ*, etc., T. & T. Clark, Edinburgh.

Commentary, and is rather an additional proof that he is the author of it. Sometimes he applies to his citation the word "Scripture" and sometimes "Gospel." Zahn examined these passages, and came to the conclusion that in all cases they were quoted directly from the *Diatessaron*, and that his readings agreed closely with the Curetonian Syriac. A still closer agreement has since been found between them and the old Syriac version discovered on Mt. Sinai.[1] But to other passages S. Ephraem applies the term "Reading," or says that he obtains them from "the Greek." In these cases the extracts are found to bear a close resemblance to the Peschito. This would agree very well with the idea commonly entertained about the Peschito, that it was a translation made from the Greek not long before this time, and was beginning to meet with pretty general acceptance in Syria in the later years of Ephraem's life. Very likely it may have been known there as the Greek version or "reading," by way of distinction from the older Syriac previously in use. From the way in which he speaks of it, it seems that he thought it more accurate than the older text. And this feeling on the part of others was probably the cause of changes being subsequently made in the text of the *Diatessaron* to bring it more into accord with the Peschito, and through it with the original four Greek Gospels, from which this part of it was derived. As the Peschito came more and more into general use, attention would be more and more drawn to the differences of wording between it and the *Diatessaron*; and it would be seen that the former was the more accurate. Thereupon some, like Theodoret, would wish to banish the *Diatessaron* from public use in the churches because of its omissions, its harmonistic comments, and its inaccuracies of translation; whilst others would seek to modify its text here and there without changing the order of events, and so bring its language into agreement with the more accurate text of the Peschito. After this process was completed, copies were translated into Arabic; and two derivatives of these have come down to us, as we have seen; and they contain a text such as we might have expected—a text which agrees chiefly with the Peschito, but yet retains some readings peculiar to

[1] Cf. Mr. F. C. Burkitt's Article in the *Guardian*, October 31, 1894.

the Curetonian Syriac, and some traces of harmonistic remarks, but without some of these which we know were once in the *Diatessaron*. It is on this account that the accompanying translation of the Ephraem Fragments is of special value; because we cannot be certain to what extent the text of the Arabic MSS. represents a departure from the very words of Tatian; and we have in these Fragments, so far as they go, a much earlier and more reliable text. There is little doubt, however, that even Ephraem's *Diatessaron* differed considerably from the form in which Tatian issued it, and that before his day the process of comparison with the distinct Gospels and the resulting assimilation had begun.

There are occasional indications that the text of the Commentary has been disturbed either by the displacement of a part from its true position, or by interpolations of marginal notes or other remarks. The following instances have been observed:—

1. At p. 29, ll. 4–6, we find a passage which occurs in both MSS., but which Dr. Moesinger has placed in brackets, because it interrupts the order of the comments. It is as follows:—"And that which it saith, A sword shall pass through, that is, Thou too shalt doubt, because forsooth she [Mary] believed that he was the gardener." This was probably a remark inserted in the margin of his copy a line or two earlier by some student of the Commentary, who may have borrowed the idea from a later part of the Commentary; for at p. 269, where the words "Touch me not" are under discussion, the author, like some other early writers, supposes that it was the Virgin Mary, and not Mary Magdalene, to whom they were addressed, and explains that Mary doubted concerning His resurrection, and quotes the words, "A sword shall pass through thine own soul," as having reference to her doubt.

2. At p. 40, ll. 6–12, the singular position occupied by the allusion to the visit of the child Jesus to the temple seems to suggest a displacement, of which there is no sign in the MSS. As it is historically impossible that this visit could have taken place after S. John the Baptist had begun to

preach, and equally incredible that it could have been represented as happening so in Ephraem's copy of the *Diatessaron*, so, on the other hand, there seems no reason why, if he had dropped the subject of the Baptist's preaching in order to comment upon that visit, he should immediately go back (ll. 12–14) to describe S. John's dress. As the passage is too short to fill a leaf, the displacement of a leaf will not account for the position.

3. An examination of pp. 58, 59 suggests that there may be a displacement there, since Christ's disciples are represented as baptizing before the final calling of some of the principal disciples. The paragraph, p. 59, ll. 18–24, certainly seems out of its true place.

4. At p. 124, l. 13, after "*seminaret*," the words "*aliud cecidit prope viam et*" seem to have been accidentally omitted by the copyist; for the citation is introduced by the statement (ll. 10, 11): "Three sowings fell into three hearings, and brought forth no fruit"; but the quotation contains only two without fruit. Again, at l. 16 "four parts" are mentioned; and the words above suggested are partly quoted at ll. 22, 32.

5. At p. 129, l. 9, Bethsaida is put for Nazareth. This is an error, and not an intentional reading, as Nazareth is put on the following page, ll. 16, 32, where the same occurrence is still under discussion. Moesinger, in his note on this passage, points out that the words "in Bethsaida" occur in the course of an argument of the Marcionites which Ephraem is quoting. He therefore concludes that the mistake was made by the Marcionites, especially as Ephraem has "Nazareth" in his own remarks. But, on the other hand, in all that we know from other sources respecting *Marcion's Gospel*, there is no reason to believe that it contained this singular reading, nor is it conceivable that it could have done so without attracting the attention of Tertullian and others who wrote against it. See the present author's translation of *Marcion's Gospel*.[1]

[1] *Marcion's Gospel*; Parker, Oxford and London.

6. In a note at p. 140, Moesinger expresses the opinion that the first paragraph of that page, owing to its allusion to the unclean spirit and his seven companions, must have been thrust in here by displacement from pp. 120–122, where that parable is under discussion. This, however, does not necessarily follow; and we are inclined to think that there is no displacement here. The line of thought, beginning on p. 139, starts with the casting out of an unclean spirit from the daughter of the woman of Canaan. Then it proceeds to another Jesus (Joshua) who cast out the unclean spirit from the Canaanites, when he conquered Canaan; and the two cases are compared to the end of the page. It is in this connection that mention is made on p. 140 of the parable of the unclean spirit and his seven companions, and this is proved by the allusion (l. 9) to the Canaanites, and to " his name," the name Jesus with its double reference.

There is also a remarkable case of repetition. A passage, beginning on p. 108 with the commencement of Chapter X. and extending to p. 109 as far as the word "Deum" in l. 16, is repeated with only slight variations at p. 179, l. 10 to end.

The comments of Ephraem contain some allusions to stories of an apocryphal nature, of which the following seem worthy of notice:—

1. At p. 23, l. 14, he refers to the death of Zacharias, the father of S. John the Baptist, as follows:—"And therefore, as some say, they killed Zacharias because he was preserving Mary at the side of the temple [or, 'among the virgins'], for those virgins congregated at one part of the temple. Others say that Zacharias, when his son was demanded of him during the slaughter of the infants, because he had preserved him by flight into the desert, *was slain before the altar, as the Lord said.*" The latter of these two accounts of the death of Zacharias agrees with the statement given in greater detail in a well-known apocryphal work of very early date, called *The Protevangelium of James*;[1] and, as references in the works of the Fathers show that the fabulous narratives of

[1] S. Ephraem's reference to the early life of the Virgin at B, 590, sec. 7, also points to an acquaintance with this work.

this book found ready acceptance among the early Christians, it is not surprising to find Ephraem acquainted with them. He seems to have had no doubt that this Zacharias was put to death in the temple, but doubted whether it was his action towards the Virgin or towards his son that provoked his murderers to the act. It would be too much to ascribe positively to S. Ephraem the opinion that Jesus was referring to this Zacharias in the expression, "Zacharias, son of Barachias, whom ye slew between the temple and the altar" (Matt. xxiii. 35; cf. Luke xi. 51); for the sentence referring to it is introduced by the words, "Others say." If we refer to pp. 211, 212, where that verse is noticed, we find nothing definite; and the same is the case at I. 546, 547, where S. Ephraem mentions the death of Zacharias, the son of Jehoiada. But at I. 344 he says: "From the blood of righteous Abel to the blood of Zacharias, whom they knew, being the last of the prophets, to have been slain by their ancestors. The Jews killed the Lord of the prophets, and killed the prophets themselves, who lived and spoke in him." It is of course possible that he counted the father of the Baptist as the last of the prophets; but it is not probable. If we reject the words "son of Barachias," which occur only in Matthew, as an interpolation, which in almost any interpretation we must do, it may be well to consider whether this Zacharias might not have been intended; for there is no foundation for the suggestion that our Lord used the future tense; and the usual explanation that the son of Jehoiada is meant is open to two objections: (*a*) that the name Jehoiada was too well known for anyone to have put Barachias in its place, even if, as is suggested, Jehoiada had borne that name as well, which there is no reason to believe that he did; and (*b*) it seems more in accordance with the *meaning* of Christ, that, if he mentioned any person at all as completing the series of martyrs, it should be a man of his own day. This objection applies also to Zechariah the prophet, whose father had the name Berechiah, but who does not appear to have met a violent death. It seems very possible that even the name Zacharias was not given by the Saviour, but was interpolated after the story of the death of Zacharias, the father of John, had become current.

2. At p. 43, l. 10, Ephraem has an allusion to the supernatural light said to have sprung up from the waters of Jordan immediately after the baptism of Jesus. This is referred to by Justin Martyr (*Dial.* c. 88), and therefore was probably known to and believed by Tatian. It does not follow, however, that he inserted it in the *Diatessaron*, as it was not in the Gospels which he was harmonising. The language of Ephraem does not imply that it was in his copy, and therefore we think it better to regard it as something which he accepted on the strength of tradition. We shall hereafter show, when treating of it as a parallelism, what allusions he has made to it in his other works. The story is said to have been in the Ebionite Gospel as well as in the *Preaching of Paul* [or *Peter*] and in Pseudo-Cyprian. It is in two Old Latin MSS.

3. At p. 132, ll. 4–6, Ephraem mentions a story, introducing it by "And they say," to the effect that, whilst the daughter of Herodias was dancing before Herod, Herodias and Herod planned out the scheme that Herod should swear to give the dancer whatever she asked, and that her mother should cause her to ask for the head of S. John.

4. At p. 240, ll. 28–31, he gives a peculiar explanation, introduced by the words "Others say," reconciling the divergent accounts (Matt. xxvii. 5 and Acts i. 18) of the death of Judas. It is to the effect that Judas hanged himself in a house, having previously shut the door and fastened it on the inside, the result being that no one opened the door or knew of his death, until decay had set in and his body had burst asunder through decomposition. Ephraem does not seem to have been acquainted with the other account of the death of Judas, which Oecumenius asserted was given by Papias, but which Theophylact quoted in a shorter form. (Routh, *Reliquiae Sacrae*, i. 9.)

Among shorter remarks of this class we may notice the statement, p. 42, l. 1, that, owing to the humility of S. John at Christ's baptism, "Our Lord took his right hand[1] and

[1] Cf. A, 122, sec. 29; 126, sec. 37.

placed it upon his own head." At p. 47, l. 7, it is further stated that Jesus was dipped three times on that occasion.

Some remarkable interpretations, explanations, and arguments may be noticed here.

1. At p. 50, l. 29, he quotes a peculiar reading of John i. 47: "Behold, indeed a scribe, an Israelite, in whom is no guile." Understanding that Nathanael was a scribe, he compares him with the rest of the scribes, and finds in his question, "Can it be that any good thing should come out of Nazareth?" the honest doubt of a careful scribe who knew that Bethlehem was foretold as the birthplace of the Messiah; for he was not one that interpreted Scripture to suit his own ends, as other scribes. And as soon as he saw Him, he did not reject Him as the other scribes, nor question Him on other points, "but confessed, 'This is the Christ,' and recognised that in Him was fulfilled what was written of Bethlehem and what was written of Nazareth, namely, 'Out of Bethlehem went forth a Governor,' and, "Upon the Galilaeans hath the light sprung up.'"

2. At p. 88, l. 27, he says: "When the woman with the issue of blood had heard Christ say to the ruler of the synagogue, 'Believe, and thy daughter shall live,' she thought within herself that He, who has the power to bring back into the body the soul of a girl of twelve years, can also remove from the body and drive out a plague of twelve years. And when she heard Him saying, 'By faith believe, and thy daughter shall live,' she understood from that, that she could give faith to the physician for payment." This interesting explanation is not supported by S. Mark or S. Luke, who alone give Christ's words of encouragement to the ruler; for they both place the saying immediately after He had completed the cure of the woman. This is the case also in the Arabic *Diatessaron*.

3. At p. 145, l. 6, in the course of a lengthy exposition of the healing of the leper, we are startled by this statement: "Indeed the Lord by no means touched the leper, but He

stretched out His health-bearing right hand towards him." But when we come to look over the rest of his remarks, we find him distinctly saying (p. 143, ll. 15, 22) that Jesus did touch him. Further examination makes it clear that Ephraem had a theory, by which he accounted for our Lord's apparent breach of the Mosaic law in touching a leper. According to him, as the hand of Jesus was on its way towards the sufferer, the work of cleansing was completely effected, so that by the time the hand reached him he was no longer a leper; and thus the Saviour committed no offence against the law; for He touched indeed the *man*, but not the *leper*.

Yet inasmuch as seven days of cleansing in a prescribed manner were appointed in the law (Lev. xiv. 8) to one who recovered from leprosy before he might re-enter the camp and mix with his fellow-men without conveying defilement, it may be doubted whether the ingenious explanation of our author would have been held to be an answer to the charge of breaking the law.

4. At p. 180, l. 1, he suggests an ingenious explanation of the workings of the mind of Zacchaeus after he had climbed into the tree: "Zacchaeus was praying in his heart, and said, 'Blessed is he, whosoever shall be found worthy, that this just *man* may enter into his house.' And the Lord said unto him, 'Make haste, *and* come down from thence, Zacchaeus.'" Curiously enough he does not quote the remaining clause, "for to-day I must abide at thy house," although it is the very ground of his theory, which is this: The statement of Jesus that He would abide at *his* house, following closely upon his own thought of the blessedness of the man who should be so honoured, showed Zacchaeus that Jesus had read his thought. Thereupon he said to himself, "If He knew this thought, He understands also all things that I have ever done." Therefore he answered, "All things that I have ever taken from any man wrongfully I will restore them fourfold."

5. At p. 182, l. 10, S. Ephraem thus explains the cursing of the fig-tree: "He cursed the fig-tree because it is

thus written:[1] 'When thou shalt gather the harvest of thy field, leave whatsoever shall remain behind; and when thou shalt beat off thine olives, thou shalt do likewise; and thus shalt thou do in all things that thou possessest.' But the owner of this fig-tree disobeyed and despised this law; and when the Lord had come, and found no fruit left on it, He cursed it, in order that the owner might not eat of it any more, because he had left nothing for the orphans and widows." This, however, is not the only explanation which he offers.

After considering these specimens of S. Ephraem's arguments and explanations of difficult passages, it may not be out of place to conclude this Introduction with some short extracts illustrative of the eloquence for which this Father was so celebrated.

1. As he strongly insisted on the Davidic descent of Mary at pp. 15–17, it is surprising to find him speaking of Jesus as a Levite at pp. 161, 162. Probably he based this idea on the intermarriages between the tribes of Levi and Judah described on p. 17. He is dealing with the demand for tribute money, and he gives two reasons why Jesus should be exempt from the tax: (1) as the King of Israel, so that both He and His servants should be free, and the tax demanded from strangers only; and (2) because He was a Levite, and therefore free from such exactions. In this connection Ephraem thus paraphrases our Lord's words to show their meaning: "Go to the sea, and cast a net there. Because they thought me a stranger, let the sea teach them that I am not only priest, but also king." He adds that, when Simon went to cast the net, the Pharisees also went with him. "And when he had drawn out the fish, which had in its mouth a stater, the symbol of dominion, those haughty ones were reproved and confounded, because they believed not that He was a Levite, to whom the sea and the fishes were witnesses that He is king and priest. The advent then of this High Priest all created things acknowledged; and all things hastened to Him to bring Him tributes in their own way. The heavenly

---

[1] A paraphrase of *Deut.* xxiv. 19–21.

host sent Him greeting by Gabriel, and the powers of the heavens by a star; the Gentiles commissioned the Magi; and the prophets, then already for some time silent, sent off the scribes, saying, 'Out of the town of Bethlehem shall He arise.' The stater, which was being coined in the throat of the fish, and receiving the image of the king in those waters, was a proof to those who were seeking strifes and stumblingblocks, that even the obedience of the sea was turned towards this stranger."

2. At p. 260, l. 28, in the course of a passage on the piercing of the Saviour's side, he says: "Envy persecuted David, and hatred and envy the Son of David. David was besieged in the inside of a cave, and the Son of David in the inside of a sepulchre. David seemed to be condemned, and the Son of David conquered; but Saul was condemned and convicted, and death was conquered and destroyed. David exclaimed, 'Where is thy spear, O king?' and the Son of David exclaimed, 'Where is thy victory, O death?' Saul cast his spear at David, and though it had not struck him, yet the wall was a witness of his striking; so also the crucifiers struck the Son of David with a spear, and though the power of Christ was not injured, yet His body bears witness of His torments. David was not pierced, and the Son of David was not injured. The wall, the spear, and the cave accuse Saul; and the body and the cross and the sepulchre convict the Hebrews. There is no one that so exalted himself as man; and there is no one that so humbled himself as God. No one hath so exalted himself as the man who stretched forth his hands towards the tree and wished to make himself equal to his Creator; and no one hath so humbled himself as the God who stretched forth His hands upon the tree, and blotted out the transgressions which by the stretching out of the first hand had entered in."

3. On the sealing of Christ's sepulchre, p. 266, l. 22, he says: "A stone was placed at the door of the sepulchre, a stone to a stone, that a stone might guard the stone which the builders refused. A stone, which was laid hold upon by hands, was applied to shut in that stone which was cut out

without a hand. The stone, on which the angel sat, was applied to shut in that stone which Jacob placed beneath his head. A stone secured with a seal was applied to guard that stone, by whose seal the faithful are guarded. The gate of life, then, went out from the gate of death. 'This,' it saith, 'is the gate through which the righteous enter.' When the Lord was shut in, He released those who were shut in; and through His death the dead lived; through His voice the silent cried out; in His resurrection the earth was moved; and by going out of the sepulchre He brought in the Gentiles into the Church."

After a close and prolonged examination of the acknowledged works of S. Ephraem, the present writer is unable to conceive how anyone else could have written these and other passages of the Gospel Commentary, which are so exactly in the peculiar style of that Father.

WESTBURY-ON-TRYM, BRISTOL, *May* 1896.

PARALLELISMS.

WE now proceed to give some comparisons—sixty-one in number—between passages of the Armenian Commentary and similar passages in other works ascribed to S. Ephraem, tending to show in a variety of ways that they are from the same author. These will be found to vary very much in their nature, sometimes depending on peculiar readings or translations; sometimes on strange conceptions of historical records, traditional legends, or apocryphal stories; sometimes on a curious combination and juxtaposition of texts; sometimes on singular arguments, or solutions of difficulties; sometimes on repetitions of the same mistake; and sometimes on resemblances in phraseology, especially in figurative language.

Accordingly, they will be found to vary very much in evidential value, some being such as no two men would be likely to have concurred in writing, whilst others are less strange and exceptional. In a few cases they are such as *any Syrian about the time of S. Ephraem* might have written. Their cumulative effect is considerable, and, joined to the other evidence already described, cannot fail to convince any unprejudiced mind that S. Ephraem was the author of the Commentary in question.

These parallelisms are arranged in the order in which they occur in the Armenian Commentary, the extracts from which are given first, with any remarks that seemed necessary; and then in a fresh paragraph the corresponding extracts from other works of S. Ephraem are given in order—first those from the Syriac volumes of the Roman edition, then those from the Greek, then those from Dr. Lamy's volumes, and lastly those from the Pauline Commentary. In the references, which accompany these parallelisms, the page and line of Dr. Moesinger's work are given. But in the case of the Roman edition, each page is divided into sections of about ten lines each, lettered from A to F; and in quoting from these, the volume, page, and letter are shown, as I. 188 E, or β, 427 F, where I. and β, as before explained, represent the first Syriac and second Greek volumes respectively. Dr. Lamy's volumes are called A, B, C; but as they are numbered in columns, not pages, the number of the column—the Latin one except in the case of notes—is here given, together with the line of the column at which the extract begins, excepting where the column is divided into sections, in which case the section is given. In the Pauline Commentary the page and line are given.

1. The Jews had a tradition that when Moses smote the rock in the wilderness, the water came out in twelve springs, forming twelve streams, one for each tribe, and that the rock afterwards followed the Israelites through the desert, supplying the tribes in the same manner at each resting-place (cf. 1 Cor. x. 4). The movement of the rock is not mentioned in our Commentary, but allusion is made to the twelve springs at Moes. p. 12, l. 2: "The Word of God is the tree of life, which offers thee blessed fruit from all its parts, even as that rock, which was opened in the desert, that it might supply spiritual drink to all men out of all its parts." That there were twelve such parts is not expressly mentioned, but is to some extent implied in the comparison with the tree of life which "bare twelve manner of fruits, and yielded her fruit every month" (Rev. xxii. 2). At Moes. p. 87, l. 17, the number is given: "The rock in the wilderness poured forth the hallowing waters, wherewith it supplied drink to the twelve tribes of the people."

Turning to the admitted works of S. Ephraem, we find both parts of the legend at I. 263 D: "They relate that the rock followed the Hebrews, as they wandered through the deserts, and did not even deny its waters to them, when they were journeying, but collected them into a well; and when the people had discontinued their advance, and settled down, immediately it poured forth twelve torrents from its full channels, as it was wont, Moses and the heads of tribes exciting the water with the rod and with the singing of psalms." Again at III. 574 A, we read: "The saying of the chief Workman seemed to me, as I considered its effects, like the rock that followed the people wandering through the deserts, which, though it contained no moisture in itself, nevertheless poured forth rushing streams of water; in fact the hard flint, in its own nature destitute of any liquid, cast up streams reproducing the sea: so the speech of God constructed all things out of nothing." At A, 246, l. 24, we find: "They drank waters [drawn forth from the rock] into streams." But the MS. is defective here, the bracketed part being supplied by the editor.

2. At Moes. p. 16, l. 8, in the midst of a long argument to prove that the Virgin Mary, although related to Elizabeth, was of the tribe of Judah, not Levi, we read: "But if, because the scripture said, 'Elizabeth thy sister,'[1] you therefore think that this was said, that it might be made manifest that Mary was of the house of Levi, in another passage the same scripture said that they were both, Joseph and Mary, of the house of David." Dr. Moesinger expressed his opinion that this was merely an interpretation of the words of Luke i. 27: "of the house of David"; but there the words are applied to Joseph only. The opinion of Zahn appears more reasonable, that the writer had a different reading at Luke ii. 4: "*they both were* of the house and lineage of David," instead of "*he was*," etc. This reading has since been discovered in the Sinaitic palimpsest.

The Davidic descent of Mary is repeatedly asserted by S. Ephraem. At I. 357 D, he says: "At last the Son of God, the descendant of David in the flesh, born of a virgin of the stock of David, has succoured the wretched." At II. 40 A, his comment on the words "a rod out of the stem of Jesse" (Isa. xi. 1) is as follows: "from his latest sons, who were kinsmen of Joseph and Mary." At III. 601 E, he says: "Joseph, David's son, espoused to himself a daughter of David"; and at III. 602 B: "Christ, conceived out of a daughter of David, and nourished in the bosom of a son of David, was worshipped in the city of David." See also B, 436, sec. 13; 550, sec. 2; 568, sec. 2; 582, sec. 1; 592, sec. 7;

[1] Luke i. 36.

606, secs. 1 and 5. It is in the Pauline Commentary alone that we find reference to the supposed various reading. In the course of an explanation of 2 Tim. ii. 8, "Remember that Jesus Christ of the seed of David was raised from the dead according to my gospel," he says, P, 260, l. 12: "Either what is said concerning Mary and Joseph, that they were both of the house of David; or that which saith, 'The Lord God shall give unto Him the throne of His father David.'" Here we find the same idea of an actual text openly asserting the Davidic descent of Mary.

3. In explaining how Mary of the tribe of Judah could be related to Elizabeth of the tribe of Levi, the writer mentions (Moes. p. 16, l. 25) the marriage of Aaron with the sister of Naasson, the leader of the house of Judah, and that of Jehoiada the priest with Jehosheba the daughter of King Joram.

The latter only of these marriages is mentioned elsewhere by S. Ephraem, I. 544 C, but with a remark that this intermarriage contrary to the law was a privilege of the royal family only. This statement suggests that he knew also of the case of Naasson's sister, Naasson being an ancestor of David.

The mother of Hezekiah was "Abi the daughter of Zachariah" (2 Kings xviii. 2). Zachariah was a prophet; but it is not known whether he was a Levite. On her marriage nothing is said in these books.

4. At Moes. p. 18, l. 17, we read: "The Annunciation of Mary took place on the tenth day of the month Arek," *i.e.* Nisan. At l. 20 it proceeds: "The law commanded that they should enclose the [paschal] lamb on the tenth day of the month Arek. On the same day the true Lamb was enclosed in the womb of the Virgin at the time when light gains the empire, and thereby He taught that He was come to cover up the nakedness of Adam. But He was born on the sixth day of the month Chaloz, according to the Greek reckoning, at the time when the sun begins to conquer, showing that the Devil was conquered, and man had conquered in Him who conquers all things."

At I. 212 F, in his comment on Ex. xii. 3 (the setting apart of the paschal lamb), S. Ephraem says: "The lamb is a type of the Lord, who came down into the Virgin's womb on the tenth day of the month Nisan." At II. 415 A, he says: "Moses enclosed the lamb in the month Nisan on the tenth day of the same, and described a type of the coming Son of God, who in this very month came down into the belly of the Virgin, and hid within her entrails confined Himself, when the tenth day was passed. Moreover, in the month wherein He was born, the space of night was shortened, and the darkness overcome, in order that we might understand that the Devil had been overcome by Him; and, the day being lengthened, the light conquered, that we might applaud the triumph of the Only-begotten." At β, 427 F, the month Xanthicus (April) is mentioned, but no day; and at β, 428 A, it says: "The month of His conception interpreted for us the type which Moses revealed by signs. And the month of His birth in like manner made the mystery clear to us." In this passage we also find allusions to the vernal equinox and winter solstice as the times of conception and birth. At β, 427 F, we read: "Then indeed the darkness running swiftly was unable to obscure the bright conception. But in the month Apellaeus[1] took place the birth of light, dispersing this our darkness. For in the month in which darkness fails, the triumphant light arose for us." At B, 446, sec. 6, we read: "The Lord of months chose for Himself two months for His own affairs. His conception was accomplished in the month Nisan, and His birth in the month Conun."

5. The writer of the Commentary makes frequent comparisons between Jesus and S. John the Baptist, employing for this purpose various titles applied to them in Scripture. Thus at p. 19, l. 31, we find: "The elder [Elizabeth] kindled in the house of her father Jacob a lamp, which is John himself; and the younger [Mary] made the Sun of Righteousness arise for all nations." And at p. 20, l. 5: "The lamp by no means dim proclaimed the Sun of Righteousness" . . . "the voice proclaimed the Word." At p. 30, l. 9, it says: "After the star had led them to the Sun, it stood still in its

[1] December.

limit; and after it had proclaimed concerning Him, it put an end to its own life. In like manner John was the voice, which proclaimed concerning the Word; but when the Word had begun to be heard, and had been made flesh, and had appeared, the voice, which had prepared the way, cried out, He must increase, and I must decrease." Again, at p. 38, l. 34, it says: "As the voice announcing light at the door of the ears, so also the brightness of the lamp knocks at the door of the eyes, even as a writing is the companion of the voice. For the lamp and the cock are one, even as Elijah and John." After further reference to S. John as the lamp and the cock, it proceeds at p. 39, l. 20: "John then is the voice, but the Word, which sounds in the voice, is the Lord. The voice aroused them, the voice called them, and brought them back; but the Word distributed to them its own gifts." At p. 49, l. 31, it says: "Because the voice could not keep disciples with himself, therefore he sent them to the Word. It was indeed fitting that on the appearance of the light of the sun the gleam of the lamp should sink." Also at p. 151, l. 16: "This is the lamp that shone, that after increase was put out; for it shone by night that it might be known, that when the brightness of the sun is risen the rays of the lamp pass away and are extinguished."

With these extracts we may compare what S. Ephraem says at A, 8, sec. 9: "John proclaimed, 'He that cometh after me was before me'; I am the voice, not the Word, the lamp, not the Light; the star arising before the Sun of Righteousness." And at A, 116, sec. 3, we read: "My mind admires now the Word, now the voice. John indeed is the voice; but the Lord is revealed as the Word, that He who had been concealed might come forth openly." At A, 126, sec. 43, S. John is represented as saying: "Lo, they that were invited by the Bridegroom are witnesses that I daily said among them, 'I am the voice, not the Word.'" Again, at B, 802, sec. 5, he says: "After the priest became dumb before the voice, and the Word came into the ear," etc.

6. At Moes. p. 22, l. 9, we read: "But if you doubt, hear Isaiah the prophet saying, 'Behold a virgin shall conceive'; and Daniel saith, 'A stone cut out without hand.'

And this is not like that saying, 'Look unto mountain and valley,' in which passage he signifies man and woman; but here he said, 'without hand.' Even as Adam filled the place of father and mother in the creation of Eve, so did Mary also in the generating of our Lord."

Compare with this the words of S. Ephraem at II. 206 E: "And accordingly the stone cut out without hands is the Lord, who in His emptying is called a little stone cut from the mountain, being born in fact of the stock of Abraham. And by the same figure of a mountain was the holy Virgin equally designated, out of whom that mystic stone has been cut without hands, *i.e.* without the seed of man." It seems as if the thought here expressed must underlie the passage in the Commentary. So, too, at B, 272, l. 29, he says: "That spiritual mountain [1] signifies to us the holy Virgin, in whom God dwelt, and from whom He was cut out without hands, that is, without connection, according to Daniel's vision of the stone that was cut out without hands."

7. At Moes. p. 24, l. 3, we read: "But just as the Lord entered when the doors were shut, in the same manner He went forth out of the Virgin's womb, for this Virgin really and truly brought forth without birth-pangs."

At β, 265 A, S. Ephraem says: "Mary neither suffered, as a woman, nor felt the birth-pang in bringing forth, as a virgin."

8. At Moes. p. 24, l. 5, we read: "If for Noah's sake the beasts were made chaste and gentle in the Ark, it was also fitting that the Virgin, foretold by a prophet, in whom Emmanuel dwelt, should not come near to marriage. Noah's beasts did it of necessity, Mary of free will."

The gentleness of the animals is mentioned by S. Ephraem at I. 52 D, where he describes hostile animals as meeting in the Ark without anger or fear, lions with oxen, wolves with lambs, hawks with small birds, etc. Their chastity is explained at I. 150 C: "He separated the males from the females in order that they might understand that all the time they were to sojourn in the Ark they ought to

[1] Cf. Hab. iii. 3.

lead a celibate life and preserve continency." At III. 128 D, he says: "Rivalry and envy have made men savage in the Church; madly they bite one another; and the wild beasts kept peace in the Ark." Also at III. 603 B, he dwells at some length on the peacefulness of the animals in the Ark. At *a*, 44 A, the reference is to the gradual and peaceful assembly of fierce animals from distant lands.

9. At Moes. p. 26, l. 21, we read: "But why was this first enrolment of the land made at the time when the Lord was born? Because it was written, 'There shall not fail a prince of Judah, nor a ruler out of his loins, until He shall come whose property he [Judah] is.' From the fact that the enrolment was made at His appearing, let it become evident that at the time of His birth the Gentiles ruled over the people, which itself reigned before, that it might be fulfilled, which he said, 'And in Him shall the Gentiles trust.' At that time, therefore, He came, because the king had failed and the prophet."

A similar explanation is given by S. Ephraem at II. 33 D: " But if the Jews do not believe our gospel, let them unroll the records of the Romans; from them they will surely learn that in that year in which the Lord was born, their republic was already forsaken by God, and the Jews, subdued by the Romans, were also subjected at the same time to a poll-tax." And at II. 414 F: "At the birthday feast of the Son of God a king imposed a census on the whole world, that he might make Him a debtor to himself."

10. At Moes. p. 33, l. 5, we find: "But Pharaoh, because the family and time of the deliverer, who was to be born to the Hebrews, had not been revealed, began to destroy many infants, that with the many that one might die whom it seemed necessary to him to destroy." This is said in connection with the murder of the innocents by Herod, which is then under comment.

At I. 543 E, in connection with the murder of the royal children by Athaliah, the same two events are again brought together: "And in the time of Moses he [Satan] induced Pharaoh to destroy the male infants of the Hebrews, because he knew that in Abraham's seed all nations of the earth were to be blessed; and after Christ's coming he suggested to Herod the slaughter of the infants of Bethlehem." So again, at II. 430 E, he says: "The Devil, who once, in seeking the destruction of Moses, stifled the offspring of the Hebrews, killed the infants of Bethlehem, in order that he might snatch away life from the living God."

11. At Moes. p. 33, l. 16, it says: "Yea, and Cain his disciple thought that he could deceive God, when he said, 'Am I my brother's keeper?'" And at p. 205, l. 32: "But Cain also thought, 'I kill a man, and I deceive God.' The man was killed, for he was mortal; but God was not deceived, for He was omniscient."

The same thought is expressed at II. 475 E: "By his speech Cain tried to deceive God." But at γ, 186 F, S. Ephraem says: "Cain was mocking God, excusing himself no doubt; therefore also he is held accountable for murder, and is punished with seven torments."

12. At Moes. p. 34, l. 4, we read: "As Moses also in his blessing says of Benjamin, 'He shall dwell between his shoulders,' because the Ark of the Covenant was laid up in the city of Jerusalem, which was the inheritance of Benjamin."

S. Ephraem, at I. 188 E, says: "Moses [saith,] 'Benjamin, the beloved of the Lord, shall dwell between his shoulders.' He calls Jerusalem, which the Benjamites inhabited, a place situated between the Lord's shoulders. In fact, Jerusalem was placed in the middle between the boundaries of two tribes." Discussing the same verse at I. 288 F, after applying the words to S. Paul, he proceeds: "Again, since the position in which Jerusalem lies touches the territory assigned to the tribe of Benjamin, and Christ has been crucified there, the same is rightly said to have leaned upon the tribe of Benjamin. And He tarried between his shoulders on that day particularly, when He hung on Mount Calvary, and held up even until the evening hands stretched out after the manner of one that is leaning."

13. At Moes. p. 35, the fleece of Gideon is represented as a type of the birth of Christ from the Virgin; and it is asserted that Gideon knew this hidden meaning though he was not free to communicate it to others. The writer is discussing the sign promised by Isaiah (vii. 14)—the virgin-birth—and at l. 4 he says: "To Moses was this sign given, that he alone, and, as it were, in private, might be persuaded through the mystery, even as both to Gideon and to Ezekiel the same sign was revealed."

This figure is employed by S. Ephraem at I. 317 B: "The fleece of Gideon, in which he received the dew from heaven, typified the Virgin who conceived God the Word." The meaning of these references to Gideon is shown by S. Ephraem at III. 214 C, to turn upon Ps. lxxii. 6: "He shall come down like the rain into a fleece of wool." This is the Prayer-Book version, and agrees with the Septuagint: but the Hebrew means, "into the mown grass." S. Ephraem's words are: "Another related that the descent of the Son of God had been shadowed forth to him by the sign of rain coming down without noise, and that Mary had been represented in a shining and pure fleece." At γ, 529 F, in a prayer to the Virgin, he addresses her in a series of figurative titles as: "Fleece of Gideon dripping with dew." And again at γ, 575 E, in a similar passage he says: "Glory of Aaron, brightness of Moses, and fleece of Gideon." But the genuineness of these prayers to the Virgin is doubtful.

14. At Moes. p. 36, l. 16, the statement, "He shall be called a Nazarene" (Matt. ii. 23), is explained as derived from Isa. xi. 1, "a Branch shall grow out of his roots," the Hebrew word for branch, "Netser," being pronounced Nazor: "for, indeed, 'branch' in Hebrew sounds Nazor, and the prophet calls Him the son of Nazor (son of the branch), for in truth He is the Son of the Branch. But the evangelist, because He was brought up in Nazareth, seeing that it was like this, said, 'He shall be called a Nazarene.'" Cf. Dr. Rendel Harris's remarks in the *Contemporary Review*, August 1895, pp. 277, 278. At Moes. p. 40, l. 2, the subject is again referred to: "And when did this take place, but at the rising of that True one in the law whose name [*i.e.* Nazarene] is

denoted by Branch and Flower, on whom," etc. Dr. Moesinger in a note points out that branch and flower are alternative renderings of the Hebrew word already mentioned.

S. Ephraem refers to the passage in Isaiah at II. 40 A and III. 214 A, without alluding to this point; but at B, 540, sec. 8, he says: "Mary was the vine, from which, as it is written, for the fulfilment of the sacrament of prophecy, the Nazarene Branch shot forth, who was brought up in Nazareth, that He might fulfil all things." See Dr. Lamy's note *in loco*.

15. At Moes. p. 40, l. 10, speaking of Herod's attempt to kill the Saviour, it says: "But when He was two years old, they had intended to do this to Him with Herod their prince." Cf. Matt. ii. 16.

S. Ephraem also places the visit of the Magi and the slaughter of the innocents in the second year of Christ's life, saying, at B, 496, sec. 2: "In the second year of the nativity of our Saviour the Magi leap for joy, the Pharisees are sad, the treasures are opened, the kings make haste, the infants are slaughtered."

16. At Moes. p. 40, l. 24, we read: "At a well Eliezer betrothed Rebecca, at a well Jacob betrothed Rachel, at a well Moses betrothed Zipporah. And all these were types of our Lord, who made the Church a bride unto Himself in the baptism of Jordan."

At I. 82 E, S. Ephraem connects the first two of these events, saying: "Jacob understood that the poor Rachel was prepared for him at the well by Him who had offered the beautiful Rebecca to Isaac at the fountain." At γ, 90, he brings together in a lengthy passage the cases of Rebecca, Rachel, and Zipporah, but with a lesson on helping others and no reference to Holy Baptism. At A, 64, sec. 4, we have the case of Rebecca compared with baptism, and in the following section that of Zipporah similarly compared. The absence of Rachel may be due to the mention already made of Jacob bringing the sheep to a fountain, and putting the rods before them. The passage runs thus: "To the well

Rebecca comes to meet *him*; she wears the earrings and the armlets. The bride of Christ has clothed herself in precious things in the waters; in her hands she bears the living body, and in her ears the promises. Moses drew, and watered the sheep of Jethro the priest of sin. Our Shepherd dipped the sheep of the High Priest of truth in the waters of baptism. At the well the flocks were dumb; but here the sheep are endowed with reason."

17. The story of the light (or fire) appearing on the waters of Jordan at Christ's baptism is alluded to at Moes. p. 43, l. 10, where Satan is represented as discovering something of His true nature and mission "from the light that sprang up upon the waters."

The same story is referred to by S. Ephraem at II. 328 E: "The river, in which He was baptized, became bright, when the Light was let in." And at III. 15 C, he says: "While He was glistening, the entire Jordan gleamed." At A, 12, sec. 18, we read: "John approached with his parents and worshipped the Son, whose person an unusual brightness was lighting up." This refers to the time of the Magi; but Dr. Lamy suggests that the idea of this illumination was borrowed from the story we are considering. At A, 98, sec. 5, he says: "In His baptism a light shone forth from the waters." At A, 128, sec. 48, we find: "The holiest Bridegroom went down into Jordan; when He had received baptism, He soon came up; and His light shone forth upon the world." And at B, 470, l. 2: "He put on the waters in baptism; and from them there shone forth rays of light."

18. At Moes. p. 57, l. 22, it is implied that the Ark rested upon a mountain in the district afterwards inhabited by the Carduchi or Cardui, Noah being said to have built the altar "in monte Carduacorum."

S. Ephraem thus quotes Gen. viii. 4 at I. 53 E, and again at I. 152 A: "And the Ark rested 'super montes Cardoos.'" At I. 560 E, commenting on the murder of Sennacherib by his sons, he says: "'And they escaped into the land of Ararath.' There are mountains in Armenia, the same that by a different name are also called Cardui, to which Noah moored the Ark." At II. 82 A, speaking of the same persons, he says: "They escaped into the lands of the Cardui, which are also Ararat." At III. 564 C, we find: "They were conveyed from the Ark unto the Cardui mountains." At γ, 3 F, he speaks of "Noah, who was saved in the Ark, when the water abated, and settled above on the mountains of Ararat." . . . And at A, 712, sec. 7, he says: "The Ark from the mountains of Cardu gathered for Him the fairest flowers."

This opinion was common in Syria; and the parallelism helps to confirm the Syriac origin of the Armenian Commentary.

19. At Gen. xxii. 2, the writer of the Commentary seems to have had a reading, "the land of the Amorites" instead of "the land of Moriah"; for at p. 57, l. 24, he speaks of "the sacrifice of Abraham on the mountain of the Amorites."

S. Ephraem quotes this verse at I. 76 E, and puts "the land of the Amorites" instead of "the land of Moriah." Again, at I. 457 E, he identifies the spot where Isaac was offered up with the site of Solomon's temple; and he proceeds to describe the purchase of it from Araunah the Jebusite, and adds: "Wherefore the site of the temple pertained to the Gentiles; for it had been received from the Amorites." A similar account is given at II. 23 F; but the Amorites are not mentioned there.

20. At Moes. p. 59, l. 21, we read: "And that 'they beckoned unto their partners' (Luke v. 7) is the mystery of the seventy-two disciples; for the Apostles were not enough for the fishing and the harvest." At p. 160, l. 17, we find: "Immediately He chose seventy-two, and sent them far away from Himself." On the other hand, at p. 287, l. 4, it says: "Thaddaeus, one of the seventy." This, however, is not in the Commentary; and the text seems corrupt at that point; for Thaddaeus was one of the Twelve.

Turning to S. Ephraem, at B, 154, l. 3, we read: "In the days of the seventy disciples"; but this seems the only instance; whilst at C, 238, l. 1; P, 78, l. 18; 104, l. 6; 110, l. 5; and 150, l. 11, we find the number seventy-two.

21. At Moes. p. 75, l. 22, we find "Legio" used as the proper name of the Gadarene demoniac.

S. Ephraem so uses it at A, 20, sec. 18; B, 662, sec. 5; 674, sec. 4; and at 720, l. 2, where the similarity of thought between "Legionem sui exercitus ducem" and the words "Legione, duce ejus" in our Commentary as above is remarkable, and points to a common authorship. At III. 575 B and A, 444, l. 21, "Legio" is not used as a proper name; but the allusions are of a more passing character; and the devils, and not the man, are spoken of.

22. At Moes. p. 81, l. 20, we read: "So also Rachel having stolen the idol was praised, and clinging to righteousness was crowned." This suggests that in the writer's opinion Rachel did not steal the images to worship them herself.

This was S. Ephraem's opinion; for he says, at I. 86 B: "Here, moreover, it was evident that Rachel had not been undeservedly beloved by Jacob, and preferred to the rest of his wives, since she also preferred the God that he worshipped to her father's gods, and clung to Him alone. Moreover, whilst she steals them, she violates them, and bears witness that they are vain images, and a useless incumbrance to her father's house," adding that she sat upon them, when the custom of women was upon her. And at C, 564, l. 22, he says of her: "For she did not steal her father's idols for her own advantage, but in order that she might remove heathenism from her father's house."

23. At Moes. p. 102, l. 28, in commenting upon the words, "Behold, I send my messenger [angel] before thee," it says: "If you reply, 'Even among the twelve prophets one[1] was called My angel,' I answer, that this man was so named by his parents, just as a name is given to the rest of mankind. The name that is given by parents is one thing; the honourable name that is bestowed by God as a recompense for works is another. But if you say that that prophet was called 'My angel' by his parents because of his heavenly manner of life, we will not dispute further on this matter."

[1] Malachi means "Angel of God."

At II. 312 A, S. Ephraem shows the same knowledge of the meaning of the name Malachi, but expresses himself differently as to how he received it: "The people, greatly admiring him for his remarkable uprightness and most holy teaching, called him Malachi, *i.e.* Angel of God, because he carried out the idea of an angel."

24. At Moes. p. 109, l. 2, it says regarding the petition of the sons of Zebedee: "Because they had come to receive by election without works, the Lord repelled them from Him, openly asserting that He had not the power, that He might not distress them, like that *saying*, 'That hour knoweth no man,' that they might not question Him any more about it. 'It is not given to you,' it says, 'to know the hour and the time.'" This passage is repeated almost verbatim at p. 179, l. 22. The writer was greatly exercised by the statement (S. Mark xiii. 32) that even the Son did not know the hour. This, in view of His divine nature, he felt could not be the case; and therefore he asserted that this statement was not true, and was only said to prevent further inquiry. In a lengthy argument beginning at p. 215, l. 20, he maintains this view, and illustrates it in a variety of ways, including an argument, p. 216, l. 22, that He, who knows the Father (Matt. xi. 27), must know all lesser things, and the time of His own coming cannot be a greater thing to know than the Father.

S. Ephraem took the same view, and was greatly interested in it, as is shown by a lengthy argument extending from III. 142 B to 148 F. Besides the identity of opinion shown, the chief correspondence in argument is at III. 142 C, where the same reasoning on the Son's knowledge of the Father, as we have seen in the Commentary, is to be found.

25. At Moes. p. 115, l. 9, we read: "The tears of the sinful *woman* came down and washed the place, where those five hundred pence of their own debts had been written down."

The language of S. Ephraem at III. 384 D, is very similar: "The tears which the sinful woman shed, restored to her and blotted out the great bond of crimes committed;

settle for me, I pray, the accounts of my debts in like manner."

26. At Moes. p. 122, l. 6, in dealing with the case of the evil spirit taking unto himself seven other spirits more wicked than himself, we find the following: "Moreover, these seven, that dwelt in him, are those of whom Jeremiah[1] said, 'She hath conceived and brought forth seven; her belly was puffed up.' She brought forth one calf in the desert, the two calves of Jeroboam, and the image with four faces of Manasseh."

This singular method of counting up the seven is given also by S. Ephraem in his Commentary on this passage of Jeremiah, II. 127 E. After explaining that by the mother of seven may be understood Leah, who bore to Jacob seven sons, or the tribe of Ephraim on account of its prosperity, he adds: "or thirdly, the whole synagogue of the children of Israel, which brought forth one calf in the desert, two in the land of promise made by Jeroboam the son of Nebat, and set up one in Dan and the other in Bethel, and the four-faced image."

Dr. Rendel Harris, in the article already referred to, shows that the passage in Jeremiah is quoted in Moesinger's work according to the Syriac version. What fourfaced image S. Ephraem here referred to may be gathered from his comment on Isa. xliii. 28 at B, 110, sec. 28: "'Thy princes have profaned the sanctuary.' They that were of the house of Manasseh profaned the sanctuary by an image of a fourfaced thing, which they brought into the sanctuary. And for these crimes, especially for that of Manasseh, 'I have devoted Jacob to the curse, and Israel to reproach.'"

Note.—S. Ephraem ascribes a similar image to Micah (Judg. xvii. 4, 5), saying, at II. 384 A: "Micah invented a fourfaced God."

27. At Moes. p. 127, l. 10, we find: "'Again, the kingdom is like a grain of mustard seed, which is the least of all seeds.' This He said of the small beginning of preaching, as that, 'Fear not, little flock.' 'And when it groweth, it

[1] xv. 9.

increaseth and becometh a tree, and becometh greater than all herbs.'"

These two sayings of Christ are similarly connected together by S. Ephraem at II. 201 D, as follows: "Now survey the beginnings of the preaching of the gospel, when there were very few that adopted the teaching and commandments of Christ. Accordingly, addressing His disciples, the Lord saith, 'Fear not, little flock,' and compares His kingdom to a grain of mustard seed, which is the least of all seeds, but, when it is grown, it is the greatest of all herbs."

28. In the account of the rejection of Jesus at Nazareth, Moes. pp. 129–131, it is asserted that the Lord was actually cast from the cliff, but miraculously sustained by the air, so that He did not fall. The statement at p. 129, l. 11, does not go beyond the Gospel narrative; but at p. 130, l. 7, we read: "Because of their liberty they cast Him down; because of His divinity He fell not. When liberty would thrust Him down, the air placing itself beneath sustained Him with its wings. He fell not, that in this way He might perhaps teach the unbelieving faith." Again, at l. 34, it says: "But the Nazarenes, seeing that in them He was rejecting the whole land of Israel, but honouring the Gentiles excessively, rose up against Him, and seized Him, and led Him forth, and thrust Him down." And again, at p. 131, l. 18: "Moreover, He permitted them to cast Him down headlong, because Satan thought that the Lord out of fear had not cast Himself down from the pinnacle of the temple. But after the Lord being thrown down had not fallen, Satan fell from his princedom." Also at p. 212, l. 27, we read: "Nor did the Nazarenes deprive Him of life, when they cast Him down headlong from the mountain."

The language of S. Ephraem is very similar. At A, 194, l. 20, he says: "They thought that He was not God; and they cast Him forth from the high ground to the bottom." And at A, 614, sec. 10: "When they cast Him forth from the top of the mountain, He would neither resist nor injure them. Cast forth from the mountain, at once He sprang up, showing how bodies would be caught up in the end. He made the air His chariot, and gave it His body as charioteer."

29. At Moes. p. 147, l. 33, in a list of cases in which the sabbath is broken by God in nature, it says: "Yea rather on the sabbath day men are brought forth, as if no commandment stands in the way, and on the eighth day [another sabbath!] they are circumcised."

In like manner S. Ephraem, at B, 734, sec. 16, says: "As often as an infant is born on the sabbath, this happens through necessity on the part of the agent, who breaks the sabbath; but when the sabbath returns, circumcision breaks it again."

30. At Moes. p. 155, l. 21, speaking of the Transfiguration, it says: "Moreover the Lord called unto Himself Elijah that was caught up into heaven, and Moses raised to life, and of the heralds themselves the three witnesses, who are pillars, *i.e.* who support the evidence of the kingdom." No doubt the "pillars" meant are "James, Cephas, and John, who seemed to be pillars" (Gal. ii. 9). This is a curious error, for the James mentioned by S. Paul was the same that he called "James the Lord's brother" (Gal. i. 19); whereas James the son of Zebedee, who witnessed the Transfiguration, was put to death by Herod before the date of this Epistle, and before the date of S. Paul's visit to Jerusalem, at which he observed that these disciples seemed to be pillars. At p. 177, l. 26, we read: "Because James and John had seen Moses and Elijah with the Lord, they were kindled with longing, and said: 'Give us authority to sit one on Thy right and the other on the left.'" It would seem, therefore, that James the son of Zebedee was supposed by the writer to be alive at the date of S. Paul's visit to Jerusalem. And so, too, in the supplementary matter at p. 286, l. 26, this disciple is represented as preaching in Gaul. There is also an allusion to the pillars at p. 274, l. 13, but not in a form to throw light on this mistake.

Now S. Ephraem says the same thing with reference to the Transfiguration at III. 15 C: "He kindled a little torch on the mountain; the three pillars, whom the evangelist numbers, struck by a sudden movement, trembled, penetrated with fear, quaking and shuddering, although He had tempered the brightness of His hidden majesty to the weak eyes of the

beholders." And again, in his comments on Gal. ii. 9, at
P, 128, l. 12, he says: "But when Peter and James and
John, the chief of the Apostles, who in truth were the pillars
of the Churches, knew them, they diminished nothing and
added nothing to those things which I revealed to them
on account of my preaching among the Gentiles." This
passage would not be decisive alone; but the words "the
chief of the Apostles" seem to point to the same mistake,
since "James the Lord's brother" was not an Apostle.

31. At Moes. p. 156, l. 35, we read: "But why did
Moses and Elijah appear to Him? Because, when He asked
them, 'What do men say concerning Me, that I am?' they
said unto Him, 'Some say that Thou art Elijah; others
Jeremiah, and others one of the prophets,' in order that He
might show them that He was neither Elijah nor one of the
prophets, Moses and Elijah appeared unto them, that they
might know that He was the Lord of the prophets."

A like statement is made by S. Ephraem at β, 42 B:
"But He led them to the mountain, that He might show them
what Son He was, and whose. For when He asked them,
'Who do men say that I the Son of Man am?' they say unto
Him, 'Some indeed Elijah, but others Jeremiah, or one of the
prophets.' Therefore He brings them up into the mountain,
and shows them that He is not Elijah, but the God of Elijah;
nor again Jeremiah, but He that sanctified Jeremiah in his
mother's womb; nor one of the prophets, but the Lord of the
prophets, who also sent them." This passage is repeated
almost verbatim at β, 427 A.

32. At Moes. p. 157, l. 4, a further reason is given why
Christ showed His glory on the Mount of Transfiguration: "He
transfigured His face on the mountain before death, that they
might not doubt concerning the transfiguration of His face
after death."

Nearly the same line of thought is expressed by S.
Ephraem at β, 43 C, and β, 427 D: "He led them unto the
mountain, and shows them before the resurrection the glory
of His divinity, that, when He rose from the dead in the same
glory of the divinity of His nature, they might know that He

did not receive the glory in return for His labour, as one in need; but it was His before the ages with the Father, and in the Father's presence, even as He said, when He was now approaching His voluntary suffering, 'Father, glorify Me with the glory which I had with Thee before the world was.'"

This may have been the doubt about the resurrection referred to above.

33. At Moes. p. 157, l. 12, allusion is made to the different positions of the bodies of Moses and Elijah, when summoned to the Transfiguration, the former being dead and buried, and the latter in heaven: "Is not He the Christ, who called Moses to life and Elijah from heaven?" See also p. 155, l. 21, quoted at No. 30.

S. Ephraem has a similar allusion at β, 42 C: "And He shows them that He is the creator of heaven and earth, and He is the Lord of the living and the dead. For He commanded the heaven, and brought down Elijah; and He signed to the earth, and raised up Moses."

34. At Moes. p. 175, l. 24, a contrast is drawn between Abraham pitying and pleading for the Sodomites and Abraham refusing the entreaties of Dives: "For if Abraham, who was a friend of strangers, and showed compassion to the Sodomites, could not pity him who felt no pity for Lazarus, how can we hope for forgiveness? For though that rich man called Abraham his father, and Abraham addressed him, 'My son,' still he could not assist him." So, too, at p. 196, l. 31: "'This did not Abraham,' but rather pitied those who were doing evil, i.e. the Sodomites."

S. Ephraem has the same thought at III. 564 E: "The unhappy man beseeches Abraham to bring help to the afflicted one; but he, than whom surely no other was gentler, and who had left nothing untried to avert from the Sodomites a pitiable slaughter, yet in severity pitied not the fall of the rich man, deeming it unjust to render pity to him who had denied it to his brother." At a, 68 E, also he says: "There the compassionate Abraham was shown forth compassionless and merciless to the rich man: and he, who had prayed on behalf of Sodom, prayed not there for one sinner, that he might obtain mercy." This passage is found again in nearly the same words at β, 374 D, and identically at γ, 481 C.

35. At Moes. p. 176, l. 28, in the explanation of the parable of the Labourers in the Vineyard, we read: "Moreover, the fact that he went out in the morning, at the third, sixth, ninth, and eleventh hour, and at sunset, may be understood of the beginning of His preaching, which He continued even unto His cross, for at the eleventh hour the thief entered into the vineyard, *i.e.* into paradise."
A similar reference to the dying thief is found at III. 539 B, where, after mentioning prophets, righteous men, and Apostles, as those who were called at the third, sixth, and ninth hours, he continues: "Lastly, at the eleventh *hour* Thou calledst the thief, to whom, under the very jaws of death, after the blessing had been promised in bright words, Thou gavest the power of entering the gates of paradise, which Adam had blocked up."

36. At Moes. p. 181, l. 4, in reference to blind Bartimaeus, we find: "'Jesus,' saith he, 'Thou Son of David, have mercy on me.' Well did he think that He was the Son of David, who showed mercy on the blind and lame Jebusites."
This strange interpretation of 2 Sam. v. 6 and 8 agrees with that given by S. Ephraem at I. 401 D: "He loves not David, who is hostile to the lame and blind; and he is friendly to the Jebusites, who wishes this class of men exterminated." This is based upon a different reading of 2 Sam. v. 8, given just before.

37. At Moes. p. 187, l. 7, in reference to the withering of the fig-tree, we read: "Therefore He made it to wither, that the Israelites might blossom again, but they would not."
The same thought is expressed more clearly by S. Ephraem at II. 525 F: "He dried up the fig-tree, in order that the vine of the Jews might come to life again." Thus it appears that in both cases the fig-tree actually withered by our Lord is made to correspond with the fig-tree of the parable, which was planted in a vineyard, but cumbered the ground,

and interfered with the growth of the vines. Cf. S. Luke xiii. 6–9.

38. At Moes. p. 187, l. 10, it says: "The Scripture relates that Adam, after he sinned, and was stripped of the glory wherewith he had been clothed, covered his nakedness with fig leaves. Therefore the Lord came, and endured torment for Adam, that He might heal his wounds and stripes, and restore to his nakedness a garment of glory."

The reasoning of S. Ephraem at III. 578 B, is very similar: "It is not possible to see anyone naked in that people, for they have all put on glory; nor wrapped in coverings of leaves, overspread with blushes, for they have all, under the favour of the Lord's grace, recovered the robe of Adam lost by a crime." In some passages the robe is represented as restored to Adam by the Virgin, since by her Christ came into the world. Thus at B, 522, sec. 12: "Mary wove a robe of glory, and gave it to our first parent. He, who had been stripped among the trees, being clothed with it, was adorned with modesty and the beauty of virtue." And again at B, 526, sec. 9: "Because the mother [Eve] had put on the leaves of shame, the daughter [Mary] wove for her and gave her a robe of glory." At B, 618, sec. 39, the thought is varied: "In Thee, O Lord, let there be comfort and strengthening to the afflicted first parents, who, when their glory was stripped off, put on leaves in the garden; behold, for them Thou hast put on thorns, that they may in fact return into Eden."

39. At Moes. p. 188, l. 5, discussing the words, "Art thou a master in Israel, and knowest not these things?" it says: "We ask what he ought to have known, except that which was contained in the law and the prophets, namely, to dip the hyssop and sprinkle with water, and to baptize unto sanctification, and other things of this kind." And at l. 29: "Likewise also Mary, the sister of Moses, is she not an evident sign of baptism, which was given to the Gentiles? For the hyssop purified her spotted sores."

Turning to S. Ephraem, we find at A, 6, sec. 3: "But the hyssop and the blood are a great symbol," probably meaning a symbol of baptism, of which he has just been speaking. At A, 118, sec. 9, in a supposed dialogue between the Saviour and the Baptist, the latter is made to say: "'I have need to be baptized of Thee': by Thy hyssop indeed Thou purifiest all things." And at P, 207, l. 16, in discussing Heb. ii. 17, he says: "But he called Him 'high priest,' not because of the things which are bestowed upon us through sacrifices, even as through Eleazar, but because of those things which are granted unto us spiritually in Him, that is, 'that He may be a propitiator' through baptism, but not through sprinkling."

40. At Moes. p. 193, l. 2, after quoting Christ's application of the Psalmist's words, "The stone which the builders rejected, the same is made the head of the corner," it proceeds: "What sort of stone? That which is called adamantine in these words, 'I lay an adamant[1] in the midst of the children of Israel.' And to teach that He Himself was this stone because of its strength, He says, 'Whosoever stumbleth on it shall be broken to pieces,'" etc.

S. Ephraem, in showing at III. 219 D, how Christ fulfilled all things, says: "The prophet likewise says that he saw the Lord standing upon an adamantine wall, holding in His hand an adamantine stone, and that he at once heard the same addressing him thus, 'Behold, I will lay an adamant in the midst of My people Israel,' wherewith plainly agree those words of David, 'The stone which the builders disapproved, the same is made into the head of the building.'"

41. At Moes. p. 194, l. 10, in commenting upon our Lord's statement, that those who are accounted worthy of that world do not marry, but are as the angels, occasion is taken to rebuke those who think that the sons of God who took wives of the daughters of men (Gen. vi. 2) were angels: "If men who become like the angels do not enter into marriages, what shall we say of those who dare to slander even angels on this account?"

S. Ephraem, in his Commentary on Genesis, at I. 48 C, etc., explains that the "sons of God" were the descendants of Seth, and the "sons of men" those of Cain. See also his

[1] Cf. Amos vii. 8, Septuagint version.

remarks at I. 145 B. At II. 455 F, in an argument against the opinions of Manes, he says: "For if angels fallen from heaven propagated the race of giants, let the authors of the fable explain whence, or from what parent sown, the nation of dwarfs has issued." And a few lines further on he says: "Hence once more the fable of the descent of heavenly beings is exploded." Again, at II. 477 B, he says: "Also that overflow of angels which having fallen from heaven some have falsely accused of having longed for marriage with women." And again, at II. 478 A, he says: "But if, moreover, they go further, and contend that angels once gave their attention to the procreation of children, let them reflect that it would not be difficult even to-day for runaway angels to oppress a woman, and beget sons. Here are devils, and here are women; let them spy out whether they are begetting children."

42. In connection with the statement (S. John viii. 56), "Abraham rejoiced to see My day, and he saw it, and was glad," we find assertions that Abraham knew that Isaac on Mount Moriah was a type of the Lamb of God. Thus at Moes. p. 197, l. 12, we have: "Now he saw it, and was glad, because he knew the mystery of the Lamb, the salvation of all nations." And at p. 207, l. 19: "'Abraham saw My day, and was glad,' no doubt by means of the lamb in the tree, which loosed and set Isaac free when bound, even as the Lord loosed the bonds of the Gentiles by means of the cross."

Compare with this the language of S. Ephraem at II. 400 A: "By the Spirit Abraham perceived beforehand the rising of the Son of God put off into the years, and therefore he desired for himself to see His day; he saw it, and was glad. Just so with like desire Isaac burned, but then especially when he saw himself preserved by Him: and truly, if when absent by offering the semblance of Himself He had laid claim to life for him, how much rather did he believe that He would benefit him, if instead of the semblance He had produced the reality." Again, at β, 318 D, he says: "And therefore God showed to Abraham as to a friend a great and wonderful mystery. For by the sacrifice he became a priest;

and He made him a prophet in the figure: and the Most High God made known to him that He also was going to give the only-begotten Son for the world, God having become man in order to save the race of men from error." And a little further on, at 319 A, he adds: "But again the Lord said to the Jews, 'Abraham desired to see My day, and he saw it, and was glad,' evidently that of the suffering in the figure of Isaac on the holy mount."

At B, 537, Dr. Lamy has a note on S. Ephraem's interpretation of the offering of Isaac.

43. In the case of the man born blind, and the clay which Jesus made to anoint his eyes, we find at Moes. p. 198, l. 6: "And He made eyes in this clay, and light sprang up in the ground, even as He made it from the beginning when the shadow of the heavens, or darkness, was scattered over all things, and He gave a command to light, and it was born out of the darkness."

This idea, that Christ formed eyes out of the clay, is expressed by S. Ephraem at II. 431 F: "He is indeed the Son of the highest workman, and possesses the most abundant treasures crammed with all resources; he then that, being blinded, desires eyes, let him approach Him; He will change the clay, out of the clay He will fashion flesh; He will restore light to the eyes." The formation of light in the clay is less distinctly indicated at III. 23 A: "The spittle cast forth from Thy mouth and mixed with earth was clay, surely a very little thing, yet endued with wonderful power: in this clay the blind man found light."

44. At Moes. p. 198, l. 7, quoted in the last parallel, the darkness at the creation is spoken of as being "the shadow of the heavens."

This idea is discussed by S. Ephraem at I. 7 A: "Nor indeed have there been wanting those who have related that the darkness covering the abyss of waters was the shadow of the heavenly bodies. And truly, if the firmament had been placed in position on the first day, this would not seem to have been said either offensively or inappropriately." He then argues at considerable length against this view.

45. At Moes. p. 204, l. 27, reasons are given why Jesus did not Himself open the sepulchre of Lazarus and remove the gravecloths: "But because Lazarus was His friend, He said, 'Open *it* yourselves,' in order that the smell of his stench might touch their nostrils, and 'Loose him yourselves from those things wherewith ye have bound him, that ye may recognise the work of your hands.'"

These ideas are put forth more fully by S. Ephraem in a sermon on the raising of Lazarus. At II. 394 A, he says: "A multitude of Jews was standing round, for many had assembled to console the mournful sisters, when Jesus ordered the stone to be removed. And this indeed was most wisely arranged, for it was of great importance that the care of opening the sepulchre should be given up to the Jews, men distinguished for their faithlessness, in order that the stench exhaling from thence on the removal of that obstacle might seize the nearest and smite them grievously; and this was done in order that by the same act by which they opened the sepulchre they might be punished by the feeling of the offensive smell, and that it should result therefrom, that they should carry the witness of decay in their own garments, as well as behold with their eyes the miracle of the resurrection." Further on, at II. 395 C, he says: "In fact, He who imparted life and loosed the bond of death, did not unwind the wrappings of the bandages, in order that the hands which before had swathed him that was dead and soon to be carried to the sepulchre, from whom they were afterwards removing the bandages, might repress the scoffs of the mockers."

46. At Moes. p. 213, l. 23, in explaining "the abomination of desolation spoken of by Daniel the prophet" (S. Matt. xxiv. 15), it says: "Whilst the city of Jerusalem was frequently demolished but built up again, in this passage the Lord spoke of the complete ruin of its demolition and of the profaning of its sanctuary, since after this it will remain in its ruin, *i.e.* be abandoned to forgetfulness. The Romans set up within the temple their standards, on which was the figure of an eagle, as it was also said, 'Upon the wings of uncleanness and destruction.'" These closing words appear

to be a variation of Dan. ix. 27, and stand thus in the Latin: "Super alis immunditiei et perditionis."

S. Ephraem also has a variation of this verse at II. 222 D, which stands thus in the Latin: "Et super alas abominationis desolatio," *i.e.* "And upon the wings of abomination desolation." Thus both in S. Ephraem and in our Commentary there is a various reading "wings," and in both it is quoted to give force to the application of the passage to the Roman eagle; for S. Ephraem, after quoting it at II. 222 D, continues: "Since the Romans, when Judaea had been brought into their dominion, placed in the temple the eagle and the image of their emperor. And this is what is read, 'When ye shall see the abominable sign spoken of by Daniel the prophet.'"

47. At Moes. p. 218, l. 31, in explaining the parable of the Talents, it says: "'Take away the talent from him,' that is faith, for he did not acquire for himself the righteous life of faith."

Compare with this what S. Ephraem says at γ, 100 F: "For to such a man God says,[1] 'Why declarest thou Mine ordinances, and takest up My covenant through thy mouth?' He therefore commands to be taken from him even that which he seemeth to have. Such an one seemeth to have faith, because he calls himself a Christian; but in works he denies *it*, and is worse than an infidel. Therefore He commands the Holy Spirit to be taken from him which he received in the day of redemption, and which he seemeth to have."

48. At Moes. p. 221, l. 9, it is suggested that our Lord, by dipping in water the sop which He gave to Judas at the Last Supper, deprived it of its consecration, so that it ceased to be sacramental: "Or on that account He dipped the bread, that He might not with the bread give the testament also. He first washed the bread and then gave it to him. The testament was first washed away from this bread, for it had been prepared through the new testament." And again, at l. 22: "In the same way the Lord separated Judas from the disciples through water when He gave him the bread

[1] Ps. l. 16.

dipped in water, because he was not worthy of that bread which was given along with the wine to the twelve disciples. For it was not permissible that he, who was betraying Him to death, should by bread receive Him who saves from death."

The same idea is expressed by S. Ephraem at A, 422, l. 17: "For when Jesus distributed bread to the eleven without distinction, Judas came near to receive as his companions had received who had come near; but Jesus dipped the bread into water, deprived it of consecration, and by this plan distinguished the morsel of Judas. Thenceforth it was known to the Apostles that Judas was he that would betray Jesus. Jesus therefore dipped the bread that its consecration might be taken away, and gave it to Judas." Again, at A, 604, sec. 15, we read: "Dipped bread He gave to him who secretly had died, but the bread was deprived by washing of the medicine of life. He who furnishes life to all blessed this food, which was made the medicine of life in the presence of the eaters. But bread deprived by washing of its blessings this second cursed serpent received." And at A, 624, sec. 16: "Christ washed away the unleavened *bread* from the medicine of life, and gave it to Judas as the medicine of death."

In an interesting note at A, 423, Dr. Lamy says this opinion was peculiar to S. Ephraem.

49. At Moes. p. 221, l. 30, attention is called to the fact that Adam lived many years after the Fall, notwithstanding the warning, "In the day that thou eatest thereof thou shalt surely die" (Gen. ii. 17): "Even as Adam, who, after he ate of that tree, lived many years, although for transgression of the commandment he was numbered with the dead; for God spake thus, 'In the day that thou eatest thou shalt die.'" And at p. 268, l. 14: "But like as it was said to Adam, 'In the day that thou eatest thou shalt die the death,' and in that day whereon he ate he did not die, but received the pledges of death, when he appeared naked, and was despoiled of his glory, and constantly foresaw death and feared it; in the same way we also have received life in Christ."

S. Ephraem has a paragraph on this subject at I. 137 D, headed: "Why did Adam not die according to God's sentence on the same day whereon he ate of the tree?" And at B, 500, sec. 9, he briefly says: "The mortal tasted it and lived."

50. At Moes. p. 221, l. 34, we find a peculiar mode adopted of reckoning the four hundred years of the sojourn of Abraham's descendants in Egypt, namely, from the day when God foretold it to Abraham: "and as that [saying], 'For four hundred years may thy seed be in Egypt' (Gen. xv. 13); for these years are reckoned from that day whereon these words were spoken."

This is a singular method of computation, considering that the Israelites did not begin their sojourn in Egypt for more than two hundred years from this time; nor did their oppression there begin for nearly two hundred and eighty years, according to the received chronology. Yet we find the same calculation employed by S. Ephraem more than once. It is to be noted that the time in question is called four hundred years at Gen. xv. 13 and Acts vii. 6; but at Ex. xii. 40, 41 and Gal. iii. 17 it is called four hundred and thirty years. The first three of these passages are against this computation, as they all speak of the whole time as one of affliction in Egypt. But the last supports it, speaking of the law as *four hundred and thirty years after the promise*. This, then, is probably the source[1] of the theory. At I. 158 C, after quoting the promise, S. Ephraem goes on: "I am of opinion that this total of years, to which thirty years must also be added, does not include descendants of Abraham only, but also Abraham himself. Wherefore into this calculation there ought to come fifteen years of Abraham, sixty of Isaac, and a hundred and thirty of Jacob, in which space of time they dwelt in their own land." And at I. 158 E, he shows how he makes up the number, namely, from the promise to the birth of Isaac, fifteen years; from thence to the birth of Jacob, sixty years; to the birth of Levi, eighty-one years; to Kohath, forty; to Amram, sixty-eight; to Moses, eighty; and to the Exodus, eighty; making a total of four hundred and twenty-four, not four hundred and thirty as there stated. Then at I. 195 C, he states that the time of residence in

[1] See the reference to S. Paul at I. 158 E.

Egypt, during which seventy souls, including little children, increased to six hundred thousand armed men, was two hundred and twenty-five years. At I. 201 B, he describes the Israelites just before their deliverance as calling to mind God's covenant with Abraham, counting up the intervening years, and finding that the four hundred had already been exceeded by thirty years, whereupon they implore God for deliverance, and are heard. A further allusion to an excess of thirty years is made at I. 201 E. Turning to I. 214 A, we find: "Moreover, their exile in Egypt was prolonged unto four hundred and thirty-six years; but this number of years must not be reckoned from the entrance of Jacob, but from the day whereon God entered into a covenant with Abraham."

51. At Moes. p. 237, l. 26, we read: "In the month Arech [*i.e.* Nisan] the flowers burst their folds and come forth, and, leaving their folds naked and empty, they become the crown of others. So also in the month Arech the High Priest tore his priesthood asunder, and left it naked and empty; and the priesthood passed over and was conferred upon our Saviour."

Compare with this the words of S. Ephraem at B, 762, sec. 8: "In Nisan the flowers burst forth from their cups; they are plucked and leave the stem naked, and serve for crowning others. As Nisan, so his feast. In it indeed the High Priest rent his clothes; and the priesthood fled from him, and left him stripped, and spread itself out upon our Saviour."

At Moes. p. 256, l. 33, and Eph. A, 682, l. 4, the High Priest is again said to have divested himself of the priesthood when he rent his clothes at the trial of Jesus.

52. At Moes. p. 239, l. 16, we find: "And in the crown of thorns prepared in mockery of Him the opposite took place; and their unfaithfulness was turned to good, clearly in order that the enemy might be overcome by it; for the Lord by means of His crown took away the curses of the first Adam. 'Thorns and thistles shall it bring forth to thee.'"

The same idea is expressed by S. Ephraem at A, 482, l. 28: "They plaited for Him a crown of thorns, thus bearing witness to the curse of Adam. They gathered choice thorns and placed them on His head. On His head the curse was extinguished and removed from the face of the earth; for immediately the thorns touched His head, the curse was transformed into a blessing; and the curse of the thorns no longer existed, because it was entwined on the head of the Son." At B, 618, sec. 39, in a passage already quoted under No. 38, the idea is much the same, though the nature of Adam's curse is not expressly mentioned.

53. A similarity of thought is noticeable in some remarks made upon the dying thief. At Moes. p. 244, l. 32, we read: "He poured forth His treasures freely before him" (thesauros suos gratis coram eo effudit).

And at A, 688, sec. 7, S. Ephraem has: "And He opened His treasure before him" (et aperuit coram eo thesaurum suum).

54. At Moes. p. 249, l. 13, it says: "Because death had entered through the ear of Eve, life entered through the ear of Mary; and because a man had contracted debts through a tree, Christ came and paid them through a tree." At p. 49, l. 4, the idea that the conception of Jesus was due to the message of the angel Gabriel entering through the ear of Mary, is thus expressed: "Observe that, in fact, the angel, who came to cast it down like seed in the ears of Mary, began to scatter the seed thus with a loud voice, 'Health *be* with thee,' he saith, 'thou blessed among women.'"

Compare with these passages the language of S. Ephraem at II. 324 E: "O fact to be admired, Thy conception from Mary! For as death entered by the narrow bend of the ear, and poured itself in, so into the young ear of Mary life penetrated, and poured itself. And just as a tree brought on death, so another tree brought back life, that death might conquer by the one, and life might triumph by the other." At III. 607 E, also, we read: "In the beginning the serpent, after taking possession of the ears of Eve, spread out the poison from thence into her whole body. To-day Mary has received from her ears the restorer of everlasting happiness." So at B, 302, sec. 5, we read: "After the priest became dumb before the voice, and the Word came into the ear into which the will of the speaker expressed it," etc. See also B, 516, l. 26; 570, sec. 6; and 608, secs. 7–10.

55. At Moes. p. 252, l. 27, it is implied that Moses held up his hands and his rod in the form of a cross during the battle with the Amalekites: "By the rod of Moses, a type of the cross, nations were forewarned: the Egyptians learnt the proof of the cross in the signs of the plagues, and the Amalekites in the battle. While they were yet untrained, they were ruled by a type of the cross; but when the cross had appeared to them, by its teaching and arrangement they were found as if enlightened and wise." The allusion at p. 262, l. 1, is less definite: "God held the arms of Moses spread out, until his enemies had fallen and perished. The Jews also stretched out the hands of the Son of God on the tree of the cross."

This thought is more precisely expressed by S. Ephraem in speaking of the same battle at I. 219 D: "Moses, moreover, with hands outstretched, and wearing at the same time the rod applied to his breast, exhibited a manifest image of the cross."

56. At Moes. p. 253, l. 13, it says: "They did not recognise that body, whose shadow covered them in the wilderness. By the tree,[1] its image, their water was made sweet." And at l. 21: "All the prophets had shown only the likeness of his beauties; for the image of the rod was not perfect as a sign of the cross; and the beauty of the tree, which sweetened the waters, was not perfect as the beauty of that tree by which the Gentiles were made sweet and gentle."

The tree that sweetened the waters is spoken of by S. Ephraem as a type of the cross at I. 218 A: "This tree shadowed forth the Lord's cross, by whose touch the bitterness of the Gentiles was marked beforehand to be cured." Also at II. 435 A, he says: "The people, indeed, and the peoples wandering through deserts, contracted bitterness, and were forsaken; they became sweet by means of the cross; for the Crucified redeemed them both."

[1] Cf. Ex. xv. 25.

57. At Moes. p. 256, l. 29, we read: "Or in the veil that was rent He set forth an image of the demolition of the temple, because His Spirit had gone out of it. And, because the High Priest had unjustly rent his garment, the Spirit rent the veil, that in this way through created things it might show the daring and pride of the Jews. Because the former had rent the priesthood, and divested himself of it, the latter also rent the veil, and departing took all things with Him." The rending of the veil of the temple is again ascribed to the Holy Ghost at p. 257, l. 6: "For the rent sea the Spirit rent the veil." And again, at p. 257, l. 23: "And the Spirit, seeing his beloved suspended and mocked, seized the veil, the ornament of the temple, and rent it." At p. 268, l. 10, there may be an allusion to the same idea in the words: "The wind rent the veil."

S. Ephraem in like manner says, at III. 189 F: "The Spirit rent the veil of the temple, that the unbeliever might rend his own heart." And again, at γ, 246 B: "Again, the Holy Spirit, who is in the Father, beholding the beloved Son on the tree of the cross, rent the well-ordered veil of the temple from the top to the bottom, and immediately went out in the form of a dove."

58. At Moes. p. 257, l. 19, the answer of Jesus, "If these should hold their peace, the stones would immediately cry out" (S. Luke xix. 40), is represented as receiving a fulfilment at the Crucifixion, when all forsook Him and were silent; but the rocks were rent: "They held their peace, and the stones spoke, as the Lord had foretold."

The same thought is expressed by S. Ephraem at B, 724, sec. 10: "In the time of praise and confession, when the deaf and the dumb glorified the Lord, and the closed mouths gave praise, the deniers held their peace. But, because the former held their peace, the stones cried out, as it had been promised. The rocks of the sepulchres were rent, and increased the praise; the earth, being agitated, uttered a cry upon its inhabitants, who refused praise; the veil by its cleavage rent their hardened ears."

59. At Moes. p. 259, l. 6, we are told that the rods

which Jacob set before Laban's flocks were a type of the cross: "Jacob the servant also showed the tree [*i.e.* the cross], which was united with water."

S. Ephraem expresses the same thought more fully at A, 64, sec. 1: "Jacob's sheep leaped up and surrounded the spring of water. In the waters they put on the appearances of the tree that was dipped in the waters. These were symbols and types of the cross, wherein the meaning of figures is declared. In the rods a figure was expressed, and in the sheep similitudes. The cross was figured by the rods, and souls by the sheep. Jacob's tree was a symbol of the tree of the cross, and his flock a symbol of our flock. The sheep of Christ leap up and surround the baptistery. In the waters they put on the form of the beautiful and living cross, whereby the world is rendered pure, and by whose sign it is sealed."

60. At Moes. p. 262, l. 23, we find the opinion which some early writers based upon Ps. lxxiv. 12 and Ezek. xxxviii. 12, that Jerusalem was in the middle of the earth: "They[1] say that Jerusalem is in the midst of the earth because of the just God, for there He gave the law, whose rays sent forth illuminated all the ends of the earth. And because His justice was there, His mercy also set up the cross there, that He might spread out His arms in all directions, and receive and embrace the souls and spirits of the whole world."

The same idea that Jerusalem was so situated, and therefore convenient as a centre for spreading the gospel, is expressed by S. Ephraem at III. 196 D: "He placed Jerusalem[2] in the midst, that the whole creation might perceive it" [*i.e.* the gospel].

61. At Moes. p. 277, l. 9, we read: "For a few words the Lord justified the publican, and made him go down with the praise of the heavenly sons that rejoice over them that repent."

[1] Apparently Marcionites, from the mention of the "just God."
[2] Latin, "the Hebrews"; but we follow here the translation of Mr. Morris from the Syriac.

The idea that the publican, who "went down to his house justified rather than the other" (Luke xviii. 14), was one of those repentant sinners over whom angels are said to rejoice (Luke xv. 10), seems to have been in the mind of S. Ephraem when he wrote at γ, 589 D: "And whilst they hear the evangelist, how that that parable of the Pharisee and publican praying in the temple was brought out to those who, trusting in themselves as righteous, despised others, they shut at once the hearing of their ears and the observation of their eyes, and are most severe condemners of others' sins of a hundred pence. But whether they will or not, they hear from the very searcher of hearts and decider of events, how that even the very holders of the key of knowledge enter not in, and suffer not others to enter. For in the same Gospel they read that the angels in heaven rejoice more over one sinner that repents, than over ninety and nine just persons which need no repentance."

THE EPHRAEM FRAGMENTS, OR THE PORTIONS OF THE DIATESSARON CITED BY S. EPHRAEM THE SYRIAN IN THE COURSE OF A COMMENTARY WHICH HE WROTE UPON IT.

THESE fragments are here presented throughout in the order in which they occur in the Arabic *Diatessaron*. References to the corresponding passages of the English version of the Arabic are given in the margin to the left; and in the margin to the right are placed the numbers of the pages of Dr. Moesinger's Latin version of Ephraem's Commentary at which the fragments are to be found. By observing the sequence of these numbers, the reader can see for himself where Ephraem quotes in a different order from the Arabic. In a few instances this may be due to the existence of a different order in his copy of the *Diatessaron*; but in general it arises from his having quoted a passage from a distant part of the *Diatessaron* by way of illustrating a point or giving force to an argument. Thus at xii. 52 we find 63 in the midst of a series steadily increasing from 88 to 94; and, on referring to Moes. p. 63, we find that this fragment, containing the words, "Peace be to the house," is quoted to illustrate the beatitude, "Blessed are the peacemakers," etc., and does not intimate that the Instructions to the Twelve occurred in the middle of the beatitudes. In this case the fragment is quoted again in its true order at p. 92.

The entire text of these fragments has been revised by Professor Robinson, who has examined both the Armenian MSS., and has expressed his willingness to be responsible for the renderings given to them here, as well as for such portions of the notes as deal with the Armenian text. A brief explanation of the reasons for a particular reading is sometimes offered in the notes; but in a few cases, where the reasons were of a complex nature, or involved points of controversy too lengthy for a note, it has been thought better to say nothing.

Brackets are used in this translation as follows : < > enclose words not in the Armenian, but almost certain to have been in Tatian; [ ] words in the Armenian, but idiomatic and not implying a various reading;) words in the Armenian, but probably a paraphrase and not an actual quotation. Words not in the Armenian, but necessary in English to complete the sentence, are printed in italics. In very obvious cases, however, these indications are omitted.

In the notes Codex A signifies the MS. from which the Armenian text was printed in A.D. 1836, and Codex B the MS. written by Nerses. Simple page references thus, p. 13, refer to Dr. Moesinger's work; simple references to chapter and verses thus, vi. 14, refer to the left hand margin of this translation; similar references with the prefix "*Diat.*" apply to the English text of the Arabic *Diatessaron*; Arm. Vulg. means the Armenian Vulgate.

Diatessaron.   Moesinger.

1 1   In the beginning was the Word, <and>   3, 4, 5, 168
       [itself] the Word was with God, and the Word
   2 was God. The same was in the beginning   5
   3 with God. All things were made by him;
     and without him was not anything made.
   4 And that which was made, by him was life,
   5 and the life was the light of men. And   5, 6
     [itself] the light was shining in darkness; and
     darkness overcame it not.
   6 But[1] there was in the days of Herod, king   6, 7
     of Judaea, a certain priest, and his name was
   7 Zacharias, and his wife Elizabeth. . . . They   7
     were blameless in all their habitation . . .
14,15 thy prayer is heard before God. . . . And   8, 12, 14 : 7
     there shall be joy and gladness unto thee.
  16 . . . and wine and strong drink he shall not   7
  18 drink . . . with the power and spirit of   37, 14
     Elijah to turn the hearts of *the* fathers
     to *the* children . . . he shall make ready
  19 for the Lord a perfected people. . . . How   8, 9, 13
  25 should this be? . . . Elizabeth hid herself   14, 15
  27 five months . . . in the sixth month . . .   15
  29[2]Health *be* with thee, thou blessed among   49

---

[1] Codex B omits, "But;" the Arm. Vulg. has, "And;" there is no corresponding Greek.

[2] At p. 16 Ephraem cites as a quotation concerning Joseph and Mary: "they were both of the house of David." Moesinger thinks he is referring to *Diat.* i. 28; but Zahn thinks it more likely that he has in view *Diat.* ii. 12, 13, with a slightly different reading from our own. In his Commentary on 2 Tim. ii. 8, Ephraem again cites the same words.

Diatessaron.	Moesinger.

1 33 women. . . . the Lord God shall give unto 15, 16
   36 him the throne of David his father. . . . The 255–6
      Spirit shall come, and the power of the
      Highest shall overshadow thee: because that
      which shall be born of thee, shall surely be
   37 called *the* Son of God. And Elizabeth thy 15, 16
      sister hath conceived in her old age; <and> 18
   39 this is the sixth month with her. . . . Mary 15
      saith, Behold, I am the handmaid of the
      Lord: be it unto me according to thy word.
   40 . . . Mary arose and went (to Elizabeth) . . . 17
   42, 43 <the babe> leaped for joy. . . . Blessed art 19: 19, 49
      thou among women, and blessed is the fruit
   44 of thy womb. <And> whence is this to 17
      me, that the mother of my Lord should come
   46 to me? . . . Blessed is she, which believed, 17, 18
      that there should be a fulfilment of all the
      words, which were with her from the Lord.
   47, 49 . . . (Bless the Lord, O my soul.) . . . from 18: 17, 18
      henceforth all generations shall call me
   57 blessed. . . . (after three months) she re- 18
   64 turned to her own house. . . . (The fingers 12
      wrote on the tablet,) His name *is* John.
   77 . . . And thou, child, shalt be called the 7
      prophet of the Highest: thou shalt go before
      the face of the Lord to prepare his ways,
   78 to give perfect knowledge of salvation. . . .
   79 whereby the sun[1] from on high shall appear 20, 30
   80 unto us, <to give light to them>, which sat in
      darkness and in the shadow of death, <and>
      to guide our feet into the way of peace.

2 1   The generation of Jesus Christ was on this
      wise: When his mother Mary was espoused
      to Joseph, and before she was given to a
      husband,[2] she was found with child of the

---

[1] "Sun;" so in the Arm. Vulg. here. At p. 30 Ephraem quotes it thus: "The sunrise from on high shall give light." Cod. B reads, "hath appeared." After "unto us" Cod. A adds, "to lighten our darkness."

[2] "She . . . husband" differs from the Arm. Vulg.

Diatessaron.		Moesinger.
2	2 Holy Ghost. Joseph, because he was a just man, was not[1] willing to make Mary a public example, and was minded to put her away	22
	3 quietly. . . . (the) angel appeared unto him, and saith, Fear not to take Mary. . . .	22–3
	5, 6 (Isaiah the prophet, that he saith,) Behold,	22
	7 the virgin shall conceive . . . he took her.	25
	8 . . . He dwelt with her in purity,[2] until	23, 25–6
	11 she brought forth the first-born. . . . They were written,[3] each in his own city. . . .	26
	19 Unto you is born this day a Saviour, who is	27
	22 the Anointed of[4] the Lord. . . . Glory to God in the highest, and peace on earth, good	27, 63
	31 hope[5] to the sons of men. . . . Every first-born, that openeth the womb, shall be called	25
	34 holy to the Lord. . . . And it was revealed[6] unto him by the Holy Ghost, that he should not taste[7] death, until he should see the	226
	36 Lord Christ. . . . He took up (our Lord)	
	37 into his arms . . . and said, Lord, now lettest thou thy servant depart in peace	28, 226
	38 according to thy word. . . . Behold, mine	28
	39 eyes have seen thy mercy, which thou hast	
	42 prepared before all Gentiles.[8] . . . Behold, this *child* standeth for falling and for rising	28, 119
	43 again, <and> for a sign of contradiction even in thine own soul: thou shalt cause a sword to pass away.[9]	28–9, 269

[1] Cod. B has, "and was not." "Quietly," as in the Curetonian Syriac.
[2] So in the Curetonian Syriac; the Arm. Vulg. has, "He knew her not."
[3] For "were written" the Arm. Vulg. has, "entered into the census." For ver. 12, 13, see note at i. 29.
[4] This reading is found in the Jerusalem Syriac.
[5] This is supported by Aphraates and the Arabic. Cf. *Diat.* ii. 22. Cod. A has words which may mean, "hope of good things to the sons of men," or, "hope to the good sons of men."
[6] Lit. "he received warning;" but the same as the Arm. Vulg.
[7] Cod. B has, "see."
[8] Arm. Vulg. has, "peoples." Eusebius, *On the Psalms*, p. 223, has, "Gentiles."
[9] So Cod. B; the text in Cod. A is corrupt. The reading as here given,

Diatessaron.		Moesinger.
3	3, 8[1] ... Jerusalem was moved ... I also	208 : 30, 31
	11 will come *and* worship him. ... and they	31
	opened their treasures, and presented unto	
	him an offering,[2] gold, and myrrh, and frank-	
	12 incense. And they were warned in a vision,	30
	that they should not return to (him). ...	
	15 Then was fulfilled the true word, which was	32, 36
	spoken by the prophet, *who* saith, Out of	
	16 Egypt will I call my son. And when	32, 34
	Herod saw that he was mocked of the wise	
	men, he was exceeding wroth, and sent *and*	
	17 slew every infant child. ... The word was	32
	fulfilled, which was spoken by Jeremiah the	
	18 prophet. In Rama a voice was cried[3];	32–4
	Rachel was weeping for her sons, because	
	23 they were not. ... He shall be called a	36
	32 Nazarene. ... Behold,[4] I and thy father,	24, 40
	sorrowing *and* grieving, were going about and	
	33 seeking thee. ... I must be in my Father's	40
	35 house. ... (she) kept everything in her	52
	50 heart. ... He came unto his own, and his	5
	53 own received him not. ... And the Word	6, 37
	56 was made flesh, and dwelt in us. ... For	7, 36, 55
	the law was given by Moses; grace and	
	truth[5] came by Jesus.	
4	1 No man hath been able to see God at any	3

which is supported by Ephraem's comments, is apparently the result of some confusion in the Syriac. Ephraem adds, as from "the Greek," "thoughts from many hearts shall be revealed." At p. 269 the passage is quoted quite differently, "and through thine own soul altogether shall a sword pass."

[1] At p. 162 there is a reference to iii. 5, but not a quotation. Ephraem there speaks of the scribes as saying, "out of the town of Bethlehem shall he arise."

[2] So in the Curetonian Syriac. In the Arm. Vulg. "offerings;" so here in Cod. B.

[3] In the Arm. Vulg. "lamented."

[4] Ephraem, by a curious displacement, comments on this section immediately before *Diat.* iv. 12.

[5] In one passage (p. 36) Ephraem, instead of "grace and truth," has, "and the truth of it," *i.e.* of the law; Cod. B, however, has, "and the truth of them," *i.e.* of the signs already mentioned in his remarks.

Diatessaron.   Moesinger.

	time; but the Only-begotten, which is in¹	
	the bosom of the Father, he declared to us	
4	2 concerning him. The Jews sent unto John,	37
	3 and say unto him, Who art thou? He	
	confessed *and* saith, I am not the Christ.	
	4 They say unto him, Art thou Elijah? He	37–8
	10 saith, No. ... and the latchet of his shoes	192
	12 I am not worthy to bear. ... And John	40, 101
	17 was clad in raiment of hair. ... God is	40
	able of these stones to raise up children unto	
	18 Abraham. ... Behold, the axe is come to	39
	25 the root of the trees. ... I am not worthy	41, 99
	29 to unloose the latchet of his shoes. ... And	41
	Jesus himself was about thirty years of age	
	at the time when he came² to be baptized of	
	30 John. ... Behold, this is the Lamb of God;	41, 43, 99, 101, 103, 208, 238
	this is he that cometh³ to take away the sin	
	31 of the world. ... After me shall come a	192
	33 man, who [indeed] is before *me*. ... I have	99, 104
	34 need to be baptized of thee. ... Suffer it	41–2
	now, that we may fulfil all righteousness.⁴	
38,39	... This is my beloved Son.⁵ ... (John	99 : 128
	bears record,) I saw the Spirit in the likeness	
	of the body of a dove, that it descended, and	
	40 rested upon him. <And> I knew him not:	155
	but he that sent me ... the same said unto	151
	43 me. ... Immediately the Holy⁶ Spirit took	42–3

---

¹ "In:" so the Arm. Vulg.; but immediately below Ephraem gives, as a quotation, "He was begotten from the bosom of his Father."

² "When he came" implies a variant ἐρχόμενος for ἀρχόμενος. Cf. Clem. Alex. p. 407, and Iren. p. 148, as quoted by Tischendorf.

³ So at p. 41, but the form of the quotation varies elsewhere.

⁴ The word is in the plural, as in the Arm. Vulg.

⁵ Ephraem's comment (p. 43), "By the shining of the light which was upon the waters, and by the voice which came from heaven," etc., shows that he was acquainted with the story of the fire on the Jordan, which is found in two Old Latin MSS., but leaves it uncertain whether he learnt it from the *Diatessaron* or from other sources. It is not in the Arabic.

⁶ So Cod. D at Mark i. 12; cf. Peschito and the Curetonian Syriac at Matt. iv 1.

Diatessaron.		Moesinger.
	and led him out into a desert, to be tempted	
4 44	by Satan. . . . And after forty days,[1] that he	44
45	fasted, he hungered. . . . If thou be the Son	44–7
	of God, command these stones, that they be	
46	made bread. . . . Man shall not live by bread	46
	alone, but by every word that proceedeth out	
47	of the mouth of God. . . . He brought *him*	44
	and took *him and* set him on a corner of	
48	the temple, <and> saith unto him, Cast thy-	44, 47
	self down,[2] for it is written, They shall keep	
	thee, lest at any time thy foot be dashed	
50	against a stone. . . . Again the devil brought	45
	him *and* took *him* into an exceeding high	
51	mountain . . . and saith unto him, The king-	45, 47
	doms and the glory of them will I give thee.[3]	
	All these kingdoms are mine; to me it hath	45
	been given: I have authority over all this.	
52	Thou shalt fall upon thy face, and humbly	
	worship me.	
5 1, 2	. . . Get thee behind *me*, Satan, . . . he	49
3	departed from him for a time. . . . Angels	
5	came and ministered unto him. . . . Behold,	197
10	the Lamb of God.[4] . . . We have found	50
15	Christ. . . . Can it be, that any good thing	
16	should come out of Nazareth? . . . Behold,	
	indeed a scribe, an Israelite, in whom is no	
19	guile. . . . If thou shalt believe, thou shalt	185
22	see greater things than these.[5] . . . there	52

[1] Omitting, "and forty nights;" see note to *Diat.* iv. 44.

[2] Lit. "from above down."

[3] Ephraem cites these passages in a different order from the Arabic, thus: (p. 45) "Mine are all these kingdoms. . . . To me it hath been given. . . . I have authority over all this. . . . Thou shalt fall upon thy face and humbly worship me." . . . (p. 47) "The kingdoms and the glory of them will I give thee."

[4] Ephraem alludes to this event as follows (p. 99): "When, it says, his other disciples heard that he was speaking concerning our Lord, and they saw Him, they left John without sorrow and followed him.'

[5] See note to *Diat.* v. 20.

Diatessaron.   Moesinger.

      was a marriage-feast¹ in Cana of Galilee.
5 24 . . . his mother saith unto him, Son,² they
  25 have no wine here. Jesus saith unto her,
     Woman, what have I to do with thee? my
  26 time has not come on. She saith unto the
     servants, Whatsoever my son saith unto you,
  31 do. . . . Every man setteth on first the good   55
     wine, and then that which is worse.³ . . .
  32 (For a beginning of his signs he made wine).   132
  35 . . . he⁴ entered, as his custom was, into   129
     their synagogues on the sabbath day.⁵ . . .
43,53 The times are fulfilled. . . . we have toiled 57 : 59
  55 all the night.⁶ . . . they beckoned unto their 59
     partners.
6 5 . . . His disciples were baptizing. . . .   58
  13 He *must* increase, but I *must* decrease.⁷ . . . 30, 105
  17 And not by measure gave he to his Son.⁸   105
  38 The land of Zabulon and Nephthali, the   6
     way of the sea, and the passage of the
  39 river Jordan, Galilee of the Gentiles. A   6, 51
     people which sat⁹ in darkness, saw a great
  42 light. . . . Thou art the Holy One of   113
     God.
7 16 . . . Our Lord saw their faith, *and* saith 59, 60
  28 unto him, Thy sins be forgiven thee. . . . The 61
     Pharisees and scribes murmur and say, Why
     do ye eat and drink with publicans and
  29 sinners? . . . They that are whole have no
     need of a physician, but they that are sick.
  30 . . . And I came not to call the righteous, but
  32 sinners. . . . The companions of the bride-

---

¹ As in the Arm. Vulg.: Ephraem (p. 53) says: "The Greek writes, He sat down and the wine failed."

² "Son" is found in the Old Latin versions *e* and *l*, and in Amb.

³ Lit. "the bad;" but the same is in the Arm. Vulg.

⁴ Cod. B has, "after these things he entered," etc. Cf. Appendix

⁵ This clause is quoted by Ephraem immediately after xvii. 37.

⁶ Ephraem also mentions the "two ships."

⁷ Lit. "To him to increase, and to me to decrease."

⁸ Cod. B has, "sons."   ⁹ At p. 51 Ephraem has, "walked."

Diatessaron.		Moesinger.

		groom cannot fast, while the bridegroom is	
7	37	with them. . . . began to pluck the ears,	
	38	to rub and to eat. . . . Behold, thy disciples	
		do on the sabbath day that which is not	
	39	lawful to do. . . . Have ye never read what	148
	40	David did, how he ate the shewbread, which	
		it was not lawful for him to eat, neither for	
	41	them that were with him. . . . The sabbath	62
	42	was made for man . . . their priests in the	
		temple break the sabbath, and are blame-	
	45	less. . . . Therefore the Son of man is lord	148
		of the sabbath.	
8,	14, 17	Thou art[1] the Son of God . . . much[2]	235 : 83
		power was going forth from him, and was	
	26	healing all. . . . Jesus lifted up his eyes on	62
	27	them, and began to say, Blessed are the	62, 64
	28	poor in their spirits. . . . Blessed are they	63
		that weep; for they shall laugh.[3] . . .	
	29, 30	Blessed are the meek.[4] . . . Blessed are they	62 : 63
		that hunger and thirst after righteousness.	
	32	. . . Blessed are they that are pure in *their*	63
	33	hearts; for they shall see God. Blessed are	
		the peacemakers; for they shall be called	
	34	sons of God. Blessed are they that are	
		persecuted for righteousness' sake. . . .	
	36	Rejoice ye, and be exceeding glad; for great	64
		is your reward in heaven, and in that day	
	37	rejoice. . . . Woe unto you, *that are* rich:	
	40, 41	. . . Ye are the salt of the earth. . . . Ye	
	43	are the light of the world.[5] . . . Let your	219
		light shine before men, that they may see	
		your good works, and glorify your Father,	

[1] Cod. B has, "the Christ, the Son of God."

[2] So in the Arm. Vulg. Ephraem prefaces this with, "But the evangelist writes."

[3] So in the Arm. Vulg. at Luke vi. 21.

[4] Ephraem quotes this beatitude before the preceding one, as if his *Diatessaron* had it in the order of the Curetonian Syriac and Aphraates.

[5] Ephraem puts this clause just before "Ye are the salt of the earth;" but he has probably altered the order to suit his previous remarks.

Diatessaron.   Moesinger.

8 46 which is in heaven. . . . I am not come to   64, 170
destroy the law or the prophets, but to
48 fulfil.[1] . . . And whosoever shall break one   65
49 of the commandments.[2] . . . Except your   65, 66
righteousness be found more than that of the
scribes and Pharisees, ye cannot enter into
50 the kingdom of heaven. This ye have   66
heard, that it was said: Do not kill; for he
51 that killeth is in danger of judgment. But   66, 68
I say unto you: He that calleth his brother
52 senseless.[3] . . . When thou hast offered thy   65
gift upon the altar, leave thy gift and go,
57 be reconciled.[4] . . . Ye have heard that it   66
58 was said: Do not commit adultery. But
I say unto you: Whosoever looketh and
lusteth, hath committed adultery.[5] . . .

9 6   Ye have heard that it was said: An eye   9, 69
7 for an eye.[6] . . . But I say unto you: Re-   69
sist not evil [7] at all; <but> he that smiteth   {65, 69, 70,
thy cheek, offer to him the other side also.   133, 223
32 . . . Our Father, which art in heaven. . . .   271
40 But thou, when thou fastest, wash thy face,   71
41 and anoint thine head,[8] <that> thou appear not unto men to fast . . . thy Father,
which seeth in secret, shall reward thee openly.
42, 46 Fear not, little flock. . . . Where your 127: 72, 170

---

[1] Ephraem shortly after quotes Luke xvi. 17 as if it followed at this point; but as the Arabic has at viii. 47 the similar passage Matt. v. 18, and places the former at xiv. 9, near where Ephraem places Luke xvi. 16, that was probably the order in Ephraem's *Diatessaron*.

[2] Ephraem adds, "of the New Testament," as if these words formed part of the *Diatessaron*.

[3] At p. 68 Ephraem has, "that saith to his brother, Vile or senseless *one*." The word here rendered "senseless" is that used for "Raca" in the Arm. Vulg.

[4] Cod. B, "first be reconciled."

[5] Ephraem here adds, "If thy hand or thy foot offend thee;" but cf. note at xxv. 18.

[6] Ephraem (p. 65) quotes twice, "a blow for a blow," as if it formed part of the text before him. Cf. *Ep. Polyc.* 2, γρόνθον ἀντὶ γρόνθου.

[7] Lit. "the evil," as in the Arm. Vulg.

[8] The same transposition of these clauses is found in the Arabic.

Diatessaron.   Moesinger.

       treasure is, there will your hearts be also.
9 48 . . . If the light that is in thee be darkness.   72
10 13   . . . Judge not, that ye be not judged;[1]
       forgive, and it shall be forgiven you. Con-
  16 demn[2] not. . . . He that hath, to him shall   72–3
       be given: and he that hath not, from him
       shall they take even that which he thinketh[3]
  18 he hath. . . . There is no disciple better[4]   223
  21 than his master. . . . Give not that which   73
  31 is holy[5] to *the* dogs. . . . Whatsoever ye   224
       would that the sons of men should do unto
  33 you, even so also do ye. . . . Strait is the   263
  34 gate,[6] . . . who come to you in lambs' clothing,   94
       and inwardly they are ravening wolves. . . .
  43 I know you not. . . .   97, 216
11 5,6 He came with the elders of the people,   74
       and besought him (that he would not dis-
   9 dain to come and save his servant. And
  10 when he undertook to go,) he saith unto
       him, Lord, trouble not thyself, but say *it* by
  12 a word, and he shall be healed. . . . And,
       when he heard this, he marvelled. . . . I
       have not found so great faith even in any one
  14 in Israel. . . . They shall go forth into outer
  25 darkness.[7] . . . I also[8] will follow thee. . . .
  26 Foxes have their resting-places;[9] and the
       Son of man hath no place where to lay his

---

[1] A different word is used in the second place, which may also mean "condemned;" but it is not the same as in "Condemn not."

[2] The same word as in the Arm. Vulg. (Luke vi. 37).

[3] Cf. Luke viii. 18, margin, and the Revised Version. See also xliii. 37.

[4] So in the Arm. Vulg. at Luke vi. 40. Cod. B has, "greater than the master."

[5] Lit. "holiness;" but the same as in the Arm. Vulg.

[6] But at p. 118, "Strait and narrow is the way."

[7] This is followed by, "The virgin's son met the son of the widow," showing that the raising of the widow's son at Nain followed here in Ephraem's copy, as it does in the Arabic.

[8] So in the Arm. Vulg. at Matt. viii. 19. Cod. B omits, "also."

[9] Or, "dens"—not the same word as in the Arm. Vulg.

Diatessaron.   Moesinger.

11 35 head . . . he rebuked the wind, and it   75
    47 ceased. . . . And the devils began to be-
    seech him, that he would not drive them
    out of that place, and would not send them
    49 into Gehenna before the time . . . and,
    when they had entered into the swine, im-
    mediately they choked them.
12 3 . . . he sent (the man) away, saying,   76
 4, 13 Go *and* preach . . . fearing and trembling   90
    behind him, she touched the fringe of his
    15 garment . . . and she knew in herself, that   84
    16 she was healed of her plague. . . . Who   78, 81
    17 touched my clothes? . . . multitudes sur-   77,80,86,89
    round thee and press thee, and sayest thou,
    18 Who touched me? . . . I know that some   81, 83, 88
    one hath touched me, <for> I know that
    much[1] power hath gone forth from me. . . .
    19 But when she saw that this also was not   80
    21 hid from him . . . Go in peace: thy faith
    23 hath made thee whole . . . believe, and thy   88, 89
    30 daughter shall live[2] . . . and he com-   90
    43 manded to give her food to eat. . . . He
    sent them forth two *and* two after his own
    44 likeness.[3] . . . Go not into the way of the   91
    45 Gentiles[4] . . . to the lost sheep of the
    47 house of Israel . . . freely ye have received,
48, 49 freely also[5] give. Possess[6] no gold <nor>
    50 silver . . . a staff . . . no shoes, no stick,[7]
    52 but sandals. . . . Into whatsoever house ye   63, 92
    54 enter, first say, Peace[8] to the house . . . shake   93

---

[1] "Much power" differs from the Arm. Vulg. here; but cf. viii. 17 and note.

[2] This clause must have occurred earlier in Ephraem's *Diatessaron*, as he distinctly implies (p. 88) that the woman heard it before her cure.

[3] Cf. xv. 15.

[4] The mention of Samaritans also is implied at p. 95.

[5] So in the Arm. Vulg.   [6] So in the Arm. Vulg. of Matt. x. 9.

[7] Cf. note to *Diat.* xii. 49.

[8] At p. 92 Cod. B has, "give peace," or "salutation" (the Armenian does not distinguish between these two words here).

Diatessaron.   Moesinger.

12 55 off the dust of your feet. . . . It shall be 94
more tolerable for the land of Sodom.[1] . . .

13 1   Now, behold, I send you forth as lambs[2] 91
in the midst of wolves; be ye then innocent 94
 2 as doves, and wise as serpents.[3] Beware of
men : . . . they will deliver you up. . . .
 8 Into whatsoever city ye enter, and they receive you not, remove[4] from thence into
another city; and, if from that they per- 94, 95
secute you, flee into another city. (If from 94
this land they shall persecute you, go ye
into another.) Verily I say unto you, ye 95
shall not be able to finish[5] all the cities, until
12 I come to you. . . . What I say unto you in 96
darkness, that say ye in light; <and> what
ye hear in the ear, that preach ye upon the
13 housetops. . . . And be not afraid of them 95–6, 230–1
which kill the body, and are not able to kill
15 the soul. . . . Two sparrows are sold for a 97
farthing; and one of them doth[6] not fall on
18 the ground without your Father . . . him
19 will I confess[7] before *my* Father. . . . He 97, 228
that denieth me, him will I deny. . . .
20 Think not that I am come to send peace 97
22 on earth . . . a sword. I am come to set
a man at variance against *his* father. . . .
26 He that will find his life,[8] shall lose it: 98
<and> he that loseth his life[8] for my sake

---

[1] Lit. "of the Sodomites," as in the Arm. Vulg.

[2] So in the Arabic, and in the address to the Seventy, Luke x. 3; Cod. B has, "sheep."

[3] Note the change of order here.

[4] The Armenian word here is the same as in Luke x. 7, "go not from house to house;" but it may be a mistake for "flee," as the Armenian words are nearly alike. In the second clause Cod. B has again "remove" for "flee."

[5] Lit. "exhaust," as in the Arm. Vulg.

[6] Cod. B, "shall."

[7] Lit. "I will give thanks concerning him." The Arm. Vulg. has, "confess."

[8] Or, "soul."

Diatessaron.		Moesinger.
	shall find it. He[1] that loveth me not	
13 27	more than his own life.[2] ... He that re-	91
32	ceiveth you receiveth me.[3] ... Mary came[4]	98
33	and sat at Jesus' feet ... carest thou not for me? speak to my sister, that she help	
35	me. ... hath chosen the good part ... not	
39	be taken away from her. ... Art thou he that should come, or look we for another?	99, 101
42	... Go *and* tell John what ye have seen.[5] Behold, the blind see, and the lame walk, and the lepers are cleansed, and the deaf	100
43	hear, and the dead[6] are raised. ... Blessed is he, whosoever shall not be offended in	
44	me. But when the apostles[7] of John were departed, he began to say unto the people concerning John, What went ye out to see in the wilderness? a reed shaken with the	101
45	wind? or a man adorned in soft[8] raiment? Such are found[9] in the chambers of kings.	
46, 47	... he is more than the prophets. ... Behold, I send my messenger[10] before thee. ...	101 : 102
14 1	Verily I say unto you, that there hath not arisen among them that are born of women a greater than John ... but he that is less in the kingdom of heaven is	7, 103, 104, 107 103
5	greater than he. ... The law and the prophets *were* until John: henceforth the	42, 104 57
9	kingdom of heaven[11] is preached. ... It is easier[12] for heaven and earth to pass	65

---

[1] This clause does not occur in our Gospels exactly in this form; but it is found in Aphraates; cf. Luke xiv. 26. See also p. 118.

[2] Or, "soul."   [3] Cf. note at xv. 32.

[4] Cf. *Diat.* xiii. 32, note.

[5] Ephraem says expressly, "not what ye have heard."

[6] This clause is not in the Arabic. Ephraem, however, speaks of it as closing the list like a seal; and he omits, "to the poor the gospel is preached."

[7] Different from the Arm. Vulg., which has "messengers."

[8] Lit. "garments of delicacy," as in the Arm. Vulg.

[9] Lit. "go about."   [10] Or, "angel."

[11] Cod. B, "of God."   [12] See note at viii. 46

Diatessaron.   Moesinger.

14 17 away, than for one tittle to fall from the law. . . . He through Beelzebul, the prince   160
24 of the devils, casteth out devils.[1] . . . No   44
man can enter into a strong man's house, and spoil his treasures, except he first bind the strong man, and then he may spoil his
29 treasures. . . . but he shall be guilty of the   111
30 eternal sin.[2] . . . An unclean spirit is in him.   113
31 . . . Whosoever shall speak a word against[3]   112
the Son of man, it shall be forgiven him: but whosoever shall speak against[3] the Holy Ghost, it shall not be forgiven him,   111, 112
neither[4] in this world, nor in that. . . .
41 They brought unto him a certain man pos-   113
sessed with a devil, deaf and dumb and blind; <and> he healed him, and caused him to hear,[5] to speak, and to see. . . .
48 This man, if he were a prophet, how knew he not of what manner of works this woman
15 2 is, that is,[6] that she is a sinner? . . . A   114
certain man, that was a creditor, had two debtors: the one owed five hundred pence,
5 and the other fifty. . . . he said unto Simon the Pharisee: I entered into thine house; and thou gavest me no water for my feet.
6 . . . A kiss of greeting thou gavest me not; and she, behold, since the time she came in,
8 hath not ceased to kiss my feet. . . . And therefore her sins, *which are* many, shall be forgiven her; for she loved much;[7] for he,

---

[1] So in Cod. A, as in the Arm. Vulg. But Cod. B and the margin of Cod. A have, "This is Beelzebul, the prince of the devils: he casteth out the devils." At p. 75, where there is a brief allusion to this passage, the MSS. are again at variance.

[2] Cf. the Revised Version at Mark iii. 29.

[3] Lit. "concerning," as in the Arm. Vulg.

[4] In two out of three places it is literally, "neither here nor there."

[5] Cf. the Curetonian Syriac.

[6] Cod. B omits, "that is."

[7] Cod. B omits, "for she loved much."

Diatessaron.		Moesinger.
	to whom little is forgiven, loveth[1] little ...	
15	15 (He chose seventy and two[2] and sent them forth from himself.) he sent them two and two after his own likeness to the cities ... whither he himself was	160 115 95
	20 about to come. ... <And> if a son of peace is there, it shall rest upon him;[3] but if not, your peace shall return to	105
	30 you. ... If the mighty works had been done in Sodom, which have been done in thee, it would have remained[4] until now.	230
	32 ... he that rejecteth you, rejecteth me.[5]	94
	34 ... I beheld Satan, that he fell as lightning	116
	35 from heaven. Behold, I gave unto you power to tread on serpents and scorpions	
	36 and all the power of the enemy ... rejoice not, that the spirits are subject unto you; but rejoice, that your names are written in	206
	37 heaven among the angels. ... In that time and in that hour Jesus rejoiced in his spirit. ... I thank thee, heavenly Father,[6] that thou hast hid these things from the wise and from the prudent, and hast revealed	216 116 : 117
	38 them unto babes ... no man knoweth the Father, but the Son, and[7] no man knoweth	117, 216
	39 the Son, but the Father. ... Come unto me, ye that labour and toil, and that have heavy	117, 127

[1] Cod. B has, "will love."

[2] Ephraem elsewhere (p. 59) says: "the mystery of the seventy-two," showing that his *Diatessaron* had that number instead of seventy. Cf. *Diat.* xv. 15, note.

[3] Cod. A omits, "it shall rest upon him." This passage may have occurred at xii. 52 in Ephraem's copy.

[4] Lit. "been an inhabited place."

[5] This clause is quoted by Ephraem in connection with the Mission of the Twelve. It may have occurred so in his *Diatessaron*, perhaps as a continuation of xiii. 27.

[6] Ephraem adds, "The Greek says, I thank thee, O God the Father, Lord of heaven and earth." Marcion's Gospel had simply, "I thank thee, Lord of the heaven," leaving out the allusion to earth, as Tatian seems to have done.

[7] Shortened at p. 117, "neither the Son, but the Father."

THE EPHRAEM FRAGMENTS. 91

Diatessaron.   Moesinger.

15 40 burdens, and I *will* refresh[1] you. ... learn   63
of me, for I am meek and lowly in heart[2];
and ye shall find rest unto your souls. ...
43 He that hateth not his own life cannot be my   118
45 disciple. ... Who is there of you, who
willeth to build a tower, and doth not first
sit down, and count the cost thereof? ...
16 1 ... we would see signs from thee. ...
2 This generation is an evil and adulterous
generation; it seeketh after a sign, and   118, 119
there shall no sign be given to it, but the
4 sign of Jonah the prophet. ... For, as   118, 230
Jonah was three days and three nights in
the belly of the fish,[3] so shall[4] the Son of   119
man be three days and three nights in the
5 heart of the earth. The queen of the south   120
6 shall condemn it. ... The men of Nineveh   119
7 ... But the unclean spirit, when it goeth   120
out of a man, (went) about through dry   121
places, to seek rest, (but found) none. ...
I will return to my former house. ...   122
9 The unclean spirit goeth *and* taketh seven   120, 121
others, his companions, who are more wicked
than himself, and they come *and* dwell in
him; and the last *state* of that man becometh
10 worse than the first. So shall it be also   120, 122
11 unto this generation. ... Blessed is the   122–3
12 womb that bare thee,[5] ... blessed are they   123
that hear the word of God and keep it. ...
15 Behold, thy mother and thy brethren seek   122
20 thee. ... (the) women (who went) with   120
him, who had been healed of diseases and
unclean spirits; Mary Magdalene, out of

[1] Or, "give you rest." "All ye" occurs at p. 127, but is not in Aphraates.
[2] Cod. A omits, "in heart."   [3] Not the word used in the Arm. Vulg.
[4] Cited as, "must enter into," in the first instance (p. 118), but three times afterwards as, "shall be in."
[5] Cod. B adds at p. 122, "and the paps which gave thee suck," as in the Arm. Vulg.

Diatessaron.   Moesinger.

16 21 whom he had cast seven devils, and Joanna, the wife of Chuza, Herod's steward, and
24 Susanna. . . . Behold, a sower went forth 124
25 to sow *his* seed; and in his sowing some fell
26 by the wayside . . . And some fell on rocky
28 ground . . . And some fell among thorns
29 . . . And other fell on fertile[1] and good
30 ground . . . He that hath ears to hear, let 72, 123
36 him hear. . . . The heart of this people is 113
waxed gross: they have made heavy their
ears; and they have shut their eyes, that
they should not see with their eyes, and
should not hear with their ears . . .
39 prophets and righteous men and kings[2] have 155
43 desired . . . That, which fell by the way- 124
44 side . . . And that, which was upon rocky 125
48 ground . . . thirtyfold and sixtyfold and a 124, 126
50, 51 hundredfold . . . he knoweth not. For[3]
the earth of itself bringeth forth fruit.
17 4 . . . Sir, didst not thou sow seeds of
holiness[4] of corn in thy field? from whence
5 then came[5] tares? He saith unto them, 127
10 That is the work of an enemy. . . . Again
the kingdom is like a grain <of mustard
11 seed> . . . for it is less than all seeds . . .
12 And when it groweth, it increaseth *and* becometh a tree, and becometh greater than
all herbs; and the birds of heaven come and
13–15 dwell in its branches. . . . (Again he com- 128
pared it to leaven, which was mixed with
20 meal.) . . . He that sowed the seeds of corn 174
21 of holiness,[6] he is the Son of man . . . and

---

[1] Lit. "fat;" the Arm. Vulg. (Luke) has, "good and fat." Cf. the Curetonian Syriac. Ephraem twice says, "good and fat," pp. 125–6.
[2] Cod. B, "prophets and kings and righteous men."
[3] Cod. B, "he knoweth not that," etc., as in the Arm. Vulg.
[4] A Syriac expression for "holy seeds of corn." Cf. ver. 20.
[5] Cod. B has, "hath it."
[6] Cf. note at ver.   Cod. B, "the seeds of holiness of corn."

Diatessaron.   Moesinger.

17 24 the seed of good *things are* the children of the kingdom . . . he will cleanse the house of his kingdom from everything that offends.[1]   211

30 . . . Again, it is likened unto a net, that is cast into the sea, and gathereth into itself of every kind . . . (they draw near to) choose[2]   128

37 the best,[3] and cast the bad away. . . . On account of this he came into his own city, and taught them[4] in their synagogues. . . .

42,43 Physician,[5] heal thyself. . . . A prophet is not acceptable in his own city.[6] . . .   129, 130

45 There were many widows in the house of[7]   130
46 Israel . . . and to one of them <Elijah>
47 was not sent . . . lepers in the house of[7]
48 Israel. . . . He could not do <there> any
50 mighty work. . . . They were filled with
51 anger . . . they took him out . . . and   129
brought him to the side of the mountain
. . . *and* cast him down. . . .   130–1, 212

18 12 . . . (at the dancing of the daughter of   132
14 Herodias). . . . Cause to be brought the   131
41 head of John the Baptist. . . . Gather up   134
the remains of the food, that nothing at
45 all be lost therefrom. . . . This is of a truth the prophet, of whom it was said that he
46 should come into the world. And our Lord . . . went up into the mountain to pray
47[8] apart. And when the day was toward

---

[1] Lit. "every stumbling-block."   [2] Cod. B, "gather."
[3] Lit. "the good good," as in the Arm. Vulg. and in the Curetonian Syriac. Codex Bezae and many Old Latin MSS. read, "the best."
[4] Cod. B omits, "them." Immediately after this clause Ephraem quotes Luke iv. 16; cf. v. 35 and Appendix
[5] Just before this clause Ephraem has, "He entered *into Bethsaida*," implying that this took place there. The idea that he may have quoted this from the Marcionite Gospel is not supported by anything that we know of that document; cf. *Marcion's Gospel*, Parker, London. Probably there is some error in the Armenian text at this point.   [6] So in the Arm. Vulg.
[7] A literal translation of the idiomatic Syriac rendering of "in Israel."
[8] Ephraem cites ver. 47 of the Arabic before ver. 46, as if his *Dia*-

Diatessaron.   Moesinger.

18 48 evening, his disciples arose and went up into a ship, *and* went to go unto Capernaum.
19 4,8 ... It is I, be not afraid ... of little   135 : 136
     9 faith. ... When our Lord came and went   136
    10 up into the ship with Simon, and the winds rested and ceased. And they ... came and drew near before our Lord, and began to worship him and say, Of a truth thou art
    24 the Son of God. ... What signs[1] doest thou,[2] that we may see and believe on thee?
    25 ... Our fathers did eat manna in the desert, as also it is written, He gave them
    32 bread of[3] heaven to eat. ... I came not   234 to do mine own will, but the will of him
    33 that sent me. And this is his will, that, whatsoever he hath given me, I should lose
    38 none of it. ... No man can come to me,   137 except my Father, which hath sent me, draw
    44 him unto himself.[4] ... This is the bread, which cometh down from heaven, that a man
    45 should eat of it and die.[5] ... every one that eateth of this bread shall live for ever: (for the bread of God came down from heaven, and is given to all the world.) ...
    47 Except ye eat his flesh,[6] and drink his blood,   58, 245
    49 there is no life unto you. ... My flesh is   37
    54 meat. ... This word is hard, who can hear   125 it? ...
20 7 ... (He) saith unto the twelve, Will ye   58

tessaron here followed the order of Matt. xiv. 22, 23, instead of S. John's order.

[1] Cod. B has, "sign."   [2] Cod. B adds, "for us."

[3] So in the Arm. Vulg., but perhaps only equivalent to "from" in our Authorised Version.

[4] Cod. B. has, "unto me."

[5] Cod. A omits, "not," as the Curetonian Syriac; but Cod. B has, "not." Ephraem seems to understand this clause of the manna given by Moses in the wilderness, after which all who ate it died.

[6] Paraphrased at p. 245, "if any man taketh not my flesh, he receiveth not life."

Diatessaron.	Moesinger.

20 8 also go¹ from me? Simon . . . saith unto
9 him, . . . We have believed and known
10, 23 . . . one of you is a devil. . . . God said, 206 : 138
Honour thy father and mother. He that 137
speaketh evil² of his father or his mother,
let him die the death: and he that blas-
24 phemeth God, let him be crucified. And ye 138
say, every one³ to your father and mother,
Behold,⁴ it is a gift,⁵ whatsoever thou mayest
25 be profited from me. . . . and this (son)
careth not henceforth to honour his father
36 and mother. . . . Every plant, which is not
planted by my heavenly Father, shall be rooted
42 out. . . . In the heart arise⁶ all thoughts of 63
49 wickedness. . . . The woman was crying 138
out and following him, and saying, Have
50 mercy on me. . . . And he answered her
53 not at all. . . . It is not good to take the 139
children's bread, and to cast it to dogs. . . .
54 Yea, Lord, even dogs eat⁷ of the crumbs of 139, 59, 138
55 their master's⁸ table. . . . On this account⁹ 139
I say unto thee, O woman, great¹⁰ is thy
faith.
21 7, 11 . . . He did all things well. . . . Give 186 : 140
13 me water¹¹ to drink. . . . The woman saith 140
14 unto him, Behold, thou art a Jew. . . . He
saith unto her, If thou knewest him that 141
said unto to thee, Give me water therefrom¹²

---

¹ Lit. "Is it that ye also wish to go?"
² As in the Revised Version. ³ Cf. the Curetonian Syriac.
⁴ More lit. "Come on, thou." ⁵ Or, "offering."
⁶ Lit. "come to be." Cod. B has, "from the heart," as the Arm. Vulg.
⁷ At p. 59 we have simply, "even the dogs are fed."
⁸ So in the Arm. Vulg. at Matt. xv. 27. Cod. B has, "the children's," as in the Arm. Vulg. at Mark vii. 28.
⁹ Cf. Mark vii. 29; but it is also possible to regard these words as part of Ephraem's comment.
¹⁰ Lit. "something great."
¹¹ Cod. B omits "water" in one place, and transposes it in another.
¹² Cod. B has, "Give me of this water."

Diatessaron.   Moesinger.

  to drink, thou wouldest have asked of him.
21 15 . . . The woman saith unto him, Thou,
  because [1] thou hast no bucket, and the well
 17 is deep. . . . He saith unto her, My waters
 18 come down from heaven. . . . He that
  drinketh of this water, that I shall give
 19 him, shall never thirst. . . . The woman
  saith unto him, Sir, give me of that water,
  that I thirst not, nor come any more to this
 20 well [2] to draw water from it. He saith unto
  her, Go, call thy husband unto me,[3] . . .
 22 Thou hast had in turn [4] five husbands, and   141, 142
  he whom thou now hast is not thy husband.
 23 . . . The woman saith unto him, Sir, thus   141
  thou seemest to me,[5] that thou art a prophet.
 24 Our fathers worshipped in this mountain,   141–143
  <and> ye say that in Jerusalem only is the
 25 place of worship. He saith unto her, Verily
  I say unto thee, Neither in this mountain
  nor in Jerusalem shall they worship. . . .
 27 but true worshippers shall worship [6] in spirit   141, 143
 29 and in truth. . . . Behold, Christ cometh;   141
  and, when he shall come, he will give us all
 30 things. He saith unto her, I that speak
 31 unto thee am he. . . . they marvelled, that   140
  he was [standing and] speaking with the
 46 woman. . . . They said unto the woman,   142
  Henceforth we believe on him not because
  of thy words, but because we have heard
  (his teaching, and seen his works, that he is
  God;) and we have known that this is

[1] So also in the Arm. Vulg.
[2] Cod. B omits, "any more to this well," and reads "hither" instead.
[3] Cod. B omits, "unto me."
[4] Lit. "hast changed," as in the Arm. Vulg.
[5] Cod. B, "thus it seemeth to me;" the Arm. Vulg. has, "it seemeth to me."
[6] At p. 141 Cod. B inserts, "the Father." At p. 143 Cod. A has, "shall worship the Father by the Holy Spirit in truth;" Cod. B omits this passage by homoeoteleuton.

Diatessaron.		Moesinger.
21 49	indeed the true Christ. . . . the Galilaeans received him.	130
22 1	. . . Lord, if thou wilt, thou canst heal[1]	143–145
2	me. . . . and he stretched forth *his* hand	145
5	<and> touched him. . . . (Tell) no man, <but> go, shew thyself to the priests, and offer a gift,[2] as Moses commanded,[3] for a testi-	143–145
13	mony unto them. . . . A certain man was there, which had been thirty and eight years in his	145
14	infirmity . . . Our Lord saith unto him,	
15	Wilt thou be made whole? The sick man saith unto him, I have no guardian, that, when the waters are troubled, he may take *and* bring me down; but while I delay to be moved[4] another goeth down before me.[5]	146
16	(He) saith unto him, Arise, take up thy bed	146, 148
19	and walk.[6] . . . He that made me whole,	147
	he said unto me, Arise,[7] take up thy bed	
20	and walk. They say unto him, Who said[8]	146, 147, 199
21	unto thee, Take up thy bed? He saith, I know not: for Jesus, when he beheld the multitude of the people, withdrew himself[9]	147
22	from that place. And after a while he saw him, and saith unto him, Thou art made whole, behold, sin no more,[10] lest thou have	

---

[1] Quoted several times, sometimes as "cleanse."
[2] Or, "sacrifice."
[3] In one place for "commanded" Ephraem has, "taught thee;" probably his own paraphrase.
[4] Cod. A has, "while I delay to be set in order;" the Arm. Vulg. has simply, "while I delay."
[5] Ephraem says in his comment, "If they believed that the angel by means of the waters of Siloam healed the sick folk."
[6] So the passage is first quoted; Ephraem subsequently twice gives, "Stand on thy feet," and once adds, "to thine house."
[7] Cod. B omits, "Arise."
[8] It seems a paraphrase where Ephraem says, "Who bade thee take up thy bed upon thee on the sabbath day?" In narrating the passage in its context he says simply, "They say unto him, But who is he?"
[9] Lit. "slipped away," or "escaped;" so in the Arm. Vulg.
[10] Lit. "henceforth sin not;" quoted also at p. 146.

Diatessaron.		Moesinger.

22 23 need of some one else. And then the man departed and told the Jews, It was Jesus
25 which made me whole. . . . (He) saith unto 147–149 them, My Father worketh a work unto this
26 day; on account of this I also work. But 147–148 the Jews on this account persecuted (the Saviour), not only because he healed on the sabbath day, but also because he called God his Father, and made himself equal with God.
30 . . . The Father judgeth no man, but hath 151, 213 given all judgments into the hands of his
34 Son. . . . As the Father hath life in him- 149 self, so also hath he given to the Son . . . 149, 150
35 <and> hath given him authority, that the 150 Son of man should execute[1] judgment. . . .
42 Not that[2] I receive witness from men . . . 151
43, 44 He is the lamp, that burned. . . . For I have witness, which is greater than that of John . . . the very works, that I do, bear 152
51 witness of me. . . . if another shall come 210 in his own name, him ye will believe. . . .
53, 54 Moses himself is your accuser . . . Moses 151, 152 wrote of me.

23 29, 32 . . . he saw all things clearly. . . . Who 153 : 153, 156 do men say [concerning me,] that the Son of
33 man is?[3] They said unto him, Some say[4] that he is Elijah; and some say[4] that he is Jeremiah; and some say[4] that he is a pro- 156
34 phet from among the prophets. . . . But 153 who say ye [concerning me,] that I am?
35 Simon saith Thou art Christ,[5] the Son of
36 the living God. Blessed art thou, Simon.
37 . . . Thou art a rock . . . and the gates of hell 154 : 153
39 shall not prevail against thee. . . . Tell no 154

---

[1] Lit. "judge judgments." [2] So in the Arm. Vulg.
[3] Nearly identical with the Arm. Vulg. of Matt. xvi. 13. At p. 156 Ephraem has, "that I am."
[4] Lit. "a certain saith."
[5] Cod. A has, "the Son Christ, the Son," etc.

Diatessaron.		Moesinger.
	man concerning me, that I am Christ. . . .	
23 40	Behold, we go up to Jerusalem; and all things are fulfilled, that have been written concerning me; for the Son of man must be	65, 154 230
41, 42	crucified, and die, and rise again. . . . This	154–6, 229
43	be far from thee, Lord [1] . . . he saith unto	154–5, 229
44	him, Get thee behind me,[2] Satan, thou art a stumbling-block unto me; for thou thinkest not the things that be of God, but those that be of men.	
24 1	There are some that now stand here with me, *which* shall not taste of death, till they	155, 222
2	shall see the kingdom of God. . . . After six days he took them and brought *them*	159
3	up into the mountain. . . . The fashion of	156
9	his countenance was altered. . . . Lord, if thou wilt, let us make here three tabernacles . . . he knew not, what he spake	
12	. . . (the voice came from heaven,) This is my beloved Son: hear him, and live ye. . . .	157 : 156, 157 157
17	And as they came down from the mountain, he gave them a command, and said, Take heed, that ye tell no man that vision, which ye have seen, until the Son of man be risen	154, 157–8
29	from the dead. . . . It is not meet, that a	159, 212
34	prophet perish out of Jerusalem. . . . they	160
35	could not heal him. . . . O evil generation, perverse and faithless, how long shall I be	203
39	with you, and suffer you? . . . He saith unto the man,[3] He that believeth, all things are	160
41	possible to him. . . . I say unto thee,[4] unclean spirit, deaf and dumb, go out *and* depart from him, and enter no more into	161

---

[1] Lit. "Propitiation be to thee, Lord, from this." So the Arm. Vulg.

[2] Ephraem sometimes omits "me," and once has, "Go away, Satan."

[3] At p. 70 Ephraem quotes apart from their context the words, "If thou believest."

[4] In connection with this miracle Ephraem adds: "At that time, it saith, his disciples were not as yet established in him."

Diatessaron.   Moesinger.

24 45 him. . . . Why could not we heal him? 160
46 And he saith unto them, Because of your
little faith. . . . If[1] ye had faith as a grain 204
of mustard seed, ye should say to this mountain, Be removed ; and it should be removed
50 from before you[2] . . . on the third day[3] I
rise again. . . .

25 4   (Thy master perchance, they say, does not 161
5 give). . . . he prevented Simon, and saith
unto him, Of whom do the kings of the
earth[4] take tribute? of sons[5] or of
6 strangers? . . . Go *and* give thou also as
7 one of the strangers.[6] Lest thou offend
them, go thou to the sea, and cast a net
8 there.[7] . . . Who is the greatest[8] in the 107
18 kingdom? . . . If[9] thy hand or thy foot 66
28 offend thee, . . . They came *and* drew near 162
to ask him, Is it lawful for a man to put
29 away his wife? He answered them, and
30 saith, It is not lawful. They say unto him,
Moses gave us permission: why is it not
35 lawful?[10] Moses, he saith, because of the
hardness of your heart, gave you permission;
but from the beginning of the creation it
was not so.

[1] It is not certain that Ephraem cites this from this chapter, he may be only quoting in a varied form xxxiii. 6, 7.

[2] Lit. "from your face ;" this occurs only at p. 204. Cf. pp. 184, 185, 189.

[3] Cod. B has, "after three days."

[4] Cod. B has, "of the nations of the earth."

[5] Cod. B has, "of their sons."   [6] So in the Arabic.

[7] In his remarks Ephraem says, "when he had drawn out the fish, which had a stater in its mouth."

[8] Lit. "Who [indeed] is great."

[9] Ephraem quotes this clause in connection with the Sermon on the Mount, Matt. v. 30, *Diat.* viii. 60, where, however, the hand only is referred to. Whether Tatian inserted the allusion to the foot in the Sermon, or Ephraem made the addition intentionally or inaccurately, is not certain.

[10] This clause combines into one ver. 30 and 34 of the Arabic, and so proceeds naturally to ver. 35 omitting ver. 31-33. Cod. B omits the clause probably by homoeoteleuton.

THE EPHRAEM FRAGMENTS.

Diatessaron.   Moesinger.

26 8 ... (joy[1] over sinners, that they repent, 163
more than over just persons, that they
14–15 sinned not.) ... (And when the younger
33 son had wasted his goods) ... It was meet
to be glad; for this thy brother was dead,
42 and became alive.[2] ... Make to yourselves 156
friends, that they may receive you into their
eternal dwellings.[3]
27 21 Where one is, there I also am;[4] and 165
where two are, there will I also be. ...
22 How oft, if my brother sin against me, shall[5] 163
I forgive him? until seven times <in a
23 day,[6]> is it enough?[7] He saith unto him, 163–4
Until seventy times seven seven times.[8]
27 ... I have a baptism to be baptized with. 229
28 ... In heaven their angels behold the 165
31 face of my Father. ... And it came to
pass, when they came[9] *and* told him of the
Galilaeans, whose blood Pilate mingled with
36 their sacrifices. ... A certain man had a 166, 184
37 fig-tree planted in his vineyard. And he 166, 213
saith unto the husbandman, Behold, *there*
are these three years, that I come seeking
fruit from this fig-tree, and find none: cut
38 it down. The husbandman answered, and 166
saith unto him, Let it alone this year
also. ...

[1] Cod. B adds, "of the angels." A few lines before these words Ephraem has, "Ten drachmas and a hundred sheep."
[2] Cod. A has, "and lived and became alive."
[3] The same word as in the Arm. Vulg., but not the same as "tabernacles" at xxiv. 9. Lit. "dwellings which *are* for ever." Cod. A omits, "which *are*."
[4] Cod. B has, "will be." Ephraem introduces this clause with, "He comforted them in his saying," as though he read it in his *Diatessaron*.
[5] Cod. B has, "How oft shall my brother ... and," as in the Arm. Vulg.
[6] Ephraem's comment makes it probable that these words followed.
[7] Or, "It is enough," or, "It is much;" perhaps Ephraem's comment.
[8] This is cited twice: in the first case Cod. B omits the second "seven": in the second place we have, "until seventy times seven seven," in both MSS
[9] "Came," as in the Arm. Vulg.; probably a better translation of our Greek than "were present." The Arabic has the same.

Diatessaron.   Moesinger.

28 3   . . . They say unto him, There is no man,   167
     4 that doeth anything in secret. . . . For his
     7 brethren did not believe on him. . . . I go
    20 not up in[1] this feast. . . . Why do ye seek 167, 168, 196
    21 to kill me?[2] . . . Who seeketh to kill 196
    27 thee? . . . Do our elders know, that this 210
    28 is indeed Christ?[3] . . . behold, Christ,
       when he shall come, no man knoweth
    29 whence he is. . . . I am not come of 173
    42 myself. . . . Good Master, what shall I do, 168, 172
    43 that I may live? . . . Why callest thou me ⎰ 123, 168
       good? There is none good but one only, ⎱ 173, 174
       God, the Father, which is in heaven. 168–174
    44 Knowest thou the commandments? if thou 171 : 168
       wilt enter into eternal life keep the
    47 commandments.[4] . . . All these things have 125
       I done from my youth up. What lack I 169
    48 yet? . . . (He) looked on him with love. 171–3
    49 . . . One thing thou lackest: if thou wilt 125, 170–1
       be perfect, go *and* sell all thy possessions,
       that thou hast. . . .

29 3   How hard is it *for them* that trust[5] in 170, 172
     6 riches! . . . Behold, we have left all; what 67, 178
     9 shall we have therefore? . . . shall receive 88
    14 sevenfold in this *present* time . . . a rich 173
    17 man . . . clothed in purple . . . the angels
       carried him into Abraham's bosom. . . .
    19[6],20 My father, Abraham . . . My son, remem- 173 : 175
       ber, that thou in thy lifetime receivedst thy

---

[1] The Arm. Vulg. has, "to."

[2] Ephraem continues, "a man, that speaketh the truth," thus blending John vii. 20 with John viii. 40. These verses he blends again, when discussing the latter (p. 196, cf. *Diat.* xxxv. 51). He may be there citing John viii. 40 as, "Why do ye seek to kill me?"

[3] The words which follow, "*more* true than all," appear to be Ephraem's omment.

[4] Ephraem (p. 171) quotes, "This do, and thou shalt live," as if these words followed here in his *Diatessaron*. Cf. xxxiv. 35.

[5] Lit. "have hoped;" the same verb as in the Arm. Vulg. of Mark x. 24.

[6] Or, 25.

Diatessaron.   Moesinger.

good things, and Lazarus his evil things.[1]
29 24 . . . They have[2] Moses and the prophets.   173
   26 . . . If they hear not Moses and the pro-   175
   32 phets. . . . Why stand ye all[3] the day idle?   176
   33 . . . No man came *and* hired us . . .   176, 177
   36 the first supposed, that they would receive   175
37, 41 more . . . they murmured. . . . Or have I   176 : 177
   not power in mine own house to do what I
   will? If I am good,[4] why is thine eye   174, 176–7
   42 evil? <So> the last shall be first. . . .   108
30 41   . . . Behold, we go up to Jerusalem . . .   178
44, 47 and they take and crucify him. . . . We
   would that thou shouldest do for us, whatso-
   48 ever we may ask. . . . He saith unto them,
   49 I will do *it* for you.[5] . . . Give us authority   177–8
   to sit, one on thy right hand and one on the
   50 left hand. . . . Are ye able to drink of the   108, 179, 229
   cup, that I shall drink of? . . .
31 3   . . . he, that will be your head, shall be   109
   19 your servant. . . . Zacchaeus make haste   180
   and come down (from the fig-tree, for I am
   22 to be with thee.). . . . Behold, Lord, the
   half of all my goods I will[6] give to the
   poor; and all things, that I have ever taken
   from any man wrongfully, I will restore
   23 them fourfold. . . . This day is salvation[7]   180, 205
   come to this house, forasmuch as he also is   180
   26 a son of Abraham . . . a certain blind man   181

[1] Lit. "sufferings;" the word used in the Arm. Vulg. Cod. B has, "evil things."
[2] Lit. "There are."
[3] Lit. "the day till evening," as in the Arm. Vulg. The discussion of this parable is commenced by the words, "Concerning the hired labourers, whom the lord of the vineyard hired at the third, sixth, and ninth *hours*."
[4] Lit. "generous;" the same word is used here in the Arm. Vulg.
[5] This represents the second half of the clause, "What will ye *that* I shall do for you?" Ephraem's *Diatessaron* must, like Cod. Bezae, have omitted the first part, and read the second as a promise. .
[6] So in the Arm. Vulg.
[7] In the second place Ephraem has, "life."

Diatessaron.   Moesinger.

       sat by the wayside, and his name was
31 27 Bartimaeus, the son of Timaeus[1] . . . (when)
   28 he asked, Who might[2] this be? (They say,)
   29 Jesus of Nazareth. . . . He began to cry   180–1
       out, and saith, Jesus, son of David, have
   30 mercy on me. . . . They rebuked, (and   181
       hindered this blind man, that he should not
       come to Jesus; therefore) he cried out the
       more, Son of David, have mercy on me.
   32 . . . And he cast away his garment, and
   34 came *unto him*. . . . Receive thy sight:
       thy faith hath made thee whole.
32 1 . . . (Within the temple they were selling
   8 sheep and oxen) . . . Destroy this temple,   182, 229
       and on the third day I will raise it up. . . .
   9 In forty and six years was this temple built,[3]   182
       and wilt thou raise it up on the third day?
   21 . . . This man went down justified more
       than (he) . . . every one that humbleth him-   41
24,25 self, shall be exalted. . . . He hungered, and   183, 186
       hasted *and* came to that fig-tree . . . he   183
   26 found nothing thereon. . . . (He cursed the   182–3
   30 fig-tree, and it withered away.)[4] . . . And   189
       is it possible for a man, *when he is* old, to
       enter again the second time[5] into his mother's
       womb, and again[6] be born out *of it*. . . .
   31 Except a man be born of water and of the
       Spirit, he cannot enter into the kingdom of
   32 God. That which is born of the flesh is
       flesh, and that which is born of the Spirit
   34 is spirit. . . . ye know not the spirit, whence
   36 it cometh, or whither it goeth. . . . Thou   188
       art a master of Israel,[7] and knowest thou not

---

[1] Cod. B, "Timaeus, the son of Bartimaeus."   [2] Or, "Who is this?"
[3] This clause agrees with the Arm. Vulg.
[4] Ephraem proceeds at once to discuss the finding the fig-tree withered, and the lesson of faith founded on it.
[5] So in the Arm. Vulg.   [6] Cod. B has, "thence.'
[7] So in the Arm. Vulg.

Diatessaron. Moesinger.

32 38 these things. . . . But now,[1] if I have told 187–8
you earthly things, and ye have not believed,
how shall ye believe, if I tell you heavenly
39 things? And there is none that hath 168, 187-9
ascended up to heaven, but he that came
down from heaven, *even* the Son of man.
40 . . . And as Moses lifted up the serpent in 189, 230
the wilderness, even so must[2] the Son of
42 man be lifted up. . . . God so loved the 258
world, even as[3] his only-begotten Son. . . .
33 3 . . . His disciples marvelled how it had 186
withered away so suddenly. . . . When they 184, 186
4 returned, they say unto him, Behold, the fig-
tree, which thou cursedst, how is it withered 184
6 away suddenly? He saith unto them, Ye 184, 185, 189
also, if ye have faith and doubt not in your
7 heart,[4] shall say to this mountain,[5] Go, be
cast into the sea; and it shall be removed.
8 And whatsoever in your prayers ye shall ask 189
of God with faith,[6] it shall be given you.
9, 27 . . . Increase our faith[7] . . . while he was 189 : 191
teaching the people, and preaching the gospel
28 to them, (they) came, and say unto him, By 191, 38
what authority doest thou these things? . . .
30 The baptism of John, whence was it? was it 191
31 from heaven or from men? . . . They began
to reason in their minds and to say, If we
say that it is from heaven, he will say[8] unto
32 us, Why then did ye not believe him? And

---

[1] So in the Arm. Vulg.

[2] At p. 230 "is" appears instead of "must be;" but that may be a paraphrase.

[3] Cod. B has, "that he gave;" but the reading of the text agrees with that of the first hand of ℵ, which omits, "he gave."

[4] Cod. B has, "mind."

[5] Cf. also *Diat.* xxiv. 46 and ver. 10 of this chapter in the Arabic.

[6] "Of God" may be due to Tatian, the rest of the clause is like the Arm. Vulg.

[7] Later on (p. 190) Ephraem comments on the conduct of the Unjust Judge, which follows here in the Arabic; but he does not quote the words.

[8] Lit. "saith."

Diatessaron. Moesinger.

if we say, From men, we fear the people.
33 35... What think ye? A certain man had
37, 38 two sons ... Yea, sir, I go ... Which of
of them did the will of his father? (They
say,) The second.[1] ... Therefore the publicans
and harlots shall go into the kingdom of
39 heaven before you. John came unto you in   192
40 the way of righteousness ... A certain
householder planted for himself a vineyard,
and hedged it round about, and prepared a
winepress in it, and built a tower in it. ...
42 and he sent his servants to bring him *the*
49 fruit ... Afterwards he sent his son ...
50 But when they saw the son, that he came,
they say, This is the heir[2] of the vineyard;
51 come, let us kill him; and hereafter the inheritance of the vineyard becometh ours.
53 ... (What do these husbandmen deserve?)
54 ... He shall miserably destroy those miser-
55 able men. ... Have ye never read: The   193
stone, which the builders rejected, the same
was made the head of the corner? ...
58 Whosoever stumbleth on it shall be broken to
pieces, and on whomsoever it shall fall, it
shall crush and grind him to powder.
34 2 ... They sent unto him their disciples with
3 the Herodians ... (whether they should give
7 tribute.) ... Give unto Caesar that which
is Caesar's, but that which is God's, render *to
9 him*.[3] ... The Sadducees came, and say
unto him, There is no resurrection of the
10 dead. ... Moses thus[4] commanded us: If

---

[1] The Arabic has, "first;" but Ephraem remarks, "And they justly discriminating say, The second." The Armenian MSS. of the Gospels vary here in their readings.

[2] Cf. Moes. p. 265.

[3] Lit. "But that which is God's, that which we owe, render." In Cod. B, however, the first clause of this is shorter, "But to God."

[4] Cod. A has, "Moses the patriarch."

Diatessaron.		Moesinger.
	a man die having no children, his brother	
34 11	shall take his wife. . . . Now a certain	194
13	woman became *the wife* of seven husbands.	
15	. . . In the resurrection of the dead there-	
	fore whose *wife* of them shall she be ? . . .	
16,17	Ye do greatly err . . . For the sons of the	
18	times of this world marry wives . . . but	
	they that become worthy of that world . . .	
19,26	they are as the angels . . . What command-	
27	ment is first and great in the law ? He	
	saith unto him,[1] Hear, O Israel, the Lord	152, 169
28	thy God is one Lord. <and> Love the	110, 194
29	Lord thy God. . . . That is *the* great com-	110
30	mandment. . . . Love thy neighbour as thy-	194
35	self. . . . this do, and thou shalt live [2] . . .	171
36,37	Who is my neighbour ? . . . from Jerusalem	195
43	to Jericho . . . Which of them, thinkest	
	thou, was neighbour to the wounded *man ?*	
44	He saith unto him, He that showed the	
	mercy. He saith unto him, Do thou also	
	likewise.	
35 1	. . . Our Lord cried[3] and said, If any	196
	man of you thirst, let him come unto me	
6	and drink. . . . from the town of Bethlehem	210
24	the Messiah is to be born. . . . Thou comest	86
	and bearest witness of thyself: thy witness	
44	is not true. . . . We are Abraham's children,	197
50	. . . If ye were Abraham's children, ye	196, 197
51	would do the works of Abraham. Why[4] do	168, 196
	ye seek to kill me, a man that speaketh the	
55	truth ? this did not Abraham. . . . Ye are	196
	the children of Satan, who is a murderer from	

---

[1] The actual passage (p. 194) is: "He saith unto him, Thou shalt love the Lord thy God, and thy neighbour as thyself." The other clauses are found at the references given, and are placed here in the order of the Arabic.

[2] Cf. note at xxviii. 44.

[3] Cod. B has, "stood *and* cried," as in the Arm. Vulg.

[4] Cf. note at xxviii. 20.

Diatessaron.   Moesinger.

35 57 the beginning. . . . Which of you convinceth   152, 242
    59 me of sin? . . . Thou art a Samaritan.   197
36 6   Abraham desired[1] to see my day; he saw   155,197,207
    7 it and was glad. . . . Thou art not fifty   197
      years old; and hast thou seen Abraham?
    8 He saith unto them, Before Abraham was, I
   10 was. . . . He caused himself to meet with   197, 203
      a blind man, who was blind from his mother's
   11 womb. And the disciples asked him, Whose   197
   12 sin[2] is it? . . . He saith unto them, Neither   197, 200
      this man's nor his kinsfolk's, but that the
      works of God should be made manifest in
   13 him. And I must work the works of my
      Father, that sent me, while it is day: the
   15 night cometh. . . . And when he had thus   198
      spoken, he spat on the ground, and made
      clay of his spittle, <and> anointed his eyes
   16 with the clay. . . . Go, wash thy face. . . .   199
   23,31[3](He made clay on the sabbath.) . . . They   199 : 202
      gave commandment to put him out.
37 1   . . . They which see shall be made blind.   199
    4 . . . (when he entereth in by the door into   210
   10 his sheepfold) . . . <I am> the door of the   137
   11 sheep. All that came before me were thieves   200, 210
   14 and robbers. . . . the good shepherd giveth   174
   21 his life for his sheep. . . . I have power over   242
      my life to lay it down and to take it *again*.
   35[4] . . . for which of my works do ye stone me?
   40 . . . If I do[5] not the works, believe me   210
   41 not. . . . if ye believe not me, at least   121, 191
   46 believe the works. . . . And there was there   200
      a certain sick man: Lazarus was his name.

---

[1] So in the Arm. Vulg.
[2] The Arm. Vulg. has, "whose fault is it, this man's, or his father's or mother's."
[3] Cf. Moesinger's note, p. 202. This fragment does not agree exactly with any passage in the Gospels or the Arabic. See the latter at xxxvi. 31 and 43.
[4] Cf. note at xlv. 39 for a fragment, which may come before this.
[5] Lit. "work."

Diatessaron.   Moesinger.

37 48 . . . And his sisters sent unto our Lord, and
say, Lord, behold, he, whom thou lovest, is
49 fallen sick.[1] . . . This sickness is not unto
death, but for the glory of God, that the
Son of God may be glorified thereby.[2] . . .
51, 52 he abode in that place two days. He saith   203 : 200
unto his disciples, Come,[3] let us go into
53 Judaea. They say unto him, The Jews seek[4]
to kill thee, and goest thou thither again?
54 . . . Are there not twelve hours in the   200, 201
day? If any man walk in the light, he
stumbleth not, because he seeth the light.
59, 60 . . . Lazarus, our friend,[5] is dead; and I am   201
61 glad for your sakes. . . . Come, let us go,
that we also may die with him.
38 5[6] Lord, if thou hadst been here, our brother   202, 205
9 had not died. . . . I am the resurrection and   202
the life; whosoever believeth in me, though
10 he were dead, he is alive. He that is alive,
17 and believeth in me, never dieth . . . he   203
18 was troubled. . . . Where have ye laid him?   201, 203
19, 21 . . . And[7] our Lord wept. . . . He[8] that   203 : 249
opened the eyes of the blind, could he not
have caused that[9] even this man should not
23 have died?[10] . . . Draw near and take away   204
the stone . . . by this time he stinketh;   202
<for he hath been> dead four days. . . .   204
25 I thank thee, that thou hast heard me.   234
26 And thou hearest me; but because of the   99, 234
people . . . I say[11] this, that they may

---

[1] Lit. "sick and fallen."   [2] Or, "in him."
[3] So in the Arabic, the Arm. Vulg. and the Peschito.
[4] Cod. B has, "sought."   [5] So Cod. Bezae.   [6] Or, 16.
[7] So in the Arm. Vulg., ℵ, D, and the Arabic.
[8] Ephraem also has (p. 202), "Did not this *man* open," etc.
[9] Lit. "can he not so do anything that."
[10] Or, "should not die."
[11] So at p. 99 in Cod. A; but in Cod. B, "I do *it*," as in the Arm. Vulg. Both give this latter at p. 234; but the comments at both places show that Ephraem must have had "say."

Diatessaron.		Moesinger.
38 28	believe, that thou hast sent me. . . . Loose	204
29	him. . . . Many believed on him there. . . .	200
32	And if we suffer it, all men believe[1] on him; and the Romans will presently come, and take away our nation, the law, and this	204, 205
42	place[2] . . . when the days were being fulfilled (of his work in Judaea) he turned his face to go to Jerusalem, and he sent (those	224
45	two wrathful ones) before him. . . . Wilt thou, that we command fire to come down[3] and consume them?	95
39 1,3	(He came to Bethany.[4]) . . . Simon the	204 : 205
5	leper. . . . And the chief priests[5] took counsel, that they might put Lazarus also	205
10[6]	to death. . . . This ointment might have been sold for three hundred pence, and given	
14	to the poor . . . that to the day of my	40
21	winding-sheet she may keep it.[7] . . . loose the colt, and bring *him* unto me. . . .	207
24	Rejoice, O daughter of Sion, for behold, a[8]	210
31	king cometh unto thee. . . . The children	207
32	were crying and saying, Blessing[9] to the Son of David. . . . Blessing in the highest. . . .	27
33	Peace in heaven and glory on earth. . . .	
36[10]	The chief priests and scribes were sore displeased, and say, Hearest thou not what these say? . . . Rebuke the children[11] that	207 208
37	they hold their peace. He saith unto them, If these shall hold their peace, yet the stones	
38	will cry out. When he came to Jerusalem,	207

---

[1] The Arm. Vulg., ℵ* and ff[2] have the present tense.
[2] Cod. B has, "and the law and the kingdom and this place."
[3] Lit. "that we say, and fire should come down:" Cod. B adds, "from heaven."
[4] On the order of these fragments see note to *Diat.* xxxix. 1.
[5] Cod. B, "the priests."   [6] Cf. *Diat.* xxxix. 13.
[7] The whole clause as in the Arm. Vulg.   [8] Cod. B has, "thy."
[9] So in the Arm. Vulg. for "Hosanna."   [10] Cf. *Diat.* xl. 2, 3.
[11] Cod. A has, "the men;" but the comments support the reading, "the children." The "disciples" on the road to Jerusalem are evidently meant.

THE EPHRAEM FRAGMENTS. 111

Diatessaron.   Moesinger.

	he beheld it, and began to weep[1] over it;	
39	39 and he saith unto it, If thou hadst known at least this day of thy peace[2]! but peace is hid from thine eyes.[3]	184, 207
40	16 . . . Now is the judgment of the[4] world: now also[5] the prince of this world is cast	208
	19 out. . . . We have heard out of the law, that the Christ abideth[6] for ever: and thou sayest, The Son of man must be lifted up.	209
	22 . . . The kingdom of God is[7] not by days 23 of observing . . . behold, the kingdom of	209–211
	44 God is within your heart. . . . Woe unto you, lawyers, for ye hide[8] the key.	211
41	2 . . . there shall come all the blood of righteous men from the blood of Abel the righteous unto the blood of Zacharias . . .	
	4 between the temple and the altar . . . how 12 often would I have gathered you. . . . If any man hear my words, and keep them not, I judge[9] him not: *for* I came not into the world to judge the world, but to save the 13 world. . . . He that receiveth not my words, the word that I have spoken, it judgeth him	213
	14 . . . he, which sent me, he gave me a commandment, what I should speak, and what I	173
	30 should say. . . . The days will come, when[10] there shall not remain in it one stone upon	44, 183

---

[1] At p. 184 Ephraem says, "It is written, The Lord saw it, and wept over it."

[2] At p. 184 in Cod. A it is, "this thy day;" and in Cod. B, "this day." At p. 207 in Cod. A it is, "this day of thy peace;" and in Cod. B, "to-day this day of thy peace."

[3] Lit. "face," as in the Arm. Vulg.

[4] So Cod. Bezae and many Latin MSS. Cod. B has, "this."

[5] For "now also," Cod. B has, "and."

[6] Lit. "liveth," one of the readings of the Arm. Vulg.

[7] Or, "cometh."

[8] The present tense, as in the Arm. Vulg. and in Old Latin MSS. *b c q*.

[9] Cod. A, "know."

[10] At p. 183, "when it shall be destroyed, and Jerusalem shall be overthrown."

Diatessaron.   Moesinger.

41 43 another[1] . . . they shall persecute you and   63
       deliver you up.
42 4   When ye shall see the sign of the terror 213
       of its desolation, which was spoken of by
       6 Daniel the prophet . . . he that standeth   214
       8 upon the housetops . . . Woe to them that
       are with child . . . there shall be anguish[2]
      10 unto this people. . . . If they shall say unto 211
      13 you, Lo, he is here, believe *it* not . . . go
      14 not forth. . . . As the lightning, which
      16 lighteneth. . . . Pray ye and ask, that your 214–5
       flight be not in the winter, neither on the
      18 sabbath day. . . . And except God[3] had 215
       shortened those days, no living thing[4] would
       have been saved; <but> for the elect's
      25 sake . . . From the fig-tree learn the   186
       parable: for[5] when the branches become
       tender, and the leaf springs forth and buds, 187
      31 ye know that summer is nigh. . . . pray that 215
       ye may be *accounted* worthy to escape all
       these things that shall come to pass. . . .
      32 That day[6] <and> that hour[6] knoweth no 109, 179, 215-6
       man, neither the angels, nor the Son . . .
      33 watch and pray; for ye know not the time. 216
47, 49 . . . in one bed.[7] . . . Two *men* shall be in 217
      50 a field . . . the body . . . eagles. . . . 218
43 2 . . . Who is[8] *the* overseer, *the* faithful
       8 servant, good and wise?[9] . . . He will cut
       him asunder, and will separate him, and
       appoint him his portion with the hypocrites

---

[1] Lit. "a stone upon a stone."
[2] Cod. B has, "great anguish."
[3] So in the Arm. Vulg. and some other versions. Cod. B omits, "God."
[4] Cod. A has "flesh" in the text, but not in the margin.
[5] Cod. B omits, "for."
[6] Ephraem three times has, "that day," and once (p. 216), "that hour," but not both together. They are together in the Arabic as well as in the Greek.
[7] These words come immediately after the next clause in Ephraem, but not in the Arabic.
[8] Cod. B adds, "indeed."   [9] Cod. B has, "and wise and good."

Diatessaron		Moesinger.
	and ¹ with the unbelievers; and there shall be for him ² weeping of eyes and gnashing	
43 10	of teeth. . . . Five of them were foolish	
26	and five wise. . . . his talent . . . the earth	
28	. . . he hid it. . . . He that had received five	
32	talents. . . . He that had received the one	219
36	talent. . . . Take ye away the talent from	218
37	him. . . . He that hath,³ to him shall be given, and he shall have abundance; and he that hath not, even that which he hath seized shall they take away from him. . . .	192
39	Let your loins be girded about and your	218–9
46	lamps burning. . . . Then shall the King say unto them, that are on the right hand,	88
53	Come, ye blessed of my Father. . . . Depart from me, ye cursed of my Father, into the everlasting fire,⁴ which is kept ⁵ for Satan and his angels.	97: 75, 216
44 42	With desire I have desired to eat this	230
44	⁶passover with you, before I suffer. . . . One	159, 219
47	of you, he that eateth bread with me, he it is that shall betray me. And behold, the	219
48	hand of my betrayer *is* with me at the table, dipping.⁶ And the Son of man goeth, as also	219, 230
	it is written of him; <but> woe to that	224
	man! . . . it were better for him, if he had not been born. . . .	112, 220
45 12	. . . (Our Lord) blessed and brake. . . .	222
16	I will not drink henceforth of this offspring of the vine until the kingdom of my Father.	
17	. . . Behold, Satan hath obtained⁷ permission	
18	to sift you as wheat, and I have prayed the	

---

¹ Cod. B omits, "with the hypocrites and."

² Cod. B omits, "for him."

³ Cf. a similar passage at x. 16. The wording here is different, and seems to allude to the taking away of the talent.

⁴ At p. 216 there is added, "for I know you not;" cf. x. 43.

⁵ Cod. B. has, "prepared."   ⁶ Cf. also *Diat.* xliv. 46.

⁷ Lit. "hath gained his cause," *i.e.* "asked and obtained permission," etc. Our Greek implies this, but the Arm. Vulg. has simply, "asked."

Diatessaron.　　　　　　　　　　　　　　　　　　　　　Moesinger.

　　　　Father[1] for thee, that thy faith fail not. . . .
45 20 A new commandment I give unto you: Love　224, 225
　　34 one another, as I have loved you. . . . I am　137
　　36 the way. . . . Shew us thy Father, and it　222
　　37 sufficeth us . . . have ye not known me?
　　38 . . . my Father, that is in me, he doeth　173
　　39 these works. . . . I *am* in the Father, and　271
　　　　the Father in me; and we are one.[2] . . .
　　40 He that believeth on me, the works that　223
　　　　I do shall he also do; and greater *works*
　　44 shall he do. . . . Another Advocate I send　225
　　　　unto you.
46 10 . . . and findeth nothing that is his in　223, 263
　　13 me . . . he that hath not his[3] sword, let　223
　　15 him buy himself a sword. . . . Two are　224
　　19 enough. . . . Ye *are* clean through my　58
　　　　word, which I have spoken unto you. . . .
28,29 This is my commandment. . . . Greater　224: 225
　　　　love than this can none other have, that he
　　34 lay down his life for his friends . . . know　106
　　　　that they hated me also, before *they hated*
　　35 you. . . . I chose you, before[4] the world　50
　　36 was. . . . If they have persecuted me, they　95
　　41 will persecute you also . . . as also it is　209
　　　　written in their law: They hated me with-
　　42 out a cause. . . . Behold, I send unto you　225
　　50 the Advocate.[5] . . . It is expedient for you,
　　　　that I go away; for, if I go not away, the
　　　　Advocate cometh not unto you (and all
　　　　truth is not made known unto you.[6]) . . .
　　54 and of judgment because the prince of this　227

---

[1] A remarkable addition, which Zohrab says was in one MS. of the Arm. Vulg. Cod. A has, "my Father."

[2] This clause may be a paraphrase of xxxvii. 33, and not belong to this verse, though quoted with it.

[3] Or, "a sword for himself."

[4] This clause occurs in a different connection at *Diat.* xlvii. ver. 23 and 42, with the latter of which it agrees closely.

[5] Cod. A has, "this friend," or, "the friends."

[6] Cod. A has, "knoweth you not."

Diatessaron.		Moesinger.
46	58 world is judged.[1] . . . Whatsoever my Father hath is mine.	179
47	13 . . . And I came from the Father. . . .	3
	17 I am not alone, because my[2] Father is with	271
	18 me. . . . I have overcome the world. . . .	223
	19 The hour is come: glorify thy Son; and thy	228
	23 Son will glorify thee . . . give[3] me glory from thyself, of that which thou gavest me	227
	28 before the world was . . . (and that which	179
	29 I have, is my Father's.[4]) . . . and I come	271
	30 to thee, my Father . . . and none of them perished but the son of perdition.[5]	137
48	6,9 . . . My soul is sorrowful. . . . Father, if it be possible, let this cup pass from me;	228 : 229, 231
	but not my will,[6] but thine be done. . . .	233, 234
	12 And he said unto his disciples, Watch and pray, that ye enter not into temptation. The spirit is willing and ready; but the	231
	13 flesh is weak . . . thy will be done . . .	232
	17 and his sweat became as *it were* drops of	235
	19 blood. . . . Sleep on now, and take your	
	26 rest. . . . Judas, comest thou to betray the Son of man with a kiss? Now wherefore	
	27 art thou come, friend? . . . Whom seek	236
	28 ye? . . . They say unto him, Jesus of Nazareth. Jesus said unto them, I am he.	
	29 While Judas was standing with them, they went backward, and fell[7] to the ground.	154, 236

---

[1] The same word as in the Arm. Vulg.; it might also be rendered "condemned."

[2] Cod. B has, "the."

[3] Ephraem says below: "For also the reading hath, and plainly saith, Glorify me with that glory before thee, before the world was." After "also" Cod. B adds, "in the Greek."

[4] Ephraem adds this to ver. 58, above.

[5] For part of ver. 42 to follow this, cf. xlvi. 35, and note there.

[6] Ephraem, at p. 233, has, "Nay, Father, but thy will be done;" so Cod. A. Cod. B has "O" for "Nay." At p. 234 he has, "Not as my will is, but *as* thine."

[7] The same as in the Arm. Vulg.

Diatessaron.		Moesinger.
48 37[1]	... Put up again thy sword into his	186,232,236
40	place. ... (He healed the ear) ...	232
47	they bound him, and led him away.[2] ...	237
49 36	Hereafter shall ye see the Son of man coming with bright clouds with the angels	
37	of heaven. Then the high priest laid hold of his garments, and rent his robe. ...	
43	And they took *and* led him out, and gave	238
44	him into the hands of Pilate. And they entered not into the judgment hall, lest they should be defiled, that they might	
47	first eat the lamb in holiness[3] ... he forbiddeth to give tribute to Caesar. ...	239
50 14	Away with this man from us, away with	238
40	*him* from us ... they put on him a purple	239
41	robe ... a crown of thorns ... (they put	
42	a reed in his hand.) ... And they spat in his face.	
51 3	... Shall I[4] crucify your king? ...	
7	When Judas saw, that our Lord was condemned, he repented, and went *and* brought back the thirty pieces of silver to the	
8	priests,[5] and saith, I have sinned, in that I have betrayed righteous[6] blood. They say unto him, We have no care; thou knowest.[7]	
9	And he cast the silver into the temple, and departed, and went *and* hanged himself, and	240
10	died.[8] ... It is not lawful to receive this	
11	silver into the treasury. ... (they bought	241

---

[1] On ver. 35, 36 Ephraem comments thus at p. 236: "Simon cut off the ear of one of them; but the kind Lord in his goodness took it, and fastened it on again" ...

[2] Here follow remarks on the denial of Simon, contrasting it with his confession of Christ afterwards.

[3] After this Ephraem comments on the silence of Jesus before Pilate.

[4] Lit. "Do I."   [5] Cod. B has, "chief priests."

[6] So in the Arm. Vulg. and some versions.

[7] "We ... knowest" is so in the Arm. Vulg.

[8] Ephraem refers to the other account of the death of Judas, Acts i. 18, and says, "his belly was poured forth," and, "he fell and burst asunder in the

Diatessaron.	Moesinger.

51 15 with it the place of burial.) . . . And when
he had taken up for himself[1] his cross, and
17 gone forth, . . . they found *and* took a
18 certain man, a Cyrenian, . . . and they
20 laid on him the cross . . . weep for your- 207
21 selves. For the days will come, in the
which they shall say to the mountains,
23 Cover us. . . . If they do this in the green 242
25 tree . . . the dry. . . . When they had
crucified him, they crucified with him two
26 others, malefactors . . . that that might be
accomplished, that it saith: He was reckoned
27 with the transgressors. And they gave[2] 245
28 him to drink vinegar and gall. . . . (his
raiment which was divided into four parts
31 . . . his coat was not rent.) . . . This is 243
38 the Christ, the King of the Jews. . . . He 249, 250
saved others: himself he cannot save. . . .
39 Come down from the cross, that we may see, 116
44 and believe on thee. . . . Art not thou the 242–3
Christ? save thyself and us with thee. . . .
47 Lord, remember me in thy kingdom[3] . . . 243–4
48 to-day,[4] Thou shalt be with me in the garden 244–5
50 of delight.[5] . . . Woman, behold, thy son. 54, 270
51 . . . Thou young man, behold, thy mother. 54
52, 53 . . . The sun was darkened. . . . God, my 245, 257 : 247
God,[6] why hast thou forsaken me?
52 5 . . . Let us see, whether Elijah cometh 247

midst." There can be little doubt that Tatian made use of Acts i. 18 and
1 Cor. xi. 23-25. Cf. *Diat.* xlv. 16, note.

[1] Or, "by himself." So also in the Arm. Vulg.
[2] Ephraem puts this after the conversation with the penitent thief. Cf. *Diat.* lii. 2.
[3] So given in the Acts of Pilate.
[4] In his citations Ephraem does not join "to-day" with "Thou shalt be." He merely refers to it in his comment. Probably his *Diatessaron* had it joined to, "I say unto thee," as in the Acts of Pilate. It may be so taken in the Curetonian Syriac, but not in the Peschito.
[5] *I.e.* "of Eden."
[6] Ephraem cites it below as "Eli, Eli" in Cod. A, as "El, El" in Cod. B.

| Diatessaron. | Moesinger. |

52 6 to take him down. . . . Father, forgive them, 117,256,265
7 for they know not what they do. . . . Into 254
8 thy hands I commend my spirit. . . . (The 256
12 veil was rent). . . . Woe was it, woe was it 245
to us:[1] this was the Son of God! Behold, 246
the judgments of the desolation of Jerusalem
17 are come . . . and one of the soldiers with 259
21 a spear pierced him. . . . The kinsfolk[2] of 258
25 Jesus stood afar off. . . . Joseph . . . a 266
26 just man . . . he was not consenting to the
27 counsel and deed of them . . . begged his
35 body . . . (a stone was laid at the door of
44 the sepulchre) . . . they sealed his sepulchre.
46 . . . (Mary[3] went early to the sepulchre.) 267
49 . . . (the stone on which the angel sat.) 266

53 22[4] . . . (She believed him to be the 29
gardener.) . . . If thou hast borne him 269
24 hence. . . . Touch me not; for I am not 268–271
yet ascended to my Father: <but> go, say
unto my brethren: I ascend unto my Father
and your Father, and to my God and your
27 God. . . . (They persuaded them with money 267
28 *to say*,) His disciples stole him away, while
we slept.

54 41,43 . . . Lovest thou me? . . . Follow me. 101: 271
44 . . . He turned and looked, and saw that 271
45 disciple, . . . and saith unto him, Lord, and
46 what *shall* this man *do?* He said unto him,
What is that to thee?[5]

55 5,6 . . . Go ye into all the world . . . and 226
baptize them in the name of the Father and

---

[1] Cod. B has simply, "Woe to us." In his remarks (p. 248) Ephraem again refers to the cry of "Woe," and connects it with the beating of their breasts and the desolation of the city. See note on *Diat.* lii. 13.

[2] Cod. B has, "servants."

[3] Ephraem understood this of the Virgin Mary; cf. his remarks both at p. 29 and p. 269, etc.

[4] On ver. 14 Ephraem remarks (p. 267): "The garment wherein he had been wrapped, he left there in the sepulchre."

[5] In his comment (p. 272) Ephraem quotes, "If I will."

Diatessaron.		Moesinger.
55 7 of the Son and of the Spirit. (They shall	106
do¹ and) observe all *things* that I have com-	
11 manded you . . . but ye shall tarry in	158, 274
Jerusalem, until ye receive the promise of	
my Father.²	

¹ Blending Matt. xxiii. 3 with Matt. xxviii. 20 in a paraphrase. Cod. A has, "do it."

² Here Acts i. 4 is worked in with Luke xxiv. 49. At p. 158 Ephraem cites, "ye shall tarry until ye receive power."

SCRIPTURAL INDEX TO S. EPHRAEM'S WORKS.

THE printed editions of S. Ephraem's works generally contain references to passages of Scripture to which he refers; but a careful search through his writings has resulted in the discovery of a large number of scriptural allusions that are not noticed in the margins or notes. In making a complete collection, full use has been made of those which are given in Mr. Morris's translation; and in the case of the New Testament, advantage has been taken of the MS. references of the late Dean Burgon in the British Museum.

The following table was drawn up in the first instance for the purpose of tracing parallelisms between Dr. Moesinger's book and the rest of S. Ephraem's writings; but it has been thought desirable to render it accessible to the public. For this purpose it has been carefully revised, and will be found to contain a fairly complete collection, from which it will be easy to gather our author's views on any part of Holy Scripture, and on any points of doctrine that rest on a scriptural basis, besides furnishing an opportunity, such as has not before existed, of ascertaining this Father's usage in regard to various readings.

The plan adopted in tabulating these texts has been to give the references to *each paragraph of the revised Bible*; but the poetical parts of the Old Testament are taken by chapters. Very short paragraphs, such as those which introduce the "burdens" of Isaiah, are included with what follows; whilst very long paragraphs are occasionally subdivided. In the case of the Gospels, which S. Ephraem generally quoted from his *Diatessaron*, the references are given to each paragraph of the English version of the Arabic *Diatessaron*.

As already mentioned in the Introduction, for purposes of abbreviation, I., II., III. represent the Syriac volumes of the

Roman edition; *a, β, γ,* the Greek volumes of the same edition; A, B, C, Dr. Lamy's volumes; P, the Pauline Commentary; and M, Dr. Moesinger's work.

When a reference is italicised, there is a quotation there, or a close paraphrase, from which the wording of the citation, in whole or in part, can be inferred. A reference in brackets [ ] is not given by S. Ephraem, but in the notes, etc.

GENESIS.

i. 1– 5. I. *6, 8–9, 12,* 14, *116–8, 128, 148*; II. 475, 543, 548; III. xlviii. *13,* 62; β, 157; γ, *609*; A, 86; B, *60,* 494; M, 198.
6– 8. I. 8, 11, *13,* 15, *118*; III. 50; γ, *609.*
9–13. I. *11, 15, 16, 120, 122–3, 128, 148.*
14–19. I. 7, *16, 123–5*; α, 213.
20–23. I. *12, 17, 127–8*; III. *14,* 73; β, 269; γ, 184.
24–31. I. *9,* 15, *18–9, 127–1, 133, 137,* 147; II. *316, 479*; III. *13,* 63, 191, *214,* 311, 456, *631*; α, 47, 262; B, 306; P, *251*; M, 133, 232, *279.*

ii. 1– 3. I. *20,* 139.
4–17. I. *2,* 19, *21–3, 26,* 28, *127,* 129, *131–3, 139,* 147, 228; II. 316, 481, 543, 548; III. *14,* 91, 191, 350, *543,* 562, 568, 597; β, 105, 162, *324*; γ, 190, 196, 597, 611; B, 522, 612, 790; M, 198, *221,* 268.
18–25. I. *24–6, 129*; II. 322, 457; III. *14, 119*; B, 740; P, *58,* 70; M, 21, 131, *216,* 227, 260.

iii. 1–21. I. 18, *26–30, 133–1,* 177, *531*; II. *318,* 321, 324, *327,* 338, 410, 439, 457, 463, 479, 481–2, 535; III. 110, 154, 168, 246, 319, 349, *543–4,* 571–2, 578, 582, 607, 680; α, 70, 130, 137, *222,* 317; β, 12–3, 105, 147, 283, 363, 376; γ, 2, 71, 150, 174, 176, *182,* 196, 244, 267, 440, 447, 459, 477,

GENESIS—*continued.*
504, 510, 547, 570, 578; A, 154, 178, 438, 482, 502, 694; B, 384, 456, 500, 522, 526, 618, 626, 768; C, *684,* 978; P, 7, *27–8, 123,* 154–5; M, 2, 23, 100, 116, 131, 163, 187, 220, 222, *225, 239,* 244, 249, 258, 267–9.

iii. 22–24. I. 33, *38–9, 135, 138, 142*; III. 572; β, 105, 147, 363; γ, 190, 298, 477, 530, 589; A, 114; B, 384, 626; C, 988; M, 28, 235, 245.

iv. 4–15. I. *39–5, 143–5*; II. *16,* 345, 438, 475, 536; α, 129, 207; β, 25, 147, 238, 243, 400, 404; γ, 3, 24, 45, 186, 298, *342,* 477, 504, 542, 605; C, 116, 646; P, 231; M, 21, *33, 119,* 177, 205, 280.
16–24. I. *43–5, 143,* 145–6; III. 564; β, 324–5; γ, 542; M, 57.
25–26. I. *47, 145*; III. 564; M, 57, 177.

v. 1– 8. I. *47, 131,* 145–6; II. 345, 449; III. 461; M, 57.
9–11. I. 146.
21–24. I. *47*; II. *324–5,* 345, 477, 481; α, 334; β, 184, 324, 369; γ, 45; C, 116, 816.
25–27. I. *47.*
28–31. I. *47*; II. 399; C, *116,* 232.
32. I. *48,* 147; II. 345.

vi. 1– 8. I. *46, 48–1, 145–7, 150, 362,* 543; II. *20,* 63, 455, 477–0, 509; III.

SCRIPTURAL INDEX.

GENESIS—*continued.*
280; α, 44, 129, 247; γ, *150, 236, 298*; B, 384; P, 152; M, *163*, 194, *281.*

vi. 9-12. I. *45, 48-9, 51, 153*; γ, *236-7.*
13-22. I. *51, 147*; α, 129; γ, *236-7.*
vii. 1- 5. I. *52, 148, 150*; II. 177; β, 182, 342; γ, *76*, 299, 529; A, 712; M, 281.
6-24. I. 11, 21, *52-3*, 137, 144, *149-0*; II. 367; III. 367, 568, 603; α, 129; β, 182; γ, 45, 477, 542; M, 154.
viii. 1-14. I. *53, 149-0, 152*, 560; III. 564, 602; β, 342; γ, 299; A, 712; B, 724.
15-ix. 7. I. *54-5, 147, 150, 152-3, 242*, 249, *358*; III. 531; γ, 3, *519, 596*; B, 630; C, 742; M, *57*, 212, *281-2.*
ix. 8-17. I. *55, 150-1*; γ, 3.
20-29. I. *55-7, 152-5*; III. 19, 368, 682; α, 138; β, 240, 284-5, 402; γ, 76, 299, 449, 495, 557-8, 605; A, 598; B, 770, 778; C, 116, 302.
x. 2- 5. I. 153.
6-14. I. *58-9, 153-4, 158*; II. *371*; γ, 563, 565.
15-20. I. 155.
21-31. I. 153, 466.
xi. 1- 9. I. *58-9*; III. *116, 214*; α, 129; β, 243, 404; γ, 542; B, 384; M, 154, 273.
10-11. I. *59*; P, 217.
12-13. I. *59.*
14-15. I. *59.*
16-17. I. *59.*
18-19. I. *59.*
20-21. I. *59.*
22-23. I. *59.*
24-25. I. *59.*
26. I. *59, 153, 156.*
27-32. I. *59*, 156-7.
xii. 1- 9. I. *59-0*, 67, 154-5, *170*; β, 24; A, 306.

GENESIS—*continued.*
xii. 10-20. I. *60*, 65, 157-8, 169; B, 510; C, 84.
xiii. 1-18. I. *60-1, 157, 159*; γ, 59, 299.
xiv. 1-24. I. *61, 159-0*, 175; III. 107; β, 15, 240, 402; γ, *300*, 342, 589; A, 578; M, 258.
xv. 1-21. I. *62-5*, 155, *158, 161-2, 165, 170, 173*, 201, 214, *272*, 497; II. 143, *284, 291*, 314; III. 161; γ, *477*; B, 630; M, *221.*
xvi. 1-16. I. *65-7*, 84, *158*, 161, 165, [*437*]; II. 425, 435; III. 668; α, *220*; β, 24; [A, 622]; B, 730.
xvii. 1-14. I. *67, 165, 170*, 173, [*297*]; II. 454; III. 187; β, 300; γ, *477*; B, 734; M, *40*, 57.
15-27. I. *67-8*, 511; III. 668; β, 355; γ, 590; M, 13.
xviii. 1-15. I. *68-9*, 153, *163, 166*, 169, 390, 479; III. 23; α, 310; β, *313*; γ, 424, 498; A, 626, 658; C, 116; P, 12-3; M, 13, 55, 110, 175, 256.
16-33. I. *69-0, 164*; III. 106, 174, 564; α, 24, 68, 247, 310, 317; β, 190; γ, *59*, 120, *225, 247*, 481, *516*, 578; M, 175, 196, *218.*
xix. 1-28. I. *70-2, 165, 167-8*, 430, 479; II. 21, 246; III. 178; α, *247*, 310, 334; β, 81, 126, 182-3, 190, 369; γ, 24, 32, 120, *237-8*, 297, 542; B, 374, 384; P, 152, 205; M, 55, 94, 110, 281.
30-38. I. *71-4*, 168; III. 461; β, 182, 190; γ, 76, 558.
xx. 1-18. I. 65, *74-5, 157, 169-0*, 173; γ, 476; C, 482.
xxi. 1- 7. I. 75.
8-21. I. *75-7, 173*; II. 426; α, 220; A, 24, 84.

GENESIS—*continued.*
xxi. 22-34. I. 76, *174*, 176, 302, 425,*478*,538; II.188.
xxii. 1-19. I. *76-7*, *170-1*, *173*, *177*, 321, 457-8, 525-6; II. 23, *363*; III. 106; β, 24, 300, *313-4*, *317-8*; γ, *4*, 300, *562-3*; A, 24, 380, [470], 652; B, 198, 538, 630-2; P, 7, 12-3, 175, 207; M, 57, 110, *197*, 207, 251, 258-9.
xxiii. 1-20. I. 77; III. 304; β, 237, 400; P, *242*.
xxiv. 1-67. I. *78*, 82, 90, 104, 161, *172-3*; III. 670; β, 352, 355; γ, *90*, *476*; A, 64; M, 40.
xxv. 1-11. I. 170, *172*; III. 304.
19-34. I. 61, *79-0*, *173*, 405; III. 683; β, 286-7; γ, *297*; B, 398; M, 188.
xxvi. 1-33. I. *80*, *174*, 176, 302, 538; III. 112; γ, *4*; C, 116; P, 7.
34-35. I. *174-5*.
xxvii. 1-45. I. *80-1*, *177-8*; II. 438; α, 130, *266*; β, 24, 240, 402; γ, *198*; A, 542; M, 188.
xxviii. 10-22. I. *81-2*, *85*, *87-8*, *178*, 181; III. 213; β, 24; γ, 529, 593; A, 34, 96; B, 630; C, 266-8, 288; M, 266.
xxix. 1-30. I. *82-3*, 179, 200; II. 247; α, 77; β, 82, 355; γ, 90; C, 492, 564; M, 40.
31-35. I. *83*, 106; γ, 590; M, 33.
xxx. 1-24. I. *83-4*, *179*, 192; II. *420*; III. 98, *669*; B, 398.
25-43. I. *84*, 86, 91, 179; III. 98; A, 64; C, 118, 564, 770, 888; M, 259.
xxxi. 1-21. I. *85-6*, *181*; A, 514-6; C, 118, 540, 562; M, 81.

GENESIS—*continued.*
xxxi. 22-xxxii. 2. I. *86-7*, *157*, *180*, 183; β, 38, *82*, 290; A, 516; C, 492, 540, 562-6; M, 81.
xxxii. 3-21. I. *87*, *180*, 312; II. *247*; β, 290; A, 514; C, 350, 592.
22-32. I. *87-8*, *180-4*; II. *246*; β, 24, 300.
xxxiii. 1-17. I. 88, *181*.
18-20. M, 142.
xxxiv. 1-31. I. 88; II. 241; α, 139; γ, 449, 590, 594; B, 782; C, 284, 568.
xxxv. 1-8. I. *88*; M, 57, 142.
9-22*b*. I. 105, 188, 192, 417; II. 457; α, 139; γ, 449, 592; C, 284, 566; M, *34*.
22*b*-29. I. 88, 192; III. 304; M, 33.
xxxvi. 1-19. I. 175.
20-30. I. *184*.
31-43. I. 175, *184*; II. 1-2.
xxxvii. 1-36. I. 88-9, 92, 95-6, 187, 418; III. 604; β, 25-6, 28-9, *82*; C, 258-2, 268, 274-8, 286, 290, 298, 310, 314, *336*, 346; P, 238.
xxxviii. 1-30. I. *89-1*, 187; II. [*211*], 421-2; III. 83; γ, 594-5; M, 142.
xxxix. 1-23. I. *91-2*; II. 438, 474; III. 29, 603, 611, 668, 687; α, 327; β, 29, 33, 64, 87, 129, 147, 191, 288, 299; γ, 65, 71, 150, 390; A, 438, 640; C, 120, 352-6, 360, 364-0, 378, 694, 816.
xl. 1-23. I. 92; III. 416; β, 33-4; C, 382-4, *388*, 834.
xli. 1-57. I. *92-4*; II. 409; α, 109; β, 34-5, *82*; A, 306; C, 88, *404*, 410-4, 418, 426-0.
xlii. 1-38. I. *94-7*; α, 109; β, *14*, 24, 35; C, 442,

SCRIPTURAL INDEX.

GENESIS—*continued.*
            416-4, 460-4, 468, 474, *480*, 488.
xliii. 1-14. I. *97*; β, 36; C, 488-2.
      15-34. I. *97-8*; C, 498-0, 504-6, 512-4, 518.
xliv. 1-17. I. *99-0*; β, *39*; C, 520-2, 528-0, 536, 556.
      18-34. I. 101; β, *14*, *39*; C, 556.
xlv. 1-15. I. 96, *101*; β, 40; C, *588*, *592-4*.
      16-28. I. *101-2*; β, 40; C, 600-4, 610, 616, 620.
xlvi. 1-27. I. *103*, *185-6*; II. 127; C, 632-4.
      28-34. I. *103*; β, 41.
xlvii. 1-12. I. *104*; β, 237, 400.
      13-27. I. *104*.
      28-31. I. *104*, 114, 172.
xlviii. 1-22. I. *104-5*, 188; II. 244; III. 684-5; β, 286-7; A, 542.
xlix. 1-27. I. *105-4*, *177*, *186-3*, 309, 347, *350*, 356, 363, *365*, 404, 417; II. *24*, 33, *89*, *105*, 269, 457; III. *212-3*, *218*, *224*; γ, *413*; B, 550, 564, 720; P, 204; M, *15*, *26*, 32, 80, *209*, 235, 274.
      28-33. I. *114*.
l. 1- 3. I. 381, 484; III. 270, 304.
      4-13. I. 114, 187; III. 270.
      14-21. I. *114*, 187.
      22-26. I. *115*, 484; III. 304; β, 299; γ, 390; P, 233; M, *248*.

EXODUS.
i. 1- 7. I. *195*, 250.
    8-14. I. 195-6; M, 121.
    15-22. I. *196*, 207, 212, 543; II. 430; γ, 476; C, 34; M, 33.
ii. 1-10. I. 197-8; II. 535; III. 51; γ, 566; A, 464; C, 96.
    11-22. I. *157*, *198-1*, 249, 254; β, 82; γ, *90*; 220, 302; A, 26, 66; M, 40.

EXODUS—*continued.*
iii. 1-iv. 17. I. *201-3*, 548; II. 328, 418, 465, 536, *555-6*; III. 17, 86, *104*, 118, *123*, 213, *510*, 605; α, 217; β, *95*, 299, *406*; γ, 170, *192*, 303, 320, 390, 529, 573, 575; A, 48, 648; B, 588; P, *15*, *232*, 239; M, 35, 91, 152, 252.
iv. 18-26. I. *177*, 200, *203-5*, 296, 528; II. 93; A, 462; C, 34-6.
    27-vi. 1. I. *205-6*; β, 405.
vi. 10-13. III. 17.
    14-27. M, 17.
    28-vii. 7. II. 465, 556; III. 679; β, 282; γ, *414*; C, 234; P, 239; M, 226.
vii. 8-13. I. *206-8*; II. 397, 483; α, 196; β, 296, 345; A, 464; B, 384; M, 152, 252.
    14-25. I. *207-8*; A, 464; B, 384; M, 252.
viii. 1-15. I. *208*; III. 89; A, 464; B, 384; M, 252.
    16-19. I. *209*; β, 405; B, 384; M, 252.
    20-32. I. *209*; B, 386.
ix. 1- 7. I. 209; B, 386.
    8-12. I. 207, 209; II. 464; α, 237; B, 386.
    13-21. I. *210*; α, 123; A, 464.
    22-35. I. *210*, 430; α, 237; A, 464, 598; B, 386.
x. 1-11. I. *211*; II. 93; A, 464.
    12-20. I. *211*; A, 464; B, 386; C, 8.
    21-29. I. 7, *211-2*, 215; II. 474; B, 386.
xi. 1- 3. I. 212; M, 241.
    4- 8. I. *212*.
xii. 1-20. I. *212-3*, *222*; II. 415; γ, *173*; A, 426, 618, 650-4, 694, 708; B, 676; P, 234; M, 18, 36.
    21-28. A, 388; M, 197, 239.
    29-36. I. 204, *213*; II. 464; A, 586; M, 257.

EXODUS—continued.

xii. 37–42. I. 186, 195, 201, *213–4*, 250.
43–51. I. *213*.
xiii. 1– 2. M, 25.
3–10. M, 257.
17–22. I. 214, 242; III. 234; β, 299, 347–8, *426*; γ, 390; A, 8, 246; P, 66; M, 121, 257.
xiv. 1–14. I. *214*; β, 82.
15–25. I. 20, *214–5*, 431, 548; II. 445; III. 386, 630, 632; α, 22; β, 44, 82, 282, 299, 348; γ, 390, 476, 574; A, 8; P, 66; M, 46, 121, 257.
26–31. I. 197, *215–6*, 302; II. 445, 525; III. 679, 687; β, 82, 282, 288; γ, 303; B, 140; M, 46.
xv. 1–18. I. *216–7*, 322; II. 145, 530; III. 56; β, 82, 348; γ, 574.
19–21. I. *217*, 311; β, 348.
22–26. I. 217; II. 435; A, 8; M, 36, 253.
27–xvi. 36. I. 138, 218, 249, 256; III. 189; β, *104*, 349; γ, 177, 246, 529, 574; A, 66, 246; B, 676, 772; C, 82, 120; P, 66; M, 82, 134.
xvii. 1– 7. I. *218–9*, 262, 525; III. 112; α, 65, 201; β, 232, 348, 396; γ, 177, 247; A, 246; B, 574, 816; C, 84; P, 66; M, 12, 87, 134, 139.
8–16. I. 175, 215, *219–0*, 299, 302, 314, *300–1*, 548; II. 492; III. 672; β, 180, 242, 363; γ, 477; A, 630; M, 36, 252, 262.
xviii. 1–27. I. 200–1, 205, *220*, 361; II. *24*; III. 9; C, 816; P, *239*.
xix. 1–25. I. *221*, 429; [II. *198*]; III. 6, 17, 568; β, 232, 396; γ, *168*; A, 608.

EXODUS—continued.

xx. 1–17. I. *221*; II. *256*, 483; III. *187*; α, 124; A, *246*, *462–4*, *468*; C, *654*; P, 7; M, *26*, 57.
18–21. α, 124; γ, 95, 170, 226.
22–26. I. *221*, *228*, 283, *459*; γ, 170; M, *143*.
xxi. 2– 6. I. 533; α, *306*.
7–11. I. *222*.
12–14. I. *222*, *448*; M, *168*, 212.
17. III. *629*.
22–25. I. *222*.
28–32. I. 55; III. *628*.
xxii. 16–17. β, 155.
28–31. I. *228*; M, 25, 61.
xxiii. 4– 5. γ, 591.
6– 9. γ, *105*.
18–19. I. *222*, *228*.
20–33. I. *222*, *226*.
xxiv. 1–11. I. *222–3*; III. 56.
12–18. I. *223–5*, 273; II. 369; III. 639; γ, 303; B, 672.
xxv. 1– 9. I. *223*; β, 280; γ, 171.
10–22. I. *223*; II. 495.
23–30. I. 229; γ, 597.
xxvii. 20–21. I. *230*, 246.
xxviii. 13–30. I. *231*.
xxix. 1–37. I. *232*.
38–46. I. *230*, *233*, 238.
xxx. 1–10. I. 223; A, 654.
11–16. I. *430*.
17–21. I. *233*.
22–33. I. *230*, *233–4*.
34–38. I. *234*.
xxxi. 18. III. 67; γ, 4, 476; B, 738; M, 251.
xxxii. 1– 6. I. *223–5*, 474; II. 59, 100, 127, 482, 519; III. 29, 371; α, 139, 246; γ, *132*, 284, 449, 590; A, 160, *182–4*, *246*, 356, 400, 468; B, 386, 674, 730, 758; C, 54, 84, 912, 962; P, 9. 38, 209; M, 82, 91, 122, 247.
7–14. I. *225–6*; γ, *304*; C, *914*; M, *166*.
15–35. I. 187, *225–6*, 363; II. 536; α, 139,

SCRIPTURAL INDEX. 127

EXODUS—*continued*.
246; β, 342; γ, 10-1, 304, 449, 592-3; A, 160-2; B, 732; C, 912; M, 251.
xxxiii. 1- 6. III. 30.
7-11. III. 30.
17-23. I. 227; II. 413, 488; A, 76, 210-2; C, 846.
xxxiv. 1-28. I. 227-8, 273; II. 369; III. 639; γ, 184, 303; B, 672, 732; M, 25, 61, 286.
29-35. I. 27, 223, 234; II. 328, 465, 544; III. 17, 60, 118, 606; β, 43, 46, 240, 299, 402; γ, 390; A, [212], 220; B, 274, 664, 672, 798; C, 788, 912; P, 15; M, 152.
xxxv. 4-19. β, 280; γ, 171.
20-29. III. 677; β, 280.
30-xxxvi. 1. γ, 529.
xxxvi. 8-19. I. 229; γ, 171.
20-34. I. 229.
35-38. I. 229.
xxxvii. 1- 9. I. 228; B, 794.
10-16. I. 228; γ, 464.
17-24. I. 229; B, 794.
25-29. III. 564.
xxxix. 30-31. I. 231.
xl. 17-33. I. 300.
34-38. I. 234-5; III. 30.

LEVITICUS.
i. 1- 2. I. 236; β, 189.
14-17. I. 236.
ii. 4-13. I. 237.
14-16. I. 237.
iii. 1- 5. I. 238.
6-11. β, 189.
iv. 22-26. I. 237.
27-31. I. 237.
v. 1-10. I. 236.
vi. 8-13. I. 238.
19-23. β, 342.
vii. 22-27. I. 238.
28-34. I. 336.
viii. 1-36. I. 239.
ix. 1-24. β, 189; γ, 5.
x. 1- 7. I. 239-0; III. 52, 258, 679; α, 19; β, 282;

LEVITICUS—*continued*.
γ, 5, 10, 497; A, 34; M, 24.
x. 12-15. I. 240.
16-20. I. 240; III. 258.
xi. 1- 8. I. 241; III. 184; γ, 174.
13-19. I. 241; M, 82.
20-23. I. 241.
29-38. I. 241.
41-45. α, 207; γ, 82.
xii. 1- 8. I. 242; M, 189.
xiii. 1- 8. I. 242.
45-46. I. 242; III. 52, 572; α, 223-4.
47-59. I. 243.
xiv. 1-20. I. 243, 247, 262; III. 440, 572; A, 6, 38; M, 188.
33-53. II. 397; α, 134; γ, 444.
xv. 1-15. α, 223.
31. β, 148.
xvi. 1-28. I. 244; III. 17.
xvii. 1- 7. I. 450.
13-16. I. 378.
xviii. 1- 5. I. 245.
xix. 9-37. I. 245-6, 274, 316; III. 51; γ, 112, 331; M, 65, 182.
xx. 1-21. I. 136, 245; γ, 63, 594.
27. I. 387.
xxi. 16-24. I. 246-7.
xxii. 1-16. I. 245, 247; α, 223; γ, 10.
17-25. I. 247; P, 222.
26-33. I. 228.
xxiii. 4- 8. I. 246.
9-14. I. 237, 246; II. 407; M, 61.
15-21. I. 246.
22. I. 245; M, 65, 182.
23-25. I. 246, 248.
33-36. I. 246, 461.
39-44. I. 248.
xxiv. 5- 9. I. 248, 377.
10-12. I. 248.
13-23. M, 138, 212.
xxv. 8-24. I. 508.
39-46. I. 526.
xxvi. 3-13. I. 528; α, 27.
14-26. I. 249; γ, 163.
27-45. I. 249; γ, 163; M, 158.

NUMBERS.

i. 1-21. I. *250.*
44-46. α, 24.
47-54. I. *250.*
ii. 1- 9. I. 251.
10-16. I. 251.
17. I. 251.
18-24. I. 251.
25-31. I. 251.
iii. 1- 4. III. 271; α, 124; M, 24.
11-13. M, 25.
14-20. I. *251.*
21-26. I. 251.
27-32. I. 251.
33-39. I. 251.
44-51. I. *252.*
v. 1- 4. I. *252.*
5-10. I. *252.*
11-31. I. *252*; II. 427; A, 160-2.
vi. 1-12. I. *253.*
vii. 1-11. I. *254.*
12-17. I. 254.
24-29. I. *254.*
30-35. I. *254.*
viii. 5-22. M. 25.
ix. 1- 8. I. *254.*
15-23. β, 45.
x. 1-10. III. 38.
11-28. I. *254.*
29-32. I. 361.
xi. 1- 3. I. *255.*
4-15. I. 186, *256-7,* 429; χ, 246; A, 356, 418, 466, 626; B, 676.
16-22. I. *256*; M, 30.
23-35. I. *255, 257,* 352; α, 22.
xii. 1-16. I. *258,* 512; II. 425, 536; III. 51, 677, 679; α, *25,* 116, 128, 143, 223; β, 280-2; χ, 5, 454, 590; A, 238; M, *62,* 188.
xiii. 1-33. I. *258-9,* 270; β, 166.
xiv. 1-10. I. 259, 270; A, *222*; P, 208; M, 139.
11-25. I. *255, 259,* 304; C, 914.
26-45. I. 175, *259,* 266, 363, 360; β, 82; P, 43, 209.
xv. 17-21. I. *259.*
32-36. I. *260.*
37-41. I. *257, 260.*

NUMBERS—*continued.*
xvi. 1-19. I. 187, *260-1, 325*;
III. 18, 52, 256; α, 128; C, 784.
20-35. I. 187, *260*; II. 544;
III. 18, 256, 258, 679; α, 128, 132, 138; β, 282; χ, 442, 449, 495; A, 48; C, 106; M, 110.
36-40. I. 187, *260,* 552.
41-50. I. 187; III. 488, 496, 505, 508, 528; P, 207.
xvii. 1-11. I. 169, *261*; III. 38; χ, 390, 529, 575; A, 626; B, 536; P, 212.
xviii. 8-20. I. *261*; M, 25.
21-24. P, 218.
25-32. I. *261.*
xix. 1-22. I. *261-2*; α, 133; χ, 166, 443; P, 207; M, 188.
xx. 1-13. I. *262*; III. 621, 679; α, 65, 201; β, 282; A, 54; B, 574; P, 25; M, 12, 87.
14-21. β, 189; A, 66.
22-29. I. 381; III. 236, 258, 271.
xxi. 4-16. I. 113, *262-3*; II. 483; III. 21; χ, 174, 214; C, 914; M, 36, 189, 251, 253.
17-20. I. *263.*
21-xxii. 1. I. *263*; β, 349; A, 66.
xxii. 2-41. I. 134, *264*; II. 47, 483; III. 42, 74, 156, 556; α, 24, 65, 201; C, 16, 54; M, 109, 207.
xxiii. 1-30. I. *264-5*; II. *281*; M, 110.
xxiv. 1-25. I. *264-5,* 390, *432*; II. *152, 226,* 396; III. 214; B, 474, 482; M, 210.
xxv. 1- 9. I. *265,* 291, 363; II. *363*; α, 246; β, 293; χ, 135; B, 388.
10-15. I. 106, 260, *265,* 291; χ, 4, 10; B, 388.
xxvi. 15-18. I. 110.
51. I. 110.
57-62. α, 124, 132.
63-65. P, 43.

SCRIPTURAL INDEX.   129

NUMBERS—*continued.*
xxvii. 1–11. I. *266.*
       12–23. III. 107 ; β, 240, 402.
xxxi. 1–12. I. 265, *267.*
       13–24. I. *267* ; α, 246 ; γ, 135.
       25–54. I. *267–8.*
xxxii. 28–42. I. 264.
xxxiii. 1–49. I. *268.*
xxxv. 9–34. P, 21.
xxxvi. 1–12. I. 508, 544.

DEUTERONOMY.

i.   1–18. I. *269, 425.*
     19–46. I. *270.*
ii. 1– 8ᵃ. I. *270.*
     8ᵇ–15. I. 270.
     16–25. I. 271, 303.
     26–37. I. *271.*
iii. 1–17. I. *271* ; II. 1.
iv. 1–24. I. *430* ; III. *46* ; α, *242* ; β, *62.*
     25–40. I. *271* ; II. *516.*
v.   22–33. γ, 95, 226.
vi. 4– 9. I. 237 ; II. 519 ; III. *213* ; γ, *67* ; M, *152, 169–0.*
     10–15. I. 511.
vii. 1–11. I. *272* ; II. *302.*
     12–26. I. *272* ; β, 415 ; P, *273.*
viii. 1–20. I. *273.*
ix. 1–29. I. *273, 277*, 511 ; M, *166*, 247.
x.   1–11. I. 300 ; γ, 590 ; M, *161.*
     12–22. I. *428* ; III. 185 ; γ, *468* ; P, 112, *273.*
xi. 13–25. I. *237* ; C, *676.*
xii. 1–19. I. 450 ; II. 104 ; γ, 184 ; A, *636.*
     20–28. I. *274.*
xiii. 1– 5. I. *274* ; II. 24 ; M, *152.*
     6–11. M, *22.*
xiv. 1– 2. I. *246, 274.*
     3– 8. I. *275.*
     9–10. I. *275.*
     11–20. I. *275.*
     21. I. *276.*
xv. 7–11. I. *277.*
     12–18. α, *306.*
xvi. 1– 8. A, 634 ; M, *159*, 212.
     21–22. I. *277.*
xvii. 2– 7. M, *22.*
     8–13. α, 128.

DEUTERONOMY—*continued.*
xvii. 14–20. I. *277*, 331, 348, *453.*
xviii. 9–22. I. *277* ; M, *134, 136, 209, 236.*
xix. 1–13. I. *278.*
     15–21. III. 99 ; M, *68.*
xx. 1– 9. β, *177.*
     10–18. I. *278.*
xxi. 10–14. I. *278.*
     15–17. I. *278*, 331 ; II. 420.
     18–21. I. *278–9.*
     22–23. I. *299* ; M, *138.*
xxii. 1– 3. I. *279.*
     4. III. *627–8.*
     6– 7. I. *279.*
     8– 9. I. *279* ; III. *627.*
     10–11. I. *279* ; γ, 331.
     12. I. 237.
     13–21. I. *279* ; II. 427.
     22. I. *280.*
     23–24. I. 280.
     25–27. I. 280.
xxiii. 1. II. 559.
     2. II. 559.
     3– 6. I. *280* ; II. 559.
     7– 8. I. *280, 378.*
     9–14. I. *280.*
     15–16. I. *281.*
     17–18. I. *281.*
     24. I. *281.*
     25. I. *281.*
xxiv. 1– 4. I. *281*, 398.
     5– 6. I. *281.*
     16. I. 550.
     19. I. 245, *282* ; M, 65, 182.
     20–22. I. 245, *282* ; M, 65, 182.
xxv. 5–10. I. *282* ; γ, 594.
     13–16. I. *282.*
xxvi. 1–11. I. *282.*
     12–15. I. *282–3.*
     16–19. II. *303.*
xxvii. 1– 8. I. *283*, 299, 487.
     11–14. I. *283*, 487 ; II. 220.
     15. II. 220.
     18. III. 99.
xxviii. 1–14. I. *283–4.*
     15–68. I. *284–5*, 486 ; II. 117, *234*, 283 ; III. 17, 27, 206.
xxix. 2– 9. I. *285* ; II. 465 ; A, 246.
     10–29. I. *285* ; β, 344.
xxx. 1–10. I. *286* ; II. *93, 283* ; III. 188 ; B, *308.*
     15–20. I. *286*; III. 118; γ, 67.

9

DEUTERONOMY—*continued.*
xxxi. 24-29. III. 118.
30-xxxii. 43. I. *185, 284-7, 317,* 358;
II. *27, 52, 112, 255,
348, 371,* 432; III.
66, 206, *217;* α, 211,
215, 237, 304; β, 87,
197, 202, 380, 386;
γ, *124, 217, 224, 304;*
A, 622; C, *760-2;*
M, *120, 167, 169,
253.*
xxxii. 48-52. I. *287.*
xxxiii. 1-29. I. *10, 106, 110,* 112,
187-8, 288-1; III.
271; β, 239, 401;
M, *34.*
xxxiv. 1-12. I. 242, 262, *288,* 381,
413; II. 145; III.
258, 271, 305, 572,
605, 639; α, 217;
C, 768; M, 34, 134,
157-8, 223.

JOSHUA.
i. 1- 9. I. *292;* II. 145; α, 217;
β, *119.*
10-11. I. *293;* α, 217; M,
139.
12-18. I. *293;* M, *158.*
ii. 1-24. I. *293-4;* III. 161; α,
310; γ, 574; P, 234.
iii. 1- 8. I. *294;* β, 299; γ, 574.
9-17. I. *295,* 431; III. 630;
β, 299; γ, 390, 574;
M, 57.
iv. 1-14. I. 110, 113, *295;* β, 299,
349; γ, 390; M, 57.
15-24. I. *295;* β, 299.
v. 1. β, 299; γ, 390.
2- 9. I. *295-6;* β, 349.
13-vi. 11. I. *297-8,* 390; β, 299;
γ, 319, 390.
vi. 12-27. I. *298, 486-7,* 521; III.
211, 630; α, 99, 310;
β, 299; γ, 199; A,
84.
vii. 1. I. *298;* A, 370.
2-15. I. 301, 359; II. 153.
16-26. I. *298-9,* 352; α, 245-6;
γ, 10; A, 370; B,
388; M, 91.
viii. 1- 9. I. *299.*
10-29. I. *299,* 548; II. 154.
30-35. I. *299-0.*
ix. 3-27. I. *300,* 424-5; γ, 199.

JOSHUA—*continued.*
x. 1-11. I. *301,* 430; C, 104.
12-14. I. 20, *301;* II. 445, 447,
465; III. 316, 630;
β, 299; A, 704.
16-27. I. *301.*
31-35. I. *301.*
40-43. I. *301.*
xi. 1- 9. I. *302.*
16-20. I. *302-3.*
21-23. I. 302.
xii. 1- 6. I. *303.*
7-24. I. *303,* 315; M, 223.
xiii. 1-14. I. *303.*
15-23. I. 303.
24-28. I. *303.*
29-31. I. *303.*
xiv. 1- 5. I. 187.
6-15. I. *303-4;* γ, 593.
xv. 1-12. I. 193; M, 34.
13-19. I. *304-5;* M, 139.
20. I. *305.*
21-32. I. *305.*
63. I. 304.
xvi. 1-10. I. 304.
xviii. 1-10. I. 107, 187, *305.*
11-28. I. 331, 424; M, 34.
xix. 1- 9. I. 107, 187.
17-23. II. 152.
40-50. I. 193, *305.*
xx. 1- 9. I. *306;* III. 367-8; γ,
592; P, 21.
xxi. 1- 3. I. *306.*
43-45. I. 306.
xxii. 1- 8. I. *307.*
13-20. I. *307.*
21-29. I. 307.
xxiii. 1-16. III. 206, 274; C, 902.
xxiv. 1-25. I. *307;* β, 147; M, *247.*
26-28. I. *307.*
29-33. γ, 593.

JUDGES.
i. 1- 7. I. *308-9.*
8-15. M, 139.
16-21. I. 309; M, 34, 139.
ii. 1- 5. I. *309,* 355.
iii. 7-11. I. *309-0.*
12-30. I. *310.*
31. I. *310.*
iv. 1- 3. I. *310.*
4-24. I. 110, *311,* 315, 361;
III. 687; β, 288.
v. 1-31. I. *311-6;* A, 608.
vi. 1- 6. I. *316.*
11-24. I. *316-7.*

SCRIPTURAL INDEX. 131

JUDGES—*continued*.
  vi. 25-32. I. 317 ; II. 441.
      33-40. I. *317* ; III. 214 ; γ,
        529, 575 ; A, 68, 388 ;
        C, 914 ; M, 35.
  vii. 2- 3. I. *317*.
      4- 8. I. 109, *317-8* ; A, 66.
      9-14. I. 312, *318*.
      15-18. I. *318* ; β, *187*.
      19-25. I. 109, 284, *318-9* ; α,
        99 ; γ, 179 ; A, 66.
  viii. 1- 9. I. *319*.
      10-21. I. *319-0* ; II. *245*.
      22-32. I. *320*.
  ix. 1- 5. I. *320*.
      6-21. I. *320*.
      50-57. I. 320-1.
  xi. 1- 3. I. *321*.
      4-11. I. *321*.
      29-33. I. *321* ; M, 110.
      34-40. I. *321-2* ; B, 782 ; C,
        688 ; M, 110.
  xii. 1- 6. I. *322*.
      7. I. *322*.
  xiii. 1. I. *323*.
      2-25. I. 109, *323*.
  xiv. 1-20. I. *323-5* ; II. 410 ; III.
        159 ; γ, 72, 150 ; A,
        24, 626.
  xv. 1- 8. I. 110 ; II. 469.
      9-20. I. 242, *325-6* ; α, 62 ;
        γ, 72, 150 ; M, 2.
  xvi. 1- 3. I. *325* ; γ, 595.
      4-22. I. *325-6* ; III. 387, 582 ;
        α, 62 ; γ, 70, 72, 150 ;
        A, 438 ; M, 33.
      23-31. I. 109, *326* ; A, 680.
  xvii. 1- 6. I. *327-8* ; II. 384.
  xviii. 11-31. I. *327-8* ; II. 100.
  xix. 1-30. I. 188, *327-8* ; II. 244.
  xx. 1-11. I. *328*.
      12-23. I. *328-9*, 435-6 ; III.
        371 ; β, 415.
      24-29. I. 329 ; III. 371.
      30-35. I. *329* ; III. 371.
      36-48. I. 329.
  xxi. 16-25. I. *330*.

RUTH.

  i. 1-22. I. 451 ; β, 355 ; γ, 593.
  ii. 1-23. γ, 593.
  iv. 1-17. I. 451 ; γ, 199, 594.

1 SAMUEL.

  i. 1-28. I. *331-4* ; II. 420 ;

1 SAMUEL—*continued*.
      III. 558, 561 ; β, 55,
      300, 355 ; γ, *99*, *231*,
      391, 581, *588* ; B,
      398 ; C, 78, 962.
  ii. 1-10. I. *334-6*, *536* ; III.
      558 ; β, *354* ; γ, *345*.
      11. I. *336* ; α, 97 ; β,
      126.
      12-17. I. *336* ; III. 258 ; α,
      139 ; γ, 449, 581.
      18-21. I. 377.
      22-26. I. *336-7* ; II. [*175*],
      425 ; III. 123 ; β,
      126, *163* ; γ, *6-7*,
      581.
      27-36. I. *337-9*, 448 ; II. 133 ;
      β, *95*, *152*, *171* ; γ,
      573, 590 ; M, 109.
  iii. 1-iv. 1*a*. I. *339-1* ; α, 218 ;
      β, 88, 96 ; γ, *7-9*.
  iv. 1*b*-22. I. 327, 338, *340-3* ;
      III. 258 ; α, 139 ; β,
      278 ; γ, 449.
  v. 1- 5. I. *342* ; II. 410 ; III.
      18 ; β, 278 ; M, 241,
      250.
      6-12. I. *342-3* ; II. 549 ;
      III. 52 ; M, 250.
  vi. 1-vii. 1. I. 110, *343-5* ; II. 464,
      549 ; III. 18 ; M,
      241.
  vii. 2- 4. I. *345*.
      5-17. I. *345-7*, 356 ; A, 590.
  viii. 1- 3. I. 249, 347.
      4- 9. I. 249, *347-9* ; II. 248 ;
      γ, *305*.
      10-22. I. *348*, 395.
  ix. 1-14. I. *349-0*.
      15-x. 9. I. *350-2* ; M, *34*.
  x. 10-13. I. *352* ; P, *203*.
      17-24. I. 331, *352* ; α, 107.
      25-27. I. *352-3*, 427.
  xi. 1-13. I. 348, *353*, 440.
      14-15. I. 354, 441.
  xii. 1-25. I. 348, *354-6* ; C, 900 ;
      M, 119.
  xiii. 5- 7. I. *357-8*.
      8-14. I. *356-7*.
  xiv. 1-16. I. *357-8*.
      17-46. I. 352, *358-0*, 378.
  xv. 1- 3. I. *360-1*.
      4- 9. I. 188, 314, *361*, 377.
      10-31. I. *361-3*, 381, 410,
      506 ; II. 480 ; III.
      55, 184 ; α, 139 ; γ,
      305, 449, 478, 495.

1 SAMUEL—*continued.*
xv. 32-33. I. *363*; II. 424; α, 227.
  34-35. γ, 478.
xvi. 1-13. I. *364-5*, 378, 446; II. 287; α, *209*; A, 52.
  14-23. I. *365-7*; II. 405; β, 424.
xvii. 1-11. I. *367*, 369; α, *210*, 303; γ, 593.
  12-16. I. 367-8.
  17-54. I. *367-8, 370*, 372; II. 305, 469; III. 372, 687; α, 303; β, 241, 288, 403, 418; γ, 94, 165, 171, 501, 594; A, 54, 590, 710; M, 46-7.
55-xviii. 5. I. *370-1.*
xviii. 6- 9. I. *322, 370-1*; III. 223.
  10-16. I. 8, *372-3*; A, 474; M, 261.
  17-20. I. *372*, 384; β, 110.
xix. 8-17. I. *373*, 398, 432; β, 57; M, 81, 261.
  18-24. I. *373-4*.
xx. 1-11. I. *374*; β, 110; γ, 454.
  12-23. I. 374, *391*, 426; α, 143; γ, 454.
  35-42. I. *374.*
xxi. 1- 9. I. 327, *374-7*; M, 62, 241.
  10-15. I. 377, 386-7.
xxii. 6-23. I. 360, 364, *377-8,* 435; III. 130, 258; γ, 590; M, 35-6.
xxiii. 1- 5. I. *379.*
  14-29. I. 374, *379*, 381, *391*, 429.
xxiv. 1-22. I. *363, 379-1*; II. 401; β, 122; A, 218; C, 898; M, 33, 260.
xxv. 1. I. *381-2*; III. 273; C, 900.
  2-44. I. *382-4*, 398; C, 10, 48.
xxvi. 1-25. I. *384-6*; II. 401; β, 122; A, 218; C, 898; M, 261.
xxvii. 1- 4. I. *386-7.*
  5- 6. I. 387; II. 374; γ, 566.
  7-12. I. *387.*
xxviii. 3-25. I. *387-9.*
xxxi. 1- 7. I. *391-2.*

2 SAMUEL.
i. 1-16. I. *392*; II. 425; III. 273; γ, 591; C, 898.
  17-27. I. *392-6*; γ, 591.
ii. 1-4ª. I. *396*, 446.
  8-11. I. *396*, 446.
  12-32. I. *396-7*; γ, 591.
iii. 2- 5. I. *397*, 451.
  6-11. I. *397-8*, 409.
  12-16. I. *398*; γ, 594; M, 81.
  17-30. I. 397, *399*, 409, 421, 445; γ, 591.
  31-39. I. *399-0*, 409, 431; II. 234; γ, 591.
iv. 1- 3. I. *400.*
  4. I. 405.
  5-12. I. 400.
v. 4-10. I. *401*; II. 69; M, 181.
  13-21. I. 401; [II. *211*].
  22-25. I. *401-2.*
vi. 1-23. I. 345, 377, *402-3*; II. 426; III. 18, 223, 258; A, 676; C, 816.
vii. 1-17. I. *403-4*, 433, 457.
  18-29. I. *404.*
viii. 1-14. I. *404-5*, 550.
ix. 1-13. I. *405.*
x. 1-19. I. *406*; γ, 592.
xi. 1. I. 406.
  2-27. I. 170, 372, *407-8*, 415-7, 421, 435, 442; II. 474; III. 42, 621, 627, 670; γ, 71, 150, *595-6*; A, 438.
xii. 1- 6. I. *409, 416*, 506; II. 457, 479; III. 407.
  7-15ª. I. 356, *410*, 415, 417, 419, *511*; III. 372, 407, 458, 479, 489, 670; α, 138; γ, 198, 449; P, 7; M, 111.
  15ᵇ-25. I. 397, *410-1, 414*, 416, 420, 443; γ, 199, 596.
  26-31. II. 489.
xiii. 1-22. I. *411*; II. 430; γ, 592; B, 780.
  23-37. I. 382, *411-3*, 416, 420; γ, 592.
xiv. 1-24. I. 366, *412-5*, 419; γ, 592.
  25-27. I. *414.*
  28-33. I. 420; γ, 592.
xv. 1- 6. I. *415, 424.*
  7-12. I. 410, 413, *415-6*, 432.

SCRIPTURAL INDEX.

2 SAMUEL—*continued.*
xv. 13-29. I. 414, 418, 436.
   30-37. I. 410, 418.
xvi. 1- 4. I. *416*, 422.
   5-14. I. *416-7*; III. 623, 683;
       β, *122*, 285; γ, 286.
   15-23. I. *417*; α, 139; γ, 449, 495.
xvii. 1- 4. I. *418*; α, 139; γ, 449, 495.
   5-14. I. *418*; α, 139; γ, 449, 495.
   15-23. I. *418-9*; α, 139; γ, 449, 495.
xviii. 1-18. I. 347, 413, 416, *419-0*, 445.
xix. 1-8ª. I. *420-1*.
   11-15. I. 421.
   16-23. I. *421-2*, 445.
   24-30. I. *422*.
   31-39. I. *422-3*.
   40-43. I. 423.
xx. 1- 2. I. *423*.
   3. γ, 594.
   4-22. I. *423-4*.
xxi. 1-14. I. 381, *424-7*; γ, 597.
   15-17. I. 369.
xxii. 1-51. I. *428-2*.
xxiii. 1- 7. I. *432-4*.
   8-23. I. *434-5*.
xxiv. 1- 9. I. *435-6*; γ, 49.
   10-17. I. *437-8*; γ, 49-0.
   18-25. I. 438, 457; II. 24; γ, 50.

1 KINGS.
i. 1-53. I. 170, 416, *439-5*, 447; γ, 596; A, 68; B, 798.
ii. 1-11. I. 409, 416, 421, *444-6*, 449.
   12-46. I. 338-0, 416, 441, *446-0*, 540; III. 369, 683; β, 285; M, 36.
iii. 1- 3. I. *450*.
   4-15. I. *450-1*, 464; II. *318*.
   16-28. I. *452*; M, 33.
iv. 1-20. I. *453*.
   21-28. I. 453, 471.
   29-34. I. 451, *455*; III. 600.
v. 1-12. I. *456*.
   13-18. I. *456*, 471.
vi. 1-10. I. *457-9*; β, 276, 278.
   14-38. I. *459*.
vii. 13-51. I. *459-1*.
viii. 1-11. I. *461-2*.

1 KINGS—*continued.*
viii. 22-53. I. *463*, 498.
   54-66. I. 462-3.
ix. 1- 9. I. *464*.
   15-25. I. 471.
   26-28. I. 464, 466.
x. 1-13. I. 451, *464-7*; III. 154; M, 120.
   14-29. I. 277, *466-7*, 470; II. *303*.
xi. 1- 8. I. 277, 384, 451, *453*, *468-9*, 471, 474; II. 479; III. 154, 611, 668; γ, 71; A, 438; M, 85.
   9-13. I. 464, 469.
   14-22. I. 404.
   26-40. I. 404, 464, *469*, 471, 474; M, 109.
xii. 1-20. I. *470-2*; B, 184.
   21-24. I. 472.
   25-33. I. *473*, *475-6*; II. 101, 127, 383, 536; γ, 259; M, 122.
xiii. 1-10. I. 474, *476-7*, 488, 565; II. 535.
   11-32. I. *478-9*, 566; III. 234.
xiv. 1-20. I. 475, *480*; II. 536.
   21-31. I. *481*.
xv. 1- 8. I. *481-2*.
   9-24. I. *482-4*.
   25-32. I. 480, 482.
   33-xvi. 7. I. 484, *486*.
xvi. 8-14. I. 482, 486.
   15-20. I. 482.
   21-28. I. 482, 486.
   29-34. I. 298, 481, *486-7*; II. 101; α, 139; γ, 449.
xvii. 1- 7. I. 346, *487-9*, 491, 493, 502; II. 325, 427, 466; III. 159, 630; α, 26; β, 70; γ, 70, *240-3*, 287; A, 626; B, 804; M, 82, 130.
   8-24. I. 242, *490-3*, 496, 502, 530, 549; II. 374; III. 459, 584; α, 143; β, 152, 418; γ, *240-3*, 287, 454, 566; A, 32; B, 714, 806; C, 864; P, 235; M, 153.
xviii. 1-46. I. 7, 346, 487, *489*, *494-0*, 520, 526, *531*; II. 466-7; III. 23; α, 26; β, 70, 418; γ,

1 KINGS—*continued.*
   4, 243, 287; B, 658,
   766; C, 76; P, 121,
   235; M, 14, 83.
xix. 1–21. I. 487, 497, *499–5*, 520,
   522, 539; II. 369,
   438, 466; III. 639;
   α, 280; β, 342; γ, 70,
   287; A, 438; B, 170,
   658; P, 235.
xx. 1–22. I. *505, 508*, 512.
  23–34. I. 499, 505–8; 512.
  35–43. I. *506–7*, 535.
xxi. 1–16. I. *507–8*, 510; II. 439;
   γ, 70, 150; A, 438;
   B, 706.
  17–29. I. *488, 508–9, 511–2,
   514, 541–2*; α, 139;
   γ, 80, 150, 449; B,
   388.
xxii. 1–28. I. *485, 512–4*, [*516*],
   539.
  29–40. I. 485, *513–4*, 531; γ,
   80; B, 390; M, 153.
  41–50. I. 514.

    2 KINGS.

i. 1–18. I. *517–8*, 523; II. 427;
   III. 23; α, 26, 139;
   β, 88, 358; γ, 212,
   287, 350, 449, 495;
   M, *110*.
ii. 1–18. I. 495, 504, *518–0*, 527,
   547, 550; II. 145,
   324, 423, 425, 427,[1]
   477, 544; III. 254,
   272, 274, 580, 639; α,
   218, 280; β, 44, 70,
   240, 342, 357, 402,
   425; γ, 102, 234, 243,
   287, 320; A, 614; B,
   392, 806; C, 768, 882;
   P, 235; M, 38, 223.
  19–22. I. *521–2*; II. 401; A,
   60, 84, 106; B, 536.
  23–25. I. *521–2*.
iii. 4–27. I. *523–6*; II. 257; M,
   110.
iv. 1–7. I. *526*; α, 143; γ, 454.
  8–37. I. *527–0*, 549; II. 349,
   425, 427; α, 143; γ,
   454, 590; A, *244*; C,
   698; P, 235.
  38–41. I. 530.

2 KINGS—*continued.*
iv. 42–44. I. 530.
v. 1–19. I. *169, 530–3*, 539; II.
   536; III. 24, 687;
   β, 288–9; γ, 478; A,
   6, 30, 52, 60; M, 143,
   188, 198.
  20–27. I. 529, *533*; II. 518,
   540, 544; III. 51,
   324, 622; α, 97, 220,
   245, 281; β, 126, 234,
   243, 398, 404; γ, 24,
   259, 284, 590; A,
   370; C, 10, 744; M,
   33, 91.
vi. 1–7. I. *533–4*; β, 360, A,
   82.
  8–23. I. 87, *534–5*; α, 266;
   γ, 87, 478.
  24–vii. 2. I. *545–6*; β, 282, *319*;
   γ, 563.
vii. 3–20. I. *537–8*, 548; III. 679;
   β, 282.
viii. 1–6. I. *538*.
  7–15. I. *538–9*; C, 900.
  16–24. I. 481.
ix. 1–28. I. *539–0, 542*.
  30–37. I. *540–1*; β, 70.
x. 1–14. I. *542–3*.
  15–31. I. 500, *542–3*; [II.
   144].
xi. 1–3. I. *543–4*, 546.
  4–16. I. 448, *544–5*.
  17–20. I. 545.
  21–xii. 3. I. 544, 564.
xii. 4–16. I. *545*, 565.
  17–21. I. *546–7*.
xiii. 1–9. I. *548*.
  10–13. I. 547.
  14–19. I. *547–9*; III. 274.
  20–21. I. 242, *549–0*; II. 349;
   III. 295; γ, 478, 591;
   P, 124; M, 250.
xiv. 1–7. I. *550–1*.
  8–16. I. 551.
  17–22. I. 551; II. *274*.
  23–29. I. *551–2*.
xv. 1–7. I. *552*.
  8–12. I. *552–3*.
  13–16. I. 553.
  17–22. I. 553.
  23–26. I. 553.
  27–31. I. 553–4; II. 27–8, 33,
   35, 48, 153, 160.
  32–38. I. *553*.

[1] In Morris, but not in the Latin.

SCRIPTURAL INDEX.

2 KINGS—*continued*.
xvi. 1-20. I. *555-4*; II. 32-4; B, *504*.
xvii. 1-23. I. *554*; II. 240; A, 620; B, 250, 502.
24-41. I. 554; M, 195.
xviii. 1- 8. I. 450, *555*; II. 66, 384, 483; M, 251.
9-12. II. 33, 35, 153, 160, 240; M, 275.
13-37. I. *555-7*; II. 34, 38, 61, 64, 74, 80, *251*; β, 242, 403; B, 250.
xix. 1- 7. I. *558*; II. 64, 81; C, 92.
8-19. I. 556, 558; II. 40; α, 211; B, 250; M, *208*.
20-34. I. *272, 558-9*; II. 65, *252*, 280; III. 227; C, 88; M, 153.
35-37. I. *559-0*; II. 39, 48, 81, 252, 464; III. 687; β, 288; C, 90; M, 153.
xx. 1-11. I. *561-2*; II. 445; α, *227*; γ, 20; M, 29, 31.
12-21. [I. *563*]; α, *252*; B, 504-6; C, 90.
xxi. 1-18. I. 553, *563-4*; II. 100, 114, 127; M, 122.
19-26. I. *564*.
xxii. 1- 2. I. *564*.
3-20. I. *564-6*.
xxiii. 1-20. I. 450, 479, *565-6*.
21-30. I. 555, *566*; II. *129*.
31-35. I. 567.
36-xxiv. 7. I. 567.
xxiv. 8-17. I. 518, 567; II. 120; B, 504; M, 122, 241.
18-xxv. 7. I. 567; II. 115, 198.
xxv. 8-22. I. 567; II. 120; M, 241, 252.
27-30. II. 44, 84.

1 CHRONICLES.

v. 25-26. II. 27-8, 33, 35, 48, 153, 160.
vi. 16-30. I. 331.
x. 8-14. I. 390-1.
xi. 1- 9. III. *493*.
10-25. A, 68.
xx. 1- 3. M, 241.
xxi. 1-27. I. 436-7.
28-xxii. 1. I. 450.

1 CHRONICLES—*continued*.
xxii. 6-19. I. *411*, 457; M, 241.
xxviii. 1-10. I. 457.
11-21. I. 463.
xxix. 1-25. I. 443; M, 241.

2 CHRONICLES.

v. 2-14. I. 462.
vi. 12-42. III. *213*.
vii. 11-22. III. 518.
xi. 1-23. I. 476, 478, 481; II. 104.
xii. 1-16. I. *481*.
xiii. 1-22. I. *482*, 505, 549.
xiv. 1-15. I. 112, *482-3*; C, 234.
xv. 1-19. I. *483*.
xvi. 1-14. I. *484*, 561; III. 66.
xvii. 1-19. I. 484.
xix. 1-11. I. *485*, 514.
xx. 1-30. I. 484; M, 111.
35-37. I. 485, 514.
xxi. 1-20. I. *484*, 520.
xxii. 10-12. I. 544; M, 17.
xxiii. 1-15. I. 544.
xxiv. 1-27. I. *546-7*, 564.
xxv. 1-13. I. *550*.
14-16. I. *550-1*.
xxvi. 1-15. I. 552.
16-23. I. 339, 552; II. 29; III. 18, 51, 69, 571, 598; P, 219.
xxvii. 1- 9. I. 554.
xxviii. 1-15. I. 554.
xxx. 1-27. I. *375*.
xxxii. 1- 8. I. 112.
24-33. I. 560-1.
xxxiii. 1-13. I. 511, 563; II. 103, 127; α, 139; γ, 199, 449, 548; B, 110; M, 122.
xxxv. 20-27. I. *566*; II. 306; III. 274; C, *900*.
xxxvi. 5- 8. I. 567.
11-21. I. 567; II. *118*; M, 248.
22-23. I. *567*; II. 97, 105; M, 248.

EZRA.

i. 1-11. β, 415; γ, 597; M, 248.
iv. 1- 6. II. 95.

NEHEMIAH.

iii. 1-32. γ, 597.
iv. 7-23. γ, 597.

Esther.

iii. 1-15. I. 362.
iv. 1-17. III. 667; B, 700.
v. 1-14. III. 295; B, 692.
vii. 1-10. B, 700.

Job.

i. 1- 5. II. 2; α, 132; γ, 441.
   6-12. I. 134, 513; II. 369, 535; β, 118; γ, 564; B, 494; P, 155.
   13-22. I. 137; II. 2, 369; III. 460; γ, 301, 564; C, 84.
ii. 1-10. II. 2-3, 19, 134; III. 669; α, 81, 315; β, 118, 416, 424; γ, 24, 71, 115, 301; A, 306; C, 70; P, 155.
   11-13. II. 3; C, 808.
iii.   II. 3, 352, 356; III. 205; γ, 269, 277.
iv.   II. 3.
v.   I. 536; II. 4; III. 526; γ, 7, 48.
vi.   II. 4, 419, 428.
vii.   II. 338; III. 238, 578; γ, 292, 578.
viii.   II. 4; α, 129; β, 96, 129; γ, 440.
ix.   II. 4; β, 140; γ, 47.
x.   II. 4, 352; III. 478; γ, 518, 578.
xi.   II. 5.
xii.   II. 4-5; III. 17; β, 120.
xiii.   II. 5-6.
xiv.   II. [2], 6; γ, 578.
xv.   II. 7.
xvi.   II. 7; γ, 527.
xvii.   II. 7.
xviii.   II. 8.
xix.   II. 1, 8.
xx.   II. 8-9, 33.
xxi.   II. 9, 122.
xxii.   II. 9-0, 132; III. 135.
xxiii.   II. 10; III. 7.
xxiv.   II. 10.
xxv.   II. 10; α, 31; β, 206, 390; γ, 578.
xxvi.   II. 11; γ, 47, 417.
xxvii.   II. 11.
xxviii.   II. 11-2, 86; III. 154.
xxix.   II. 12-3; γ, 301.

Job—continued.

xxx.   II. 13.
xxxi.   II. 12-4; γ, 301; C, 932; M, 238.
xxxii.   II. 14.
xxxiii.   II. 12, 15; III. 80; β, 290.
xxxiv.   II. 15; β, 243.
xxxv.   II. 15.
xxxvi.   II. 15-6.
xxxvii.   II. 16.
xxxviii.   II. 11, 16; γ, 170.
xxxix.   II. 16-8.
xl.   I. 18; II. 18; III. 125; β, 87.
xli.   II. 18; III. 125; γ, 181, 184.
xlii.   I. 134; II. 2, 19, 177.

Psalms.

i. I. 255, 421; II. 202; α, 192, 306; β, 138-9; γ, 190, 572.
ii. I. 336, 406, 432; II. 96, 105, 158, 494, 516; III. 4, 27, 213, 217; β, 78, 203, 387; γ, 12, 97, 158, 228, 402; A, 668; B, 210, 488.
iii. I. 557.
iv. II. 122, 338; γ, 186, 343.
v. II. 62; β, 149; γ, 329.
vi. II. 345; α, 22, 31; β, 205, 389; γ, 107, 156, 162-3, 186, 204, 225, 320, 517, 598.
vii. I. 189; III. 495; α, 22, 53, 64, 68, 89, 184, 199, 223, 232; β, 31, 39, 194, 215, 373; γ, 67, 147, 362, 375, 497.
viii. I. 190; III. 212, 219, 300.
ix. II. 62; β, 199, 383; γ, 97, 154, 228, 402.
x. γ, 221.
xi. II. 119; III. 128; β, 179.
xii. I. 190; γ, 102, 107, 233.
xiii. α, 28; γ, 540.
xiv. II. 116; III. 23; α, 80.
xvi. II. 105, 409; III. 523, 630; β, 76; γ, 154, 421; M. 119.
xvii. I. 365; II. 331; III. 468, 518, 525.
xviii. I. 374, 428; III. 44, 78; α, 308; β, 75, 83; γ, 86, 102, 199, 222, 233.

SCRIPTURAL INDEX.

PSALMS—continued.
  xix. II. *115, 344*, 547; III. *24*,
        138, 140, *218, 652*; α,
        110, 298-9; γ, *331*; P,
        112; M, *127*.
  xxi. γ, *516*; M, 241.
  xxii. I. *189*; II. *271, 288*, 396,
        558; III. 128; α, *25, 68*;
        β, *44, 426*; γ, *221, 330*,
        480; A, *508*, [622].
  xxiii. γ, *161*.
  xxiv. II. *167*; III. *304*; β, *102*;
        γ, *328*.
  xxv. γ, *107, 225, 286*; M, *209*.
  xxvi. I. *170*; γ, *320*.
  xxvii. α, *236, 335*; β, *146, 183-4*,
        369; γ, *87, 93-4, 359*.
  xxviii. α, *322*; γ, *225, 329*.
  xxix. III. 53; β, *378*.
  xxx. I. *490*; III. *508, 523*; β,
        238; γ, *598*.
  xxxi. III. 10; β, *87, 119, 146*, 236,
        339; γ, *93*, 574.
  xxxii. III. 60-1; α, *90*.
  xxxiii. I. *185*; α, 114, 127, *327*; β,
        141; A, 612.
  xxxiv. I. *180*; α, *28, 90, 221*; β,
        115, 118, 142; γ, *91, 262*,
        296, 330, 436, 581; B, *718*.
  xxxv. I. *189*; III. *524*; α, *68*,
        257; γ, *107*, 222, *480*,
        482; M, *209*.
  xxxvi. I. *455, 559*; II. *110, 407*;
        III. 530; β, *116*.
  xxxvii. II. *258*; α, *9*, 31, *212, 324*;
        β, 111, *117, 119, 189*; γ,
        93, 120, 225.
  xxxviii. III. *386*, 507, *517*; α, *100*;
        β, *186*; γ, *225, 540, 588*,
        593, 595; M, *258*.
  xxxix. α, 45, *253, 320*; β, *84*, 237,
        400; γ, *308*.
  xl. III. 44, 507, *518*; α, *6, 230*,
        233, *322*; β, *183*; γ, *224*,
        286.
  xli. III. *642*; β, *139*; γ, *578*;
        A, 414.
  xlii. III. *530*; α, 64, 199, *264*,
        320; γ, *30, 107, 305, 320*,
        366, 543, 555.
  xliii. α, *264, 320*.
  xliv. III. 56, 219; α, *68*, 254,
        257, 299, *307, 323*; β,
        137, 373; γ, *327*.
  xlv. I. 350, *354*, 366, *433*; II.
        401, 423; III. 58, *215*,
        224, 607; B, *186-8*.

PSALMS—continued.
  xlvi. α, *306*; γ, *99*, 154, *231*,
        572.
  xlviii. α, 240; γ, *95, 227, 402*.
  xlix. III. 66, 147, *479*; β, *84, 86*,
        116, 204, 219, *234*, 257,
        388, 397; γ, *120, 158*,
        262, 269, 277, 398, 412,
        436.
  l. I. 18; II. 418; III. 56, 58,
        185, *413, 456, 483, 489*;
        α, *116*; β, *139, 202, 205*,
        341, 386; γ, *100, 169*,
        232, 269, 278.
  li. II. 22, 357; III. *374-5, 459*,
        466, 492, 495, 501, 506;
        α, 20, *31*, *110*; β, *111*,
        135, 160; γ, *97-8*, 199,
        203, 229, 328, 496, 510,
        540-1, 595, 598; C, *224*;
        M, *63*.
  lii. β, *139*; γ, *120*.
  liii. γ, *30, 329*.
  lv. α, *91*.
  lvi. III. *631*; γ, *320*.
  lvii. III. 128.
  lviii. II. *97*; β, 31; γ, *329*; B,
        214.
  lix. II. *356*.
  lx. III. 613; β, *231, 396*; γ,
        47.
  lxi. II. 404; III. *490*.
  lxii. β, *221*.
  lxiii. α, 64, 81, 199; γ, *103, 245*,
        344.
  lxiv. III. 128; β, *118*.
  lxv. γ, *409, 482, 549*.
  lxvi. γ, *214*; C, *950*.
  lxviii. I. 290, *526*, 549; III. 154;
        β, *68*, 206, 352, 390; γ,
        529; B, *144*.
  lxix. II. 404; III. 507; α, 58,
        68, 211, *244*; β, *45*,
        111-2, 182, 242, 246, 374,
        426; γ, *107, 359, 460*,
        480, 574; A, *510*, 622;
        M, *209*.
  lxxi. α, 111.
  lxxii. I. *345, 422*; II. 428; III.
        213-4, 216; γ, *154*; B,
        554.
  lxxiii. I. *557*; β, *139, 161*; γ, *29-1*,
        99, 230.
  lxxiv. I. *405*; β, *159*.
  lxxv. III. 62; β, *149, 242, 403*.
  lxxvi. β, *94, 96, 195, 200, 378, 384*.
  lxxvii. III. 24, 358; α, *238*; γ,

PSALMS—*continued.*
162, 466-8; A, 124; M, 31, 136.
lxxviii. I. 275, 343, 479; II. 513; III. 56, 216; α, 22, 93; β, 41; γ, 174; A, 242, 540-2; M, 82.
lxxix. II. 219; β, 141; γ, 225.
lxxx. I. 108; II. 434; III. 27, 214; α, 58; γ, 165; B, 654; M, 192.
lxxxi. II. 428; III. 22, 217; α, 65, 200; β, 66, 241, 402; γ, 225.
lxxxii. II. 2, 556; γ, 120, 162; M, 1.
lxxxiii. I. 315; III. 217.
lxxxiv. β, 80; γ, 344.
lxxxv. III. 26.
lxxxvii. I. 394; II. 396; γ, 529.
lxxxviii. III. 466; α, 306; β, 45, 83, 426; γ, 572, 598.
lxxxix. β, 90; γ, 578, 597; A, 462; M, 136, 280.
xc. I. 420; II. 193; γ, 39, 557.
xci. III. 456, 483, 489; β, 9, 117, 212, 240; γ, 220; M, 44-5, 115.
xcii. α, 9; γ, 7.
xciii. B, 638.
xciv. α, 70, 236, 257, 329; β, 76, 157, 163, 424; γ, 48, 491.
xcv. β, 182, 208, 393; γ, 53, 121, 280, 579.
xcvi. α, 240.
xcvii. II. 330, 403; α, 52.
xcviii. γ, 154.
xcix. II. 432; γ, 4.
c. I. 403; γ, 409.
ci. β, 139.
cii. II. 338, 345; α, 257; β, 85, 113; γ, 107, 305, 491.
ciii. α, 327; β, 63, 169; γ, 19, 239, 557.
civ. I. 429; II. 512; III. 85, 146; α, 19, 88, 328; γ, 47, 121, 320, 528, 557; B, 406; P, 155; M, 227.
cv. I. 214, 380; α, 327.
cvi. I. 255-6, 425; III. 112, 219; α, 24; β, 147; γ, 256; B, 718; M, 14.
cvii. III. 27; α, 10; β, 180; γ, 52, 96, 227, 402; B, 40; M, 121.

PSALMS—*continued.*
cviii. I. 524.
cix. β, 112, 116; γ, 186, 413.
cx. III. 115, 120, 214-5, 607; β, 48; A, 670; B, 810; M, 16, 26.
cxi. III. 629; α, 70; β, 92.
cxii. α, 2, 96, 245, 252; β, 92, 154; γ, 119, 177.
cxiii. β, 86, 120; γ, 221.
cxiv. I. 489; γ, 363.
cxv. γ, 598; A, 164.
cxvi. III. 233, 235, 240, 316, 357, α, 26; β, 198; γ, 262, 436; M, 9.
cxviii. III. 219, 224; α, 233, 248, 327; β, 9-0, 83, 119; B, 482; M, 266.
cxix. II. 106, 168, 338; III. 352, 473, 501, 504, 637; α, 28, 79, 84, 101-2, 111, 127, 193, 221-2, 326, 335; β, 9, 79, 90, 94, 107, 110, 133-4, 144, 152, 184, 206, 296, 369, 390; γ, 31, 100, 107, 112, 153, 161, 169, 231-2, 321, 324, 328, 332, 359, 366, 482, 570; B, 638.
cxx. γ, 455.
cxxi. III. liii. 44, 173, 487.
cxxiii. γ, 153.
cxxv. β, 80, 117; M, 174.
cxxvi. α, 35, 271; γ, 63, 153, 158, 280, 320, 555.
cxxvii. γ, 317, 327, 498, 540.
cxxviii. α, 252; β, 80.
cxxx. β, 238, 400; γ, 171, 458, 522, 578.
cxxxi. γ, 51, 153.
cxxxii. I. 345; III. 220; M, 63.
cxxxiii. β, 106.
cxxxv. α, 126, 229; M, 252.
cxxxvi. II. 527; α, 26, 213; β, 111, 168.
cxxxvii. II. 254; γ, 318, 595; B, 188, 222.
cxxxix. II. 411; III. 7, 50, 313, 315, 358; α, 251, 329; β, 139, 243, 404; γ, 112, 540; M, 217.
cxl. β, 145; γ, 221.
cxli. II. 330; III. 114, 525; α, 89, 129, 247, 280; β, 90, 161-2; γ, 439; A, 298.
cxlii. I. 314.
cxliii. III. 261, 339, 458, 466, 508;

SCRIPTURAL INDEX.

Psalms—*continued*.
    α, *68*; β, *205, 230, 374,*
      389; γ, *480*; M, *173*.
cxliv. I. 429, *433*; α, 58, *256*; β,
      96, 129, 181; γ, *54,*
      490.
cxlv. I. 316; III. *215*; α, *19, 99,*
      240, *270, 326*; β, *75*; γ,
      11, 60; B, *54*.
cxlvii. III. 213; α, 51, *76*, 238; γ,
      48, 121, 574.

Proverbs.

i. α, *70, 75*; γ, *204, 582, 585,*
    587.
ii. β, *111, 145*; γ, *33*, 340.
iii. I. 7; II. 396;[1] III. 608; α,
    79, 81, 87, 89; β, *111, 146*.
iv. β, *146, 153*; γ, *73, 331*.
v. II. *336*; α, 205, 226, *234*; β,
    198, 382; γ, *65, 132*; A,
    290.
vi. II. *318*; α, *221*, 324; γ, *57,*
    73, 212.
vii. α, 235, *261*; β, *155*; γ, 43,
    58, 73.
viii. III. 100, 508.
ix. I. *280*, 434; II. 409; α, *70,*
    72, 75, 78, 246, 263; γ, *64*;
    M, *196*.
x. α, *72, 75, 95, 234*; β, *121*.
xi. α, *76, 95–6*; β, 110.
xii. α, *82, 95–6, 106*, 235; β, *127*.
xiii. α, *95–6*; β, *165, 188*.
xiv. III. *683*; α, *5, 76, 97*; β,
    285.
xv. α, *72, 74–5*; β, 360.
xvi. III. 49; α, *27, 96–7*; β, *80*;
    γ, *330, 536*.
xvii. III. 87, 96, *683*; α, 12, 70;
    γ, *103, 235*.
xviii. II. 404; III. 28; α, *18, 75,*
    96; β, *106*; γ, *204*.
xix. I. *527*; α, *73, 81, 84*.
xx. II. 409; α, *73, 91, 230*; β,
    390.
xxi. α, *74, 77*; γ, *70–1, 204*.
xxii. α, *12, 73, 75, 94*; β, *153*.
xxiii. III. 30, 66; α, *253*.
xxiv. α, *73–4*; β, 110; γ, *359*.
xxv. I. 455.
xxvi. α, *19, 73, 276*; β, *181*.
xxvii. II. *81*; α, *74*, 80–1, *95*, 108,
    275.

Proverbs—*continued*.
xxviii. α, *74, 85, 95–6*; β, *151, 177*;
    γ, *163*.
xxix. α, *95–6*, 217; β, *165*; M, *253*.
xxx. I. *281*; III. *23*, 213; α, *207*.

Ecclesiastes.

i. 2–11. II. *339*; α, *335*; β, *184,*
    369; γ, *24, 308*; A,
    286.
   12–18. I. *420*; II. *338–9*; α,
    133; γ, *443*.
ii. 1–11. α, 110.
   12–17. γ, *586*.
iii. 1–15. β, *73*.
iv. 13–16. II. *337*; γ, *569*.
v. 1– 7. III. 41; β, *157, 165*.
   8– 9. III. 173.
vii. 1–14. [I. *515*]; III. *427*; α,
    75, 94, 96; γ, *214,*
    572.
   15–18. β, *187*.
viii. 10–15. III. 152.
ix. 17–x. 20. II. *337, 348*; α, *89,*
    217, *274*; γ, *172*, 212,
    569.
xi. 1– 8. III. 50, 53, 71, 81.
   9–xii. 8. II. *339*; III. *484*; α,
    335; β, *184, 369*; γ,
    24, 213, 308; B, *324*.
xii. 13–14. α, *133*; γ, *258, 443*.

The Song of Songs.

i. II. 401; III. *436*.
ii. I. *393*; II. *272*, 430–1; III.
    159; γ, *94*.
iii. I. *229*; γ, *530*, 535.
iv. II. 430; γ, *529*.
v. I. *365*.
viii. γ, *586*.

Isaiah.

i. 1– 9. II. *20–1, 480*; III.
    156, 211, *216–7*;
    B, *246*; M, 61.
   10–17. II. *21–2*, 115, [*183*],
    414; III. 185; α,
    129; γ, *439*; B,
    204.
   18–20. II. *22*; III. 154; β,
    124.
   21–23. II. *22–3*.

---

[1] In Morris, but not in the Latin.

ISAIAH—*continued.*
i. 24–31. II. *23, 113.*
ii. 2– 4. II. *23–4, 277, 311*;
III. 213.
5–22. II. *24.*
iii. 1–15. II. *24–5*; III. 212.
16–iv. 1. II. *25–6*; B, 346.
iv. 2– 6. II. *26.*
v. 1– 7. II. *26–7*, 407; III. 211, *217*; α, *115.*
8–10. II. *27.*
11–17. II. *27*; α, *37*; β, *199*, *383*; γ, *51.*
18–19. II. *28, 262*; α, *243.*
20–21. II. *28*; α, *37.*
22–24. II. *28*; α, *37*; β, *199*, *219, 383.*
25–30. II. *28*; III. 213.
vi. 1–13. I. 305, 339, *534*; II. *29–2, 79, 92, 140*, 433; III. 23, 45, 118, 166, 214; β, 229, 252, 304; γ, 143, *146, 289*, 420, 464, 530, *608–9*; A, 16, 58, 256, 352, 418–0; B, xxii. 450; M, *72, 113.*
vii. 1– 2. II. *32.*
3– 9. II. *32*; γ, *6*; B, 506.
10–17. I. 561; II. *32–3*; III. 56, 214; γ, *413*; A, 354; B, *486*, *506, 546, 588*; M, *22*, 24, 32, 35.
18–19. II. *33.*
20. II. *33.*
21–22. II. *33.*
viii. 1– 4. I. 217; II. *34.*
5– 8. II. *34.*
9–15. II. *34–5*; M, *28*, 79.
16–18. II. *35.*
19–ix. 7. I. *160, 493*; II. *35–7*, *396*; III. 213–4, 607; β, 308; γ, *182–3, 413*; B, *552*, 568, 624; M, *50–1*, 150.
ix. 8–12. II. *37.*
13–21. II. *37*; B, *370.*
x. 1– 4. II. *37–8*; γ, *370.*
5–11. II. *38.*
12–15. II. *38*; α, *27.*
16–19. II. 396.
24–27. II. *39.*
28–32. II. *39.*
33–34. II. *39*; M, *39.*

ISAIAH—*continued.*
xi. 1– 9. I. *190*, 353, 366, *467*; II. *40*, [*287*]; III. 213; A, *614*; B, 488, 540; P, 44; M, *16*, 36, 40.
10. I. *294, 434*; II. *40–1*; III. *608*; M, *27–8*, *121.*
11–16. II. *41, 54.*
xii. 1– 6. I. *350*; II. *42*; γ, *414.*
xiii. 1–xiv. 2. II. *42–3*, 450; β, *202*, *386*; γ, *182.*
xiv. 3–23. I. *43–4*, 450; α, *27*, 116; M, *116.*
24–27. γ, *182.*
28–32. II. *37, 44.*
xv. 1– 9. II. *44–6*, 149.
xvi. 1– 5. II. 46.
6–12. II. *46–7*, 151.
13–14. II. *47, 150.*
xvii. 1– 3. II. *47.*
4–11. II. *47–8.*
12–14. II. *48.*
xviii. 1– 7. II. *48–9.*
xix. 1–15. II. *49–0, 144–5*; γ, 170.
18. II. *50.*
19–22. II. *52.*
23. II. *52.*
24–25. II. *52.*
xx. 1– 6. II. 29, *52, 102*; α, *280*; γ, 289, *359.*
xxi. 1–10. II. *52–4.*
11–12. II. *54.*
13–17. II. *54–5, 74.*
xxii. 1–14. II. *55–6*; III. *376*; α, *224.*
15–25. II. *56–7, 239*; III. 27; γ, 575.
xxiii. 1–18. II. *57–8*, 148.
xxiv. 1–15. II. *59, 282*; III. 203, 213, *216.*
16–20. II. *59–0*; III. 98.
21–23. II. 39, *60*; III. 220.
xxv. 1– 8. I. *438*; II. *60–1*; γ, *414, 531*, 576.
9–12. II. *62*; III. *213.*
xxvi. 1–10. II. *62–3, 344*; α, *252*; β, *249, 256*; γ, *120.*
11–15. II. *63.*
16–19. II. *63–4*; III. *316*; α, *319*; β, *118*; γ, *124, 128*, 596.
20–21. II. *64.*

SCRIPTURAL INDEX.

ISAIAH—*continued.*
xxvii. 1. I. *191*; II. *64*.
2- 6. II. *65*.
7-11. II. *65-6*.
12. II. *66*.
13. II. *66*.
xxviii. 1-13. II. *66-8*; III. 86.
14-22. I. *420*; II. *68*; III. *219*; M, 28.
23-29. II. *69*.
xxix. 1- 8. II. *69-0*.
9-12. II. 70.
13-14. II. *70*; α, *85*.
15-24. II. *70*.
xxx. 1- 5. II. *71*; α, *115*; γ, *413*.
6-18. II. *71-2*; γ, *125*, *162*.
19-26. II. *72*; γ, *125*, 188.
27-33. II. *72-3*; III. 66, 111; A, 88.
xxxi. 1- 9. II. *73-4*; α, *282*; β, *89*.
xxxii. 1- 8. II. *74*; III. 7.
9-20. II. *74-5*.
xxxiii. 1- 6. II. *75-6*.
7-12. II. *76*.
13-24. I. 490; II. *76-8*; III. 178; γ, *63*; A, 90.
xxxiv. 1-17. II. *78*; α, 39; β, *193*, *213*, *251*; γ, *145*, *373*, *553*, *556*.
xxxv. 1- 2. II. *79*.
3-10. II. *79-0*; III. 27, 217; γ, *290*; B, *760*.
xxxvi. 1-22. II. *80*.
xxxvii. 1- 7. II. *81*.
8-20. II. 54, 156; α, *211*; M, *208*.
21-35. II. *65*, *81*, *85*; III. 38.
36-38. II. *81*.
xxxviii. 1- 8. II. *82-4*; III. *632*; γ, 565; B, 796; C, 26; M, 29, 31.
9-20. II. *82-4*; III. *353*; γ, *204*.
21-22. II. *84*; C, 26.
xxxix. 1- 8. II. *84-5*; III. 98.
xl. 1- 2. II. *85*; III. *220*.
3- 8. II. *85-6*; III. *214*, *220*, *314*; α, *215*; β, *77*, *93*, *245*, *405*; γ, *282*; B, *314-8*, *324*, *328*, *334*.

ISAIAH—*continued.*
xl. 9-26. II. *86-7*, 434; III. 82, 110, 144, *546*; β, *202*, *386*; γ, *124*, *154*.
27-31. II. *87-8*; III. 66, 173.
xli. 1- 7. II. *88*; M, *157*.
8-20. II. *88-9*, *97*; B, *214*; M, 111, 121.
21-24. II. *89*.
25-29. II. *90*.
xlii. 1-17. II. *90-2*; III. *652*; γ, *2*, *469*.
18-25. II. *92-3*.
xliii. 1-13. II. *93*; III. *220*; α, 70, *255*; β, *343*; B, *106*.
14-xliv. 5. II. *137*; III. *220*; β, 245, 405; B, *106-0*.
xliv. 6-20. γ, *417*; B, *112*; C, *204*, *210*, *760-2*; M, *157*.
21-23. B, *112*.
24-28. B, *114*.
xlv. 1- 7. I. *451*; II. *214*; B, *116*.
8. B, *116*.
9-13. B, *118*.
14-17. B, *120*.
18-25. β, *195*, *197*, *215*, *253*, *381*; γ, *218*; B, *120*.
xlvi. 1- 2. B, *120*.
8-13. III. 518; B, *120-2*, [284].
xlvii. 1- 7. II. 450; III. 220; B, *122*, *164*, *202*.
8-15. II. 450; III. 51; γ, 52; B, *122-4*.
xlviii. 1-11. II. *308*, 450; B, *124-6*.
12-19. II. 450; B, *126*; M, *157*.
20-22. II. 450; B, *126*.
xlix. 1-13. I. *534*; II. *5*; III. 539; γ, *87*; B, *128-2*; M, *121*.
14-21. II. *267*; III. *220*; B, *132-4*.
22-26. II. 435; B, *134-6*, *174*.
l. 1- 3. III. 102; B, *136*.
4- 9. α, *115*; β, *146*; γ, *359*; B, *136-8*.
10-11. B, *138*.

ISAIAH—continued.
li. 1- 3. B, *138.*
4- 6. B, *1.38-0.*
7- 8. β, *146*; γ, *459.*
9-11. III. 69; γ, *290*; B, *140.*
12-16. γ, *87*; B, *140-2.*
17-23. B, *142-4.*
lii. 1- 2. III. 214; B, *144.*
3- 6. I. *523*; γ, 52, *104-5*; B, *144.*
7-12. III. *212*, 538; α, 27; γ, *598*; B, *144*; M, *134.*
13-15. B, *144-6.*
liii. 1- 3. I. *523*; II. *396*; III. 27, 213-4, *409*; B, *146-8.*
4- 6. II. *286*; γ, 52, *413*; B, *148.*
7- 9. I. *237*; II. 298, 425, 435; III. *9*, 213-4, 573; β, *319*; B, *150*; M, *187*, *262.*
10-12. B, *150-2*; M, *234.*
liv. 1-10. I. *384*; II. *119*; III. *219-0*; B, *152-4*, 766; M, *33*, *246.*
11-17. III. *220*; α, *216*; B, *154-6.*
lv. 1- 5. II. *33*, *387*; III. 27, 157; B, *156-8*; M, *121*, *196.*
6-13. III. *516*; B, *158-0.*
lvi. 1- 8. γ, 554; B, *158-0.*
9-12. B, *162.*
lvii. 1- 2. B, *162.*
3-14. III. 27; B, *162-4.*
15-21. B, *164.*
lviii. 1-14. III. *642*; α, 129, *256*; γ, *439*, *491*, *583*; A, 444; B, *166-8*, 686.
lix. 1-21. II. *122*; β, 137; γ, *412*; B, *168-2.*
lx. 1-22. I. 433; II. *287*; III. 122, *214*, 217, *219-0*; γ, *96*, 228, 402; B, *172-8*; C, 720, *966.*
lxi. 1- 9. III. 213, *219*; γ, *168*; B, *178-2*, [354]; M, *273.*
10-11. III. *220*; γ, *554*; B, *184.*
lxii. 1- 5. II. *140*; III. 213,

ISAIAH—continued.
220; B, *186-8*; C, 960.
lxii. 6- 9. B, *188.*
10-12. β, *202*, *386*; γ, *154*; B, *188*, *228.*
lxiii. 1- 6. I. *190*; II. *307*; γ, 554; A, 68; B, *188-0.*
7-lxiv. 12. II. *169*, 332; α, *35*, *38*, *91*, *153*, *234*, *335*; β, 179, *184*, *208*, *308*, *369*, *392*; γ, *21*, *149*, *188*, *220*, *384*, *555*, 582; B, *190-6*; C, *708.*
lxv. 1- 7. I. 508; III. 78, 518; B, *196.*
8-12. B, *198.*
13-25. II. *93-4*; β, 193, 213, 251; γ, *125*, 145, 190; B, *200-2*; M, *122.*
lxvi. 1- 4. II. *94*, 418; III. 358; α, *8*, 101, *233*, *237*; β, *145*, *291*; γ, *6*; B, *202-4*; M, *63*, 74.
5- 9. II. *94-5*; B, *204-6.*
10-24. I. *559*; II. *95-7*, *283*; III. *219*; α, 39; β, 193, 213, 251; γ, *64*, 145, 190; B, *206-4*, *296.*

JEREMIAH.
i. 1- 3. II. *98.*
4-10. II. *98-9*, *133*; III. 227; β, 42, *119*, *333*, *427*; γ, *288-9*; A, 80; M, *251.*
11-19. I. *193*; II. *99-0.*
ii. 1- 3. II. *100*; β, *168.*
4-28. II. *98*, *100-2*, 442.
29-37. II. *102-3*; M, *166.*
iii. 1- 5. II. *103-4.*
6-25. II. *104-6*; γ, 594, *596.*
iv. 1- 2. II. *106.*
3-18. II. *106-8*, *130*; III. 185, 214; M, *218.*
19-22. II. *108.*
23-31. II. *108-9*; [A, 622].
v. 1- 9. II. *109-0*, *220*, *282*; β, *147*; B, *142*, *172.*

SCRIPTURAL INDEX. 143

JEREMIAH—*continued.*
- v. 10-19. I. 284; II. 110, 159.
- 20-29. II. 110; III. 50.
- vi. 1- 8. II. 110-1, 121.
- 9-15. II. 111, 282.
- 16-21. II. 111-2.
- 22-30. II. 112.
- vii. 1-15. II. 113; III. 220; γ, 568.
- 16-20. II. 114, 127; α, 129; γ, 289, 459.
- 21-26. II. 114.
- 29-34. II. 115.
- viii. 1- 3. II. 116.
- 4-17. II. 116-7, 470; III. 156; α, 316; γ, 150, 459, 596.
- 18-22. II. 118; γ, 596.
- ix. 1- 6. II. 119, 282, 345; α, 40, 110, 146, 153, 255; γ, 490, 494.
- 7- 9. III. 67.
- 13-16. III. 219.
- 17-22. I. 267.
- 23-26. II. 119-0.
- x. 1-10. II. 120.
- 11. II. 262.
- 17-25. II. 120-1; III. 64, 476.
- xi. 15-17. II. 115, 121, 127.
- 18-23. II. 121-3; γ, 289.
- xii. 1- 6. I. 541; II. 122-3.
- 7-13. II. 121, 123-4; C, 10.
- 14-17. II. 124.
- xiii. 1-14. II. 125; A, 68.
- 15-19. II. 125.
- 20-27. II. 125-6; III. 63, 154.
- xiv. 1- 6. II. 126.
- 7- 9. II. 126, 493.
- 10-18. II. 112, 127.
- xv. 1- 9. II. 127; M, 122.
- 10-11. II. 127-8.
- 15-18. II. 128; α, 237; β, 418.
- 19-21. II. 128; III. 273; α, 282; β, 89.
- xvi. 1-13. II. 128.
- 14-21. II. 128-9; M, 51.
- xvii. 1- 4. II. 129.
- 5-11. I. 356; II. 129-0; α, 289; γ, 409-0.
- 12-18. II. 131; α, 20, 63, 172, 199; γ, 498.
- xviii. 1- 4. II. 131; β, 273.
- 5-12. II. 99, 131.
- 13-17. II. 131-2.

JEREMIAH—*continued.*
- xviii. 18. II. 132.
- 19-23. II. 132.
- xix. 1-13. I. 340; II. 133; III. 216.
- 14-15. II. 133.
- xx. 1- 6. II. 133.
- 7-13. II. 133-4, 146.
- 14-18. II. 134.
- xxi. 1- 2. II. 134.
- xxii. 1- 9. II. 135.
- 10-12. II. 135.
- 13-19. II. 135.
- 20-30. II. 136.
- xxiii. 1- 4. II. 136-7.
- 5- 8. II. 137.
- 9-14. II. 137.
- 15-29. II. 137-8; γ, 169.
- 30-40. II. 138; III. 216.
- xxiv. 1-10. I. 489; II. 138-9.
- xxv. 1-14. I. 567; II. 154.
- 15-31. II. 139, 157.
- xxvi. 10-24. P, 235.
- xxvii. 1-11. II. 148.
- 12-22. III. 377.
- xxviii. 1-17. III. 27.
- xxix. 1-20. III. 456, 483, 489.
- xxx. 4-11. II. 139-0, 146.
- 12-22. II. 118, 139-0.
- xxxi. 1- 9. II. 93, 140; α, 27.
- 15-20. II. 139, 141; M, 32-4.
- 21-22. II. 141, 412; III. 214.
- 31-40. II. 141-2; α, 27; M, 286.
- xxxii. 1- 5. II. 142.
- 6-15. II. 142.
- xxxiii. 14-26. II. 137, 142.
- xxxiv. 8-22. I. 497; II. 143.
- xxxv. 1-11. M, 275.
- 12-19. II. 143; M, 275.
- xxxvi. 9-26. III. 186; B, 512.
- xxxvii. 11-21. β, 71.
- xxxviii. 1-13. II. 177; β, 71, 418; γ, 289, 591; A, 80.
- xl. 1- 6. II. 141.
- xliii. 1-13. II. 144.
- xliv. 15-23. II. 120, 255.
- xlv. 1- 5. II. 145.
- xlvi. 1- 2. II. 146.
- 3-12. II. 146.
- 14-28. II. 146-7.
- xlvii. 1- 7. II. 147.
- xlviii. 1-47. II. 148-9; β, 95.
- xlix. 1- 6. II. 152-4.

144 DISSERTATION ON S. EPHRAEM SYRUS.

JEREMIAH—*continued.*
xlix. 7–22. II. *154–6*, 160; III. *284.*
23–27. II. *156.*
28–33. II. *157.*
34–39. II. *157–8.*
l. 1– 5. II. *158–9.*
6–16. II. *159.*
17–20. II. *160.*
21–32. II. 93, *160.*
33–46. II. *160.*
li. 1–14. II. *160*, *205.*
25–32. II. *160–1.*
33–44. II. *161–2.*
45–58. II. *163*; III. *217.*

LAMENTATIONS.

i. II. *163*; III. 212; B, *216*, *226.*
ii. II. *163*; III. 212; B, *218.*
iii. II. *164*; β, *168*; B, *218–2*, *226.*
iv. II. *133*; β, *319*; B, *222–6*, 372.
v. II. *350*; III.*509*; β, *319*; B, *226–8.*

EZEKIEL.

i. 1–28. I. 248; II. 26, *165–7*; III. 103, 146, 213, 557; γ, 420; B, 544; C, 122.
ii. 1–iii. 3. II. *167–8*, 345.
iii. 4–11. II. *89*, *168.*
12–15. II. *167–8*; III. *338.*
16–21. II. *168*; γ, *56*, *583.*
22–27. II. *168.*
iv. 1– 3. II. *169*; III. 67.
4–17. II. *169–0*, 345.
v. 1– 4. II. *170*, *232*; γ, *87.*
5–17. II. *170–1.*
vi. 1–10. II. 116, *171.*
11–14. II. *171.*
vii. 1– 4. II. *171.*
5–27. II. *108*, *172*; γ, *590.*
viii. 1–18. II. *172–3*; III. 216; B, 202.
ix. 1–11. II. *174*; B, 210.
x. 1–22. II. 26, *174*; III. 214; γ, 420; C, 122.
xi. 1–13. II. *175.*
14–25. II. *175*; III. 213.
xii. 1–16. II. *176.*
xiii. 1– 7. I. *480*; II. *176.*
8–16. II. *176.*
17–23. II. *176–7*; 440.
xiv. 1–11. I. *390*; II. *177.*
12–23. II. *177*, *183*; α, 129;

EZEKIEL—*continued.*
β, *234*, 397; γ, 83, 439.
xv. 1– 8. II. *177.*
xvi. 1–14. II. *177–8*; III. 189.
15–34. II. *178–9*; III. 190.
35–43. II. *179*; III. 190.
44–63. II. *104*, *180*; III. 190, *219*; γ, 200.
xvii. 1–10. II. *180.*
11–21. II. *181.*
22–24. II. *181.*
xviii. 1–32. II. *155*, *181–2*; III. 26, 28, 149, 261, 377, 460; α, 184, *316*; β, *88*, *149*, 206, *246*, 309; γ, 513, 565, *597–8*; A, *74*; C, *20.*
xix. 1– 9. II. *182.*
10–14. II. *182.*
xx. 1–26. II. *183*; B, 162.
27–44. II. *183*; III. 187.
45–49. II. *184.*
xxi. 1– 7. II. *184.*
8–17. II. *184.*
18–23. II. *184–5.*
24–27. II. *185*[–*6*]; III. 211.
28–32. II. *185.*
xxii. 1–16. II. *186*; III. 27; β, 147.
23–31. II. *186*; M, *166.*
xxiii. 1–21. II. *186–7*; B, 162.
36–49. II. *187*; M, *223.*
xxiv. 1– 5. II. *187.*
6–14. II. *187.*
15–24. II. *187.*
25–27. II. *187.*
xxv. 1– 7. II. *188.*
8–11. II. 148, *188.*
12–14. II. *188*, *293.*
15–17. II. *188.*
xxviii. 1–10. II. *188.*
11–19. II. *188–9.*
20–24. II. *189.*
xxix. 1–16. II. 64, 147, *189*[–*0*].
17–20. II. 148.
21. II. *189.*
xxx. 1– 5. II. 190.
6– 9. II. 190.
13–19. II. *190.*
20–26. II. *190*; γ, 592.
xxxi. 1– 9. II. *190–1.*
10–17. II. *191–2.*
xxxii. 1–16. I. 7; II. *192.*
17–32. II. *192–3.*
xxxiii. 1– 9. γ, *56*, *583.*

SCRIPTURAL INDEX. 145

EZEKIEL—*continued.*
xxxiii. 10-20. II. *193*; III. 149, 261, 377, 460; α, *184, 249, 316*; β, 206, 390; γ, 513, 565, *597-8*; A, *74*; C, *20*.
21-33. II. *193*.
xxxiv. 1-19. II. *193-4*; III. *62-4*, 114, 199, *300*; α, *267-9*; γ, *589*.
20-31. II. 97, *194*; III. 27; α, *269*.
xxxvi. 1-15. III. 376.
xxxvii. 1-14. II. *194-5*; III. 20, 53, *301*, 337; β, *355*; γ, *123-4*.
15-28. II. *195-6*; III. *220*.
xxxviii. 1-13. I. *112*; II. 20, *196*; B, 208; [C, 198].
14-23. II. *197*; B, 208; C, *200*.
xxxix. 1-10. II. 95, *197*; C, *202*.
11-16. II. *197*.
25-29. II. *198*.
xl. 1- 4. II. *198*.
5-16. II. *199*; γ, 530.
17-27. II. *199*; γ, 530.
38-47. II. *199*.
xli. 15-26. II. *200*.
xlii. 1-14. [II. *198*].
xliv. 1-14. γ, 590; B, *534, 584*; M, 35.
15-31. I. *491*; II. *200*; γ, 575.
xlv. 1- 8. II. *200*.
xlvi. 1-15. [II. *199*].
xlvii. 1-12. I. 489; II. *201-2*, 407; III. 24, 112; A, 106.
xlviii. 8-20. γ, 590.

DANIEL.
i. 1-21. II. *203-4*; III. 584, 639, 687; α, 25; β, 289, 319-0; B, 652, 664, 668.
ii. 1-16. II. 177, *204*, 463; III. 109; P, 235.
17-24. II. *204-5*.
25-49. II. *205-6*, 463, 469; III. *214*, 584; γ, 530; B, 272, 766, 816; M, *22, 193*, 266.
iii. 1-30. I. 285; II. *207-8, 225*;

DANIEL—*continued.*
III. 177, 386, 432, 508, 632, 639, 687; α, *302*; β, 68, 72, 82, 289, 319, 343, 346, 418; γ, 123, 187; A, 78, 596; B, 656, 700; C, xix.; P, 235; M, 56, 110.
iv. 4-18. I. 28; II. *206, 209*, 400; M, *49*.
19-37. II. 171, *208-0*; III. *214*; α, 129; γ, 439; M, *49*.
v. 1-12. II. *210-1*; γ, 598; M, 241.
13-31. II. *211-2*; B, 660-2.
vi. 1-24. II. *212-3*; III. 631-2, 639, 687; β, 71, 289, 346, 418; γ, 70, 290; A, 530; B, 656, 698; P, 235; M, 266.
vii. 1-14. I. 174; II. *213-6, 511*, 516; III. 56, 213-4, 522, 635; α, 33, 39, 63; β, 192, *194*, 213, *215*, 251, *253*, 256; γ, 145, *147*, *156-7, 269, 277, 281, 290, 309, 375*, 421, 553, 579; A, 136, 352, 680; B, 638.
15-28. II. *216, 218*; III. 86; γ, 143, *290, 310*.
viii. 1-14. II. 157, *216-8*; III. 522.
15-27. II. *218-0*; III. 19, 118.
ix. 1-19. II. *220[-1]*; α, *25*; γ, *488*; B, 488.
20-27. II. *220-2*, 290; III. 602; A, 354; B, 662; M, 166, *213*.
x. 1-xi. 1. II. *223-6*; A, *206-0*, 634; B, 666, 670.
xi. 2-xii. 4. II. *226-2*; III. 86, 637.
xii. 5-13. II. *232-3*; III. 19, 86; γ, 143; C, *860*.

HOSEA.
i. 1- 9. I. 549; II. *234-6*; III. 159; γ, 595.
10-ii. 1. II. *235-6*, 396; III. 214, *219*.

HOSEA—*continued.*
ii. 2-23. II. *236-7*; III. 102, 212.
iii. 1- 5. II. 103, *237-8.*
iv. 1-19. II. *238-9*; III. 151.
v.   1- 7. II. *103, 240.*
     8-15. II. *240.*
vi. 1- 3. II. *240.*
     4-11. II. [*180*], *240-1*; β, *112.*
vii. 1-16. II. *241-2*; β, *231, 395.*
viii.1-14. I. *441*; II. 115, *242-3.*
ix. 1-17. II. *243-4.*
x.   1-15. II. *244-5*; III. *xxxvi.* 43; β, *231, 395*; ɣ, *93*; B, *34.*
xi. 1-11. II. 93, *245-6*; β, *47*; M, *32.*
12-xii. 6. II. *246.*
xii. 7-14. II. *246-7.*
xiii.1-16. II. *247-8*; III. *544.*
xiv. 1- 9. II. *248*; α, *162*; ɣ, *468, 557.*

JOEL.
i.   1-20. II. *249-1.*
ii. 1-14. II. *250-1*; III. *518*; ɣ, *157, 186, 459, 468*; M, *67.*
     15-17. II. *251.*
     18-27. I. *434*; II. *251-2, 254.*
     28-iii. 8. I. *113*; II. *252-3*; M, *274.*
iii. 9-21. II. *253-4*; III. 484, 607.

AMOS.
i.   1- 2. II. *255, 259.*
     3- 5. II. *157, 255-6.*
     6- 8. II. *256.*
     9-10. II. *256.*
     11-12. II. *257.*
     13-15. II. *257.*
ii. 1- 3. II. *257.*
     4- 5. II. *257.*
     6-16. II. *258-9*; α, 129; ɣ, 439.
iii. 1- 8. II. *54, 259-0*; ɣ, *434.*
     9-16. II. *260.*
iv. 1- 3. II. *260.*
     4-13. II. *27, 260-1*; III. 213.
v.   1-27. II. *28, 261-3*; III. 185, 212; α, *69*; β, *375*; ɣ, *203, 468, 599*; A, *636.*
vi. 1-14. II. *263-4.*
vii. 1- 3. II. *264.*
     4- 6. II. *264-5.*

AMOS—*continued.*
vii. 7- 9. II. *265*; III. 213, *219*; M, *193.*
     10-17. II. *259, 265.*
viii.1-14. II. *266*; M, *63.*
ix. 1-10. II. *148, 267.*
     11-15. II. *267-8.*

OBADIAH.
i. 1-21. II. *269-1*; ɣ, *468*; B, *190.*

JONAH.
i. 1-17. I. 551; II. 359, 379, 382, 546; III. 508; α, *319*; β, 70; ɣ, 561; A, 88, 546; B, *230-4*; P, 124.
ii. 1-10. II. 331, 359, 379; III. 37, 312, 317, 385, 459; α, *319*; β, 70, 278, 346; ɣ, 20, 70, *468*, 561; A, 88, 546; B, *234-6*; P, 124.
iii.1-10. II. *359-1*, 371, 373; III. 640; ɣ, 32, *170*, 182-3, 561-2, 566-7; B, 234, *238-0*, 692; C, 964.
iv. 1-11. I. *494*; II. 373, 377-9 381; III. 203; ɣ, *555, 565-8*; B, *238-4*; C, 94.

MICAH.
i.   1-16. II. *273-4.*
ii. 1-11. II. *274-5.*
     12-13. II. *275-6.*
iii. 1-12. II. *276*; ɣ, *204*; M, *122.*
iv. 1- 5. II. *277.*
     6-v. 1. II. *277-8.*
v.   2- 9. II. *278-0*, 396, 434; III. 214, 600; B, *488-0*; M, 32.
     10-15. II. *280.*
vi. 1- 8. II. *280-1*; ɣ, *459.*
     9-16. II. *281-2.*
vii. 1- 6. II. *282*; α, *237*; ɣ, *72.*
     7-13. II. *282-3.*
     14-20. II. *283-4.*

NAHUM.
i.   1-15. B, *248-?*; M, *134-5.*
ii. 1-13. B, *252-6.*
iii. 1-19. II. 60; B, *256-0.*

SCRIPTURAL INDEX.

Habakkuk.

i. 1-17. II. 122, *128*; α, *111*; γ, *469*; B, *262-6*.
ii. 1- 8. III. 56, *149*; α, *78*; γ, *154*; B, *266-8*.
    9-11. B, *268*.
    12-14. B, *268*.
    15-17. α, *269*, *318*; β, *111*, *113*; γ, *33*; B, *268-0*.
    18-20. III. 58.
iii. 1-19. I. *193*, *301*, *465*; II. *117*; β, *202*, *386*; γ, *125*, 530; B, *270-282*.

Zephaniah.

i. 1- 6. III. 151; B, *284*.
    7-18. II. *120*; III. 58, 464; γ, *451*, *469*, *599*; B, *284-8*.
ii. 1-15. II. 148; B, *290-2*.
iii. 1-20. III. 64, *213-4*; B, *294-0*.

Haggai.

i. 1-11. B, *302-4*, *308*.
    12-15. γ, *469*; B, *302*.
ii. 1- 9. I. *350*, 467; B, *304-8*.
    10-19. B, *304-8*.
    20-23. B, *308-0*.

Zechariah.

ii. 1-13. I. 433; II. *41*; III. 155; γ, *33*.
iii. 1-10. I. *165*; II. 2, *285-8*, 396, 404; III. 214; [A, 14].
iv. 1-14. I. 229, 248; II. *288-0*; III. *20*; B, 800.
v. 1- 4. II. *290*; β, 161.
    5-11. II. *291-2*; γ, 593.
vi. 1- 8. II. *292-3*, [*294*], *297*.
    9-15. II. *294-5*, 396; III. 214; [A, 14].
vii. 1- 7. II. *295-6*.
    8-14. II. *296*; III. 217; γ, *204*.
viii. 1-17. II. *296*.
    18-23. II. *297*; III. 122.
ix. 1-17. I. 160, *190*; II. 58, 156, *297-0*; III. 23, 212, 217, 219, *222-4*; γ, *598*; A, 354, *480*; M, *135*, 210.
x. 1-12. II. *300-1*.
xi. 1-14. II. *301-4*; III. 211.
    15-17. II. *304*.

Zechariah—*continued*.

xii. 1-14. II. *304-6*.
xiii. 1- 6. I. *190*, *419*; II. *306-7*. 7- 9. II. *307-8*.
xiv. 1-21. II. 197, *308-1*; III. 484; γ, *188*, *469*.

Malachi.

i. 1- 5. II. *312*.
    6-14. II. *312-3*; M, *138*.
ii. 1- 9. II. *94*, *313*; B, *202*.
    10-16. II. *314*; γ, *469*.
    17-iii. 6. II. *314*; III. 518; β, *202*, *386*; γ, *154*, *157*, *269*, *278*, *599*.
iii. 7-12. II. *314*.
    13-iv. 3. II. *315*; III. 516, 612; M, *210*.
iv. 4- 6. II. *315*, 436; β, 228; γ, 142; C, 208; M, *159*, 248, 270.

APOCRYPHA.

1 Esdras.

v. 4-46. M, 37.
vi. 1- 6. M, 37.
viii. 68-90. γ, 590.

Tobit.

i. 3-14. γ, 187.
    15-22. γ, 591.
iii. 2- 6. A, 300.
xii. 6ᵇ-15. β, *289*.
xiii. 1-18. α, 275.

Wisdom.

i. β, *147*, *309*.
ii. III. 92; α, *13*, *329*; γ, 116.
iii. α, *256*; γ, *26*, *491*.
iv. α, *87*, *241*, *256*.
v. III. 94; α, *241-2*; β, 143; γ, *87*, *96*, *228*, *291*.
vi. α, *128*; β, *141*, *195*, *378*; γ, *158*.
vii. II. 424; III. 529; γ, *28*.
ix. III. 69, 85, 167, 169.
xi. III. 49.
xiv. γ, *598*.
xv. β, *181*.
xvi. III. 545.
xviii. β, 199.

ECCLESIASTICUS.

i. III. 71, 213; β, 120–1; γ, 221.
ii. α, 6, 70; β, 118, 327–8.
iii. III. 654; α, 85–6; γ, 587.
iv. α, 77, 92, 101, 221, 308; β, 167; γ, 65.
v. α, 92; γ, 594.
vi. α, 87, 94; β, 110; γ, 100, 231.
vii. α, 76, 104; A, 302.
viii. α, 77.
ix. γ, 73.
x. III. 643.
xi. α, 71, 92.
xiv. α, 246.
xvi. α, 300.
xviii. α, 86.
xxi. III. 518; γ, 594.
xxiii. α, 91, 300.
xxiv. II. 430; III. 52, 607, 610.
xxv. α, 83; γ, 70–1, 73.
xxvi. γ, 72.
xxvii. α, 98.
xxxi. α, 81.
xxxii. α, 76.
xxxiii. γ, 351.
xxxix. III. 521.
xliv. α, 213.
xlviii. III. 606; γ, 240.

BARUCH.

iii. 9–37. III. 213.
iv. 1–35. III. 212.
vi. 1–73. III. 216.

SONG OF THE CHILDREN.

i. 1–22. III. 459; α, 211, 302; γ, 291, 458.

HISTORY OF SUSANNAH.

i. 1–64. III. 47; α, 251; β, 65, 87, 147, 168, 191, 300; γ, 60, 65; B, 670; C, 694.

BEL AND THE DRAGON.

i. 1–22. B, 662, 668.
33–42. III. 179; β, 71; γ, 92; A, 530; B, 656.

PRAYER OF MANASSEH.

i. β, 199, 383; γ, 400, 506.

1 MACCABEES.

i. 16–19. A, 78.
20–28. II. 231.
ii. 29–38. M, 214.
vii. 26–32. M, 153.
39–50. M, 153.
ix. 1–22. II. 306.
x. 18–20. A, 590.
51–58. II. 226.
59–66. A, 590.
xi. 1–19. II. 227.
63–74. II. 228.
xvi. 11–22. II. 229.

2 MACCABEES.

ii. 1– 8. A, 510.
v. 1– 4. II. 309.
11–20. II. 308.
vi. 18–31. β, 108.
vii. 1– 6. C, 654, 686–696.
20–29. III. 285.
ix. 1–18. II. 230.
xii. 26–31. III. 396.
38–45. II. 558; β, 401.

THE DIATESSARON.

i. 1– 5. I. 18; III. 62–3; β, 49, 358, 387; γ, 410, 469; B, 514; P, 140; M, 3–6, 168, 286.
6– 8. M. 6–7, 99.
9–24. I. 213, 458; II. 315; III. 6, 21, 38, 61, 496, 556, 602; β, 47; γ, 465; B, 802; M, 7–9, 12–4, 29, 37, 188, 270.
25–26. M, 14–5, 29.
27–39. I. 213, 352, 357, 404; II. 137, 142, 216, 321, 415, 478; III. 6, 507, 601–2, 606; α, 22, 32, 33, 37; β, 268–9, 313, 359; γ, 410–3, 465, 546–7, 574, 576, 609; A, 142, 152; B, 570, 578, 586, 594, 600, 608, 802; C, 970–4, 984–6;

SCRIPTURAL INDEX.

THE DIATESSARON—*continued.*
P, *260*; M, *15–6, 18, 49,* 187, *255–6.*
i. 40–57. I. 315; II. *478*; III. 605; β, 313, *354*; γ, 422, 465; A, 270; B, *546, 576, 594, 604*; C, 984; M, *17–9,* 23, *49,* 99, 208.
58–67. M, *12.*
68–80. I. *357,* 433, *438*; β, *196, 379*; γ, *216,* 482; A, 14; B, 182; M, *7, 20, 30.*

ii. 1–8. I. *352*; III. *507,* 601–2; M, *20, 22–3, 25–6,* 266.
9–15. I. 357; II. 33, 40, 414; III. 601, 605–6; β, 47; γ, 410, 419; A, *14*; B, 272; P, *260*; M, *16, 26,* 32, 207.
16–22. II. *279*; β, 47; γ, *434*; B, *112,* 460, *558, 584*; M, *27, 63.*
23–28. II. 418; III. 33; [1] β, 47; γ, 419.
29. β, 47; γ, 465; B, 500.
30–40. α, 218, *320*; β, 47; γ, *555*; A, *258–4*; B, 146, 630–6, 744; M, *25, 28, 226.*
41–47. I. *130,* 404; γ, 574; A, *266–8*; C, 688; M, *28–9, 119, 269.*

iii. 1–12. II. 278, 450; III. 201, 605; β, 47; 208, 277; γ, 410, 419, *601–2*; A, 98, 130–2, 140; B, 130, 274, 442, 468, 474–8, 550; M, *30–2,* 35, 50, ·162, 208.
13–18. I. 543; II. 50, 141; β, *47*; B, *472–4,* 496; M, *32–4, 36,* 208, 212.
19–23. III. 601; B, 540; M, *36.*

THE DIATESSARON—*continued.*
iii. 25–35. α, *218*; β, 46, 276; A, 20; B, 746; M, *24, 40, 52.*
36. I. 562; II. 425.
37–iv. 1. I. 178, 189, *373, 426, 469–0,* 521; II. 269, 496; III. *48, 53,* 84, *498, 548, 606*; α, 4; β, *49, 318,* 387, 405; γ, 56, *82,* 112, 170, 410, 587, *596*; A, 8, 164; B, 802; C, *236*; M, *3, 5–7, 36–7,* 55, 99, 104, 264.

iv. 2–11. II. *85*; III. *22, 118*; A, 8, 116; M, *37–8, 99, 192.*
12–23. III. *383*; α, 213, 280; β, *126, 182,* 358; γ, 166, 350, 587; A, *8,* 52; M, 36, *39–0, 101.*
24–26. I. 33; II. 492; III. xxxviii. 24, 69; γ, *24, 31, 410*; A, *8,* 52, 126, 418; B, *36*; M, *41,* 99.
28–41. I. *171, 357*; II. 90, 165, 328, *417*; III. *16,* 24, 83–4, 93, *128*; β, *47, 206, 247,* 254, *390*; γ, *24,* 169, *410, 422,* 466; A, *8, 12–4, 52–6,* 90, 98, *116–0, 128,* [150]; B, 470; P, *239*; M, *41–3,* 99, 101, *103–5, 128, 151,* 155, *192, 197, 208, 238.*
42–v. 3. II. *286*; III. 54, 639; α, *36*; β, *47*; γ, *177,* 292, *385, 429*; A, 346; B, *718,* 746, 816; P, *80, 110,* 122; M, *42–7, 49,* 131, 201.
v. 4–11. III. 119; γ, 177, *465*; A, 52; M, *49–0, 99,* 108, *197.*

---

[1] In Morris, but not in the Latin.

THE DIATESSARON—*continued.*
v. 12-20. γ, *22*; C, *236*; M, *50*, *185*.
22-34. II. *409*, 532; III. 29, 101; α, 64, 199; β, 47; γ, *423*, *464*, 473, *477*, 520; A, 40, 346-8; B, 538, 746, 822; M, *52-5*, *131-2*, 206, 270.
35-38. M, *129*.
42-43. α, 221; γ, *56*, *587*; B, *180*; M, 57.
44-48. α, *40*; γ, 385, 465; A, *72*; M, 51.
49-vi. 4. γ, 3, 16; M, *59*.
vi. 5-13. II. 492; III. 24, 175; B, 794; M, *80*, *58*, *105*.
14-19. II. *90*; α, *70*; γ, *130*; M, *105*.
20-22. M, *58*.
25-34. A, 610.
35-45. I. 113; II. 482; III. *102*, *607*; β, 283; A, 130; M, *6*, *50-1*, *113*.
47-vii. 10. III. 101, 680; β, *245*, 283, *405*; γ, 574; A, 596, 610; B, 820; M, 58, 122.
vii. 11-24. III. *370*, 372; β, *160*; γ, *21*, 473, 574; A, *190-4*, 314, 330, 348; P, *21*; M, *59-0*.
25-36. I. *489*; II. *223*, 542; III. *506*, *518*; α, *30*, 100, *148*, 187, *312*; β, *86*, *112*, *149*, 161, *206*, 208, *390*, 392; γ, *386*, *541*, *573*, *589*; A, 116, *242*; B, *712*; P, *246*; M, 58, *61*, 200, 237.
37-46. I. 281, 376; III. 144, *506*; β, *112*; γ, *589*; M, *61-2*, *148*.
47-viii. 8. II. *90*, 431; γ, 473, 574; A, 610; M, 185.
viii. 9-17. β, *245*, *405*; M, *83*, *235*.
18-25. C, 236; M, 286. 7.

THE DIATESSARON—*continued.*
viii. 26-39. III. 132, 400, *473*, *484*; α, *8*, *27*, *30-1*, 33, *35-6*, *78*, *85*, 93, *98*, *116*, *203*, *226*, 254-5, *270*, *310*, *330*; β, *112*, *140*, *143-4*, *153*, *168*, 170, *207-8*, *327*, *361*, *391-2*, *418*; γ, *21*, 51, *54-5*, 107, *132*, *156*, *159*, *221*, *258*, *280*, *312*, *328-9*, 337, *348-9*, *359*, *383*, *554-5*; A, *22*; C, 10, 176, 872; M, *62-4*.
40-45. II. 401; III. *xxxvii.*; α, *59*, *279-0*; β, 79, *146*, *172*, *191*; γ, *104*, *120*, 187, *330*, *350*; B, *32-4*, *402*; C, *736*; M, *64*, *198*, *219*.
46-49. I. *300*; III. *563*; β, 88, *245*, *405*; A, 378, 444; M, *64-6*, *170*, 196.
50-56. III. *642*; α, *132*; β, *121*; γ, *20*, *442*; A, 48; M, *65-6*, *68*.
57-62. II. *174*, 410, 517; α, 132; β, *133*, *155*; γ, *72*, *149*, 177, 592; M, *65-6*.
ix. 1- 5. III. 643, α, 221, 292; β, *161*; γ, *570*; C, 654, 658, *874*; M, 158.
6-11. II. *164*; α, *42*, *308*; γ, *90*; A, *300*; B, *220*; M, *9*, *65*, *69-0*, *133*, *223*.
12-19. I. *463*; II. *484*; III. *455*, *503*; α, 19, 84; β, 199, *310*, 382; γ, *16-7*, *283*, *434*; C, 18, 58, 846; M, 70.
20-21. α, *84*, *299*; γ, *16*, *207*, *328*.
22-25. α, *129*; γ, *187*, *329*, *350*, *439*; A, *196*; P, *74*.
26-38. I. *189*; II. *333*; III.

SCRIPTURAL INDEX. 151

THE DIATESSARON—*continued.*
26, *551, 641-2* ; α,
74, 91, 267 ; β,
361, 370 ; γ, 13,
*155, 186, 202, 314,
317, 350, 352,* 565,
586, 609 ; A, *436* ;
B, *396* ; P, *133* ;
M, *271,* 277.

ix. 39–41. M, *71-2.*
42-50. I. *443* ; II. *201, 302* ;
III. 66, 88, *392* ;
β, *84* ; γ, *26, 120,*
218 ; M, *72, 127,
170.*

x. 1-12. II. *81, 342* ; III.
549 ; α, 19, *39, 91,
100, 232,* 265, 297 ;
β, *93, 112, 158,
316-7, 418, 431* ;
γ, *18, 51, 54, 107,*
111, *120,* 132, *151,
210, 282* ; B, *718* ;
C, 52.
13-16. III. *663* ; α, *80* ; β,
81, 88, 116, 195,
246, 378, 429 ; γ,
283, 589 ; M, *72-3.*
17-20. α, *80,* 111, 159 ; β,
150, 158 ; γ, 507 ;
C, 804 ; M, *223.*
21. III. 155 ; γ, *112,
174* ; M, *73.*
22-30. II. *324* ; III. *261,
369, 379,* 483, *491,
503* ; α, *56,* 138,
257, 326 ; β, *80,*
160, *181, 222* ; γ,
223-4, 448, *460,
497,* 511, 592 ; B,
714.
31. α, *42, 108* ; γ, *586* ;
M, *224.*
32-33. α, *33-4, 37, 39, 83,*
90, 168, *189, 249* ;
β, *65,* 91, 153, *175,
204-5, 218, 221,*
252, 331, *387-9,
417,* 430 ; γ, *99,
285, 398, 519, 559* ;
A, 286 ; M, 118,
263.
34-48. III. 27, *275, 334* ; α,
9, 19, *57,* 88, *123,
153, 243-4, 257,
313,* 316 ; β, *105,*

THE DIATESSARON—*continued.*
126, 169, 171, 178,
198-9, 244, 340,
382, 404, 418, *432* ;
γ, *65,* 101, 219,
233, 302, 364, 498 ;
C, 730 ; M, *94, 97,
216, 282.*

xi. 1- 2. III. 102.
4-16. III. 16, 101 ; α, 39,
110, 171, 214, 255 ;
β, 198, *333,* 382 ;
γ, *26, 256,* 490,
521, 574 ; M, *74,*
131.
17-23. II. 389, 391 ; γ, 473,
574 ; A, 328, 348 ;
B, 820 ; M, 74.
24-31. III. *149, 648* ; α,
192, 334 ; β, *81,
183,* 345, *369* ; γ,
21, 33, 151, 153,
292, *297, 560,* 574,
610 ; A, *352* ; M,
74.
32-37. II. 513 ; III. 101,
173, 192 ; α, 195 ;
β, 47 ; γ, *311,* 486,
513 ; A, *264,* 328,
346 ; B, 538, 728 ;
M, *74-5,* 202.
38–xii. 1. II. 405, 482, 525,
535 ; III. 100, *102,*
115, 575 ; β, 118,
245, 376, 424 ; A,
20, 444, 610 ; B,
136, 662, 674, 720 ;
M, 44, *75-6,* 182,
185-6, 235.

xii. 2- 5. M, *76.*
6-10. A, 328.
11-21. III. 22, 24, 27, 375,
484, 554 ; α, 195 ;
β, *160* ; γ, 223,
473 ; A, 176, 258,
328, 348 ; M, *76-1,
83-6, 88-9,* 277.
22-32. II. 389, 391 ; III.
345 ; γ, 590 ; M,
88-9.
33-37. III. 74 ; α, 257 ; β,
178 ; γ, *222.*
38-39. A, 348.
40-41. M, 99.
42-55. I. 164 ; II. *279* ; III.
622 ; β, *232, 397* ;

THE DIATESSARON—*continued.*
γ, 12, 463, *477*;
M, *63*, *90-5*, *115*,
206.

xiii. 1- 8. α, *6*, *207*, *305*, *334*;
β, *81-2*, *107*, *109*,
156, *181*, *183*, *328*,
362, *365*, *368*; γ,
39, 212, *214*, *327*,
482; M, *91*, *94-5*.

9-19. α, *35*, *132*; β, *118*,
172, *191*, *194*; γ,
65, 208, *410*, *415*,
442; P, *261*; M,
95-7, *228*, *230-1*.

20-26. α, *265*, *333*; β, *326*,
332, *355*; γ, *198*,
209; M, *97-8*.

27-29. III. *290*; β, 152,
235, *393*; γ, *4*, *21*,
170, *350*, *354*; C,
780; M, *91*.

30-35. III. 589; α, 24, *35*;
γ, *103*, *235*, *320*,
354; A, 256; M,
92, *98*, 202.

36-37. M, 206.
38-43. γ, *417*; M, 94, *99-1*.
44-47. II. 314; M, *100-2*.

xiv. 1-14. I. *287*; II. 305, *315*,
414; III. 27, 31,
43; α, 38; β, *205*,
245, *389*, *405*; γ,
208, *327*; A, 106;
B, *416*, 748; M,
7, *42*, *57*, *65*,
103-4, *107*, *288*.

15-40. I. *474*; II. *320*, 483;
III. 680; α, *9*, *51*,
91, *244*, 302; β,
94, *141*, *196*, 273,
282, *380*; γ, 60,
96, 113, *216*, 227,
370; A, 406; C,
144; M, *44*, 75,
111-3, 143, *160*,
206.

41-42. III. 553; α, 257; A,
330, 348; M, *113*.

45-xv. 11. II. 543; III. 373,
384, 389-0, 393-5,
397 - 8, 401 - 2,
404-8, 410, 538,
645-6; β, 47, 55,
160, 297-8, 302,

THE DIATESSARON—*continued.*
305-6; γ, 32, 197,
257, 387, 389, 519,
523, 581; A, 176,
180-2, *186-8*, *198*,
240, *244*, 256, 314,
332-8, 362, *366*,
602; B, *xxiii.* 788;
P, 20-1, 24; M,
84-5, 98, *113-4*,
168.

xv. 15-26. III. 580, 622; β,
109-0, *156*; P,
64; M, 59, *63*, *90*,
92, *95*, *105*, *115*,
160.

27-31. I. 164; M, *230*.
32. α, *29*; γ, *294*; M,
94.

33-36. β, *9*, *84*, *118*, *240*; γ,
104, *175*, *191*, *236*,
317, *353*; B, 456,
724; M, *115-6*,
206.

37-41. I. *189*; II. *90*, *298*;
III. 8, 87, 133,
171, *372*, *503*, 549;
α, *26*, *30-1*, *115*,
149, *162*; β, *107*,
120, *181*, *207-8*,
258, *309*, 364, *366*,
391-2; γ, *13*,
102-3, *112*, *131*,
155, *235*, *284*, *381*,
581; P, *80*; M,
63, *116-7*, *127*,
216.

42-50. II. *487*; III. 28; α,
333; β, *74*, *311*;
γ, *337*, *596*; M,
118.

xvi. 1-10. I. 464; II. *130*; α,
192, 307, *333*; γ,
104, *180*, 186, *206*,
236, *479*; B, 234;
M, *118-2*, 130,
139-0, 221, *230*,
267.

11-12. M, *122-3*.
13-18. II. 429; M, *122*.
19-21. M, *120*.
22-48. I. *435*; III. 105; α,
35, *108*, 118, *204*,
307; β, 6, *116*,
126; γ, *101*, 126,
233, *407*, *594*; B,

SCRIPTURAL INDEX. 153

THE DIATESSARON—*continued.*
xxii. 360; C, *674*;
P, *51*; M, *72*, 88,
106, *113, 123-6,
155, 192,* 215, *235.*
xvi. 49-52. M, *126.*
xvii. 1- 7. II. 409; III. 69, 533;
α, 23, 45, 70, 294;
β, 76, *200, 383*;
M, 88, *126-7,* 167.
8-12. II. 201; III. 9; M, *127.*
13-15. III. 27; γ, 463; M, *128.*
19-26. I. *466*; III. 489; β, 144, *197, 200,* 244, *381, 383*; γ, *26,* 218, *411, 553-4,* 575, *582, 598*; P, *81, 192*; M, *174, 211.*
27. α, *294*; β, 54, 260; γ, 463.
28-29. III. 11; α, 45, 294; β, 54, 260; γ, 463.
30-33. II. 407; III. *146*; γ, 463; M, *128.*
36-52. III. *33,* 80; α, *2*; γ, 199, 240; A, 194, 614; M, *128-0, 212.*
xviii. 1-21. III. 61; α, 266; β, 147, 287; γ, 70-1; A, 438, 640-2; B, 338, 430; C, 100, 150, 736; M, 37, 67, *131-2,* 165.
22-43. I. 530; II. 409; III. 101; α, 64, 81, 199; β, 47; γ, 423, 574; A, 328, 348, 444, 708; C, 74, 126; M, *132-5,* 206.
44-46. M, *134.*
47-xix. 13. II. 497, 535; III. 15, 24, 101, 385, 453, 470, 481, 503, 505, 563; γ, 473; A, 264, 348, 608; B, 422, 806; C, 880; M, *134-6,* 202, 248.
xix. 16-34. III. *336*; α, *80, 93,* 115; β, *208, 222,*

THE DIATESSARON—*continued.*
392; γ, *112*; B, *156,* 816; M, *136, 234.*
xix. 35-45. III. 80; A, *418*; M, *137.*
46-53. III. *102*; γ, *409*; M, *37, 58, 245.*
54-xx. 5. M, *125,* 270.
xx. 6-11. M, *58, 206.*
12-16. M, 138.
17-37. γ, 202; A, 252; P, *271*; M, *137-8.*
38-45. α, 133; γ, 443; M, *63.*
46-58. II. *41, 302-4*; III. *585*; α, *54,* 137, 258; β, *161, 355*; γ, *223,* 447, 574, 589; A, *164*; B, 820; M, *59,* 131, *138-9.*
xxi. 1- 7. A, 168, 172, 348; M, *186.*
8-42. II. *309*; III. 173, 530, 554; α, *43*; β, 47, *50*; γ, *168,* 206, *411*; A, *70-2*; B, *156,* 818; C, *126, 716*; M, 131, *140-3.*
43-46. II. 407; M, *142.*
47-49. M, *130.*
xxii. 1- 8. α, 257; β, *160*; A, 444; M, *143-5.*
10-37. I. *165, 167, 446*; II. *68*; III. 39, 41; α, 39, 71; β, *114, 160, 364*; γ, *123-4, 130,* 195, *283, 553*; A, 106; M, *145-1, 199,* 204, *213,* 223, 241, 261.
38-55. III. 171; β, *92*; γ, *282, 330, 341*; A, *220,* 642; M, *151-2, 210.*
xxiii. 5-12. I. 530; II. 409; A, 444.
26-30. A, 348; M, *153.*
31-39. II. *166,* 559; III. liii. 170-1, 532, 563; β, *42,* 45, *426-7*; γ, *3,* 219,

THE DIATESSARON—*continued.*
415, 474 ; A, *268* ;
B, *156, 186* ; C,
746; M, 108, *153–4,
156.*

xxiii. 40–44. III. *618* ; M, 59, *65,
154–6, 229–0.*

45–50. II. 12 ; III. *333* ; α,
29, *31, 54,* 66, *216,
244, 265, 304, 335* ;
β, *54, 56, 74, 184,*
326, *332–3, 368–9* ;
γ, *24, 40, 79, 260,
282, 285, 369, 416,
555.*

xxiv. 1. β, *41* ; M, *155, 222.*
2–16. II. *544–5* ; III. *16,*
84, *128* ; β, *42–9,
425–7* ; A, 96 ; B,
146 ; M, *156–7,
159.*
17–24. M, 37, *154, 157–8,*
248.
27–29. II. *408* ; III. 61 ; C,
736 ; M, *159, 212.*
30–44. M, 59, 70, *160–1,
203.*
45–47. II. 32 ; β, *80* ; γ,
219 ; M, *160*, 189,
204.
48–52. M, *204.*

xxv. 4– 7. B, 148, 746 ; M, 51,
161–2, 206.
8–13. III. 116 ; α, *328* ; β,
141 ; γ, *33, 63* ;
M, *107–8.*
14–26. II. 97, 354, 435 ; III.
xxvii. 243, 459,
481 ; α, 39, 111 ;
β, 51, *141,* 157,
198, *202,* 256, *385* ;
γ, *128,* 210, *506* ;
B, *14* ; M, *66–7,*
96.
27–42. I. 280 ; β, *156–7,*
164 ; M, *162.*
43–46. III. 299.

xxvi. 1– 8. I. 513 ; II. 348, 408,
543 ; III. *377,*
383–4, 412, 483,
492, *524,* 600 ; α,
29, *230,* 299 ; β,
18, *178, 206,* 247,
390 ; γ, 171, 380,

THE DIATESSARON—*continued.*
567, 589, 593 ; A,
58 ; B, 118, 358,
516, 562, 742 ; C,
28 ; M, 58–9, *162–3,
268,* 277.

xxvi. 9–11. I. 513 ; II. 348, 408,
543 ; III. *377, 412,*
483, *524* ; α, *29* ;
β, *178, 206,* 247,
390 ; γ, 463, 567,
589 ; A, 58 ; B,
118 ; M, 59, 162.
12–33. I. *562* ; III. *370,* 483 ;
α, 150, 187, 195,
292 ; β, 16, *113,
138, 160, 247* ; γ,
164, 459–0, 598 ;
C, 20 ; M, *163.*
34–45. II. 404 ; α, *264,* 335 ;
β, *141,* 184, *336,*
369 ; γ, *21, 28,
120,* 197 ; M, *156,*
163.

xxvii. 1–13. I. 526 ; III. 55, 489 ;
α, 109 ; β, *250,
370* ; γ, 216, 548 ;
C, 794.
14–25. III. 260, 359, 373,
391, *483* ; α, 71,
90, 106, *114, 299,
325,* 331 ; β, *89,
169,* 195, *197–9,
205,* 247, *370, 378,*
382, *389* ; γ, 200,
218, 363, 587, *596* ;
P, 116 ; M, *163–5.*
26–27. III. *xxxviii. xlviii.
633* ; γ, *320* ; A,
80 ; B, *36* ; M,
229.
28–29. II. 408 ; α, *328* ; γ,
589 ; M, 148, *165.*
31–35. M, *165.*
36–39. α, 227 ; β, *182* ; M,
143, *166, 184, 213.*
40–47. M, 149.

xxviii. 1– 8. M, *167.*
9–14. I. *353* ; III. 37 ; M,
167.
15–25. II. *40* ; β, *137* ; B,
734 ; M, *167–8,
196.*
26–32. M, *173,* 210.
33–41. α, 89 ; γ, *594.*

THE DIATESSARON—*continued.*
xxviii. 42–51. III. 26, 246; α, *19.3,
333*; β, *360*; γ,
296, 531, 597; M,
38, *123, 125, 168–4.*

xxix. 1–11. I. *177*; II. *113, 305*;
III. 473; α, *79*,
251; β, *111, 126*,
215; γ, *123, 151*,
159, 187, 297, 301,
307, *410*; A, 398,
430; B, 414; P,
106; M, *67*, *88*,
126, *170, 172, 178*,
223, 276.
12–13. III. *646*; α, *23*; β,
86, 93; γ, *330*,
589.
14–26. III. 26, 184, 244–5,
284, 564, 585; α, 3,
34, 231, *235,* 335; β,
93, 142–3, 184, 198,
207, 218, 256, 369,
374, 381, 391, 431;
γ, 23, 218, 460,
481, 548; C, 142,
178, 782, 830; M,
67, *173, 175.*
27–42. I. 153, *177,* 269; III.
373, 383–4, 509,
539; α, 28–9, 66,
176, 281, 334; β,
76, *111,* 183, *200,*
368, *383*; γ, *83,*
363, 571; C, 64;
M, *108,* 126, *174–7,*
277.
43–48. γ, 574; M, 200.

xxx. 1– 5. III. *646*; α, *80, 105,
116, 164, 208, 229,
254*; β, *93, 118–9,
171*; γ, *330, 339*;
M, *41.*
6– 8. γ, *12.*
10–15. III. 26; α, *51.*
16–30. I. 405; II. 344, 351;
III. 37, 417; α,
2, 38, *51,* 152, 168,
239; β, *76, 168,*
200, *383*; γ, *120,*
575; B, *286*; C,
140, 146.
31–45. I. *522*; II. 536; γ,
414; M, *65, 154,
178,* 204.

THE DIATESSARON—*continued.*
xxx. 46–xxxi. 5. I. *440*; II. 491; III.
615–6; α, *24, 76,* 89,
114–5; β, *93,* 355;
γ, *338–9, 354,* 474;
A, 428; M, *108–9,
177–9, 229.*
xxxi. 6–14. III. *334*; α, *3.1, 53,
57, 123, 153,* 168,
171, 214, 255, *257*;
β, 91, *111, 168–9,
175, 198–9, 203–4,
221, 256–7, 382–3,
387, 389*; γ, *107,
256, 302, 327, 398,*
490, *506, 555–6*;
B, *422.*
15–24. II. 455; III. 44, 110,
495; α, 137; β,
160; γ, 31, *38,*
448, 510; B, 720;
C, 808; P, 20; M,
180, 205, 277.
25–35. II. 537; III. 602,
612; α, 28, 257;
γ, *222*; A, 330;
B, 650; M, *180–1,*
206, 277.
36–52. I. *409*; II. 510; III.
27, 32, 324; α, 3,
32, 52; β, 20, *116,
164, 196, 380*; γ,
126, *216, 219,* 326,
516; B, 728, 786;
C, 842.

xxxii. 1–11. I. 108; II. 374; III.
101; β, 68; γ,
179, 566; A, 472;
B, 160; M, 131,
181–2, 229.
12–15. III. 677; α, 64, 200;
β, 152; γ, 28, 171;
B, 818.
16–21. III. 159, *375–6,* 466,
646; α, 28, *80, 91,
105, 116,* 137, *164,
208, 254, 330*; β,
83, 93, 118–9, 171,
359; γ, *126, 200,
330, 339,* 430, 447,
457, 474, 510, *578,*
589; C, 64; M,
41, 181–2, 277.
22–26. II. 525; A, 272, 388,
636; C, *xxv.*; M,
182–3, 186–7.

THE DIATESSARON—*continued.*
xxxii. 27–47. I. 263 ; II. *483* ; III.
393 ; *a*, 70, *128* ;
β, 379 ; γ, *16*, *176*,
183, *195*, *216*, *306* ;
M, *168*, *187–9*, *230*,
258.

xxxiii. 1– 8. γ, *576* ; A, 610 ; M,
183–6, *189*, *204*.
9–14. *a*, *23*, *25* ; β, *118* ; γ,
219 ; M, *189*.
15–17. β, 181 ; γ, *20*, *155*.
18–25. *a*, 138, 155 ; β, *178* ;
γ, *19*, *332*, *344*,
448, 511 ; C, 222 ;
M, 190.
26–34. M, *38*, *191*.
35–39. M, *191–2*.
40–60. I. 260, 394, *506*, *511* ;
II. 135 ; III. 64,
102, 156 ; β, *21*,
165 ; A, *254* ; B,
482 ; M, 28, 171,
192–3, 256, *265–6*.

xxxiv. 1– 7. III. 102 ; M, 158,
193.
9–21. *a*, *279*, *291* ; γ, *51*,
131, *192*, *236* ; M,
97, *193–4*.
22–45. I. *221*, *245* ; III. *188*,
253, *628* ; *a*, 22,
67, *239*, 317 ; β,
11, *209* ; γ, *15*, *41*,
67, *335*, 498, *583*,
586, 589, 591 ; A,
280 ; C, 52, *676* ;
M, *110*, *152*, *169*,
171, *194–5*.

xxxv. 1– 8. I. *524* ; *a*, 70 ; β,
297 ; γ, *387* ; A,
242 ; M, 50, *196*,
210.
17–22. III. 41 ; A, *576*.
23–xxxvi. 9. I. *168*, *311*, *560* ; II.
298, *400* ; III. 6,
97, 102, 184, *509* ;
a, 10, *64*, *115*, 149,
232, *245*, *308* ; β,
150, *203*, *319*, 322,
387, 429 ; γ, *106*,
112, 207, *414*, *593* ;
A, 472 ; B, *148* ; M,
86, *152*, *155*, *168*,
196–8, *207*, *242*.

THE DIATESSARON—*continued.*
xxxvi. 10–21. III. 23, 74, 168, 554 ;
a, 65, 137 ; β, *47*,
178, *203*, *387* ; γ,
447, 574 ; A, 72,
172, 314, 330, 598 ;
B, [354], 650 ; M,
89, 148, *197–0*,
203, 248.
22–43. γ, 207 ; A, *252* ; M,
148, *199*, *202*.
44–xxxvii. 3. M, *199*.
xxxvii. 4– 9. M, *210*.
10–21. III. 27, *113*, 608 ; β,
203, *273*, *387* ; γ,
16, *112*, 226, *412*,
414, 466 ; M, *137*,
174, *200*, *209–0*, *242*.
22–24. M, 89.
25–42. I. *168* ; II. *13* ; III.
123 ; γ, *408*, *411* ;
P, *112*, *174* ; M,
121, *191*, *210*, *242*,
271.
46–61. II. *390–3* ; III. 27,
274, *301* ; β, 355,
γ, 24 ; [A, 360] ;
C, 236, *904* ; M,
200–1, *203*.

xxxviii. 1–28. II. *387–9*, *391–5*,
416 ; III. 149, 268,
301–2, 304, 314,
345, 348, 435, 612 ;
β, 47, 160, *203*,
258, *387* ; γ, *112*,
195, *409*, *474*, 574 ;
A, 156, 328, 348 ;
C, 904, 918 ; M,
89, *98–9*, *201–5*,
234, *249*.
29–30. M, 89, *200*.
31–37. I. *475*, *534* ; II. *66* ;
A, 270, *432*, 484,
590 ; M, *204–5*.
42–47. III. 211 ; M, *95*, *224*.

xxxix. 1– 6. III. 397, 410 ; A, 360 ;
M, *203–5*.
7–17. II. *486* ; III. 397,
409–0, 468, *645–6* ;
β, *306* ; γ, *395* ;
A, 40, *256–8*, 360,
366–2, *402*, 602,
610 ; B, 720, 788 ;
C, 646–8 ; M, 40,
159, *203–6*.

SCRIPTURAL INDEX.

THE DIATESSARON—*continued.*
xxxix. 18-25. I. *108-9, 190*; III.
222-3; A, 154;
M, *207, 210.*
29-33. III. 202, *211, 220-4,*
602; β, 47, *194,*
214, 252; γ, *146,*
374; A, 154, 608,
638; B, 720, 754,
800; M,*27*,193,*207.*
34-37. α, *246, 330*; B, 724;
M, *207-8,* 257.
38-41. γ, 589; A, 154; M,
184, 207.
42-45. III. *80, 202, 223*;
M, 208.

xl. 1- 4. I. 190; III. *221,* 300,
602; B, 800; M,
27, 207.
5-21. I. 412; II. 409, 434;
α, 265; β, *355*;
M, *208-9.*
22-23. I. *459*; II. *332*; III.
550; α, *273*; γ,
344; M, *209-1.*
26-40. I. 342; II. *491*; III.
646; α, *2, 17, 80,*
105, 116, 164, 208,
254, 269; β, *93,*
118-9, 171, 365;
γ, *329-0, 339, 571*;
M, *41*, 167, 277.
43-44. γ, *412*; M, *211.*
55-56. γ, 202, 341.
57-58. II. 550; III. 660; α,
78; γ, *589.*
59-60. α, *17.*
61-xli. 3. I. 344, 546; II. *291*;
α, 236; M, 23,
[35], *211-3.*
xli. 4- 6. I. *394*; III. *224*; M,
213.
7- 8. β, *93.*
9-15. α, *29-1, 34*; β, 203,
387; γ, *133*; M,
173, 213.
18-20. β, *172, 191.*
21-26. γ, 434; M, 72.
27-30. A, *376*; M, *44, 183.*
31-49. II. *162*; β, 224, 227,
245; γ, *378, 414*;
B, *156*; C, *188*;
P, *195*; M, *63,* 209.
50-54. α, *56, 253, 334*; β,
184, 328, 365, 369;
γ, *39, 327, 415.*

THE DIATESSARON—*continued.*
xli. 55-58. III. *309*; α, *6, 305,*
334; β, *81-2, 181,*
183, 328, 362, 365,
368; γ, *39, 327,*
415.
xlii. 1- 3. M, 214.
4-24. II. *162, 222*; III. 80,
544, 634; α, 33,
39, 52, 69, 159,
168; β, *139, 193,*
213-4, 222, 224,
229,250-2, 375; γ,
24, 94, 123, *143-4,*
145-6, *155, 157,*
189, 191, *194,* 213,
226, 373-4, 414,
416, 556, *599*; B,
406-8; C, *156,*
192, *204, 208*; P,
239; M, *210-1,*
213-5, 270.
25-28. II. *320*; α, 30, *167*;
β, *245, 405*; γ,
155, 313, 570; M,
186-7.
29-37. I. 527; III. *142,144-8*;
α, 2, 51, 110; β,
94, 127, 203, 224,
227, *386-7*; γ,
140, *364,* 599; M,
109, 179, 215-6.
38-53. I. 415; III. *529*; α,
44, 69, *89,* 110,
168; β, *127, 174,*
182, 202-3, 386-7,
399; γ, *23-4, 155,*
239, 378, *556*; B,
406; P, 187; M,
217-8.
xliii. 1- 8. III. xxv. 101-2; α,
2-3, 69, *141, 303-4*;
β, *221,* 375; γ,
119, 262, *451*; M,
218.
9-21. I. *493*; II. 332;
III. 26, *306-8,*
370, 445, *500, 504,*
529; α, *33,* 39,
44-5, *52-3, 56-7,*
110, 137, 167-8,
183, 190, 197, *257*;
β, *127, 169, 174,*
182, 193, 199, 202,
214, 218-9, 230,

THE DIATESSARON—continued.
    252, 256-7, 357,
    386-7; γ, 53, 101,
    146, 155, 302, 311,
    314, 347, 374, 447,
    489, 491, 496, 506,
    510, 587; A, 638;
    C, 142-4, 166, 688;
    M, 218.
xliii. 22–38. I. 251-2, 298; III.
    11, 27, 102, 225,
    256, 489; α, 3, 230,
    322; β, 75, 108,
    116, 342, 414; γ,
    79, 85, 101, 120,
    205, 219, 232, 272,
    308, 321, 575, 582;
    C, 964; M, 73, 124,
    126, 192, 218-9.
 39–42. α, 56, 167-8, 190, 197;
    β, 97; γ, 155, 272,
    357; M, 218-9.
 43–58. I. 295; II. 332, 355,
    383, 405, 482; III.
    244, 291, 474, 477,
    498, 500, 504, 535,
    545, 637, 642-3,
    676; α, 30, 33, 53,
    57, 68, 81, 164,
    167, 226, 255, 310;
    β, 54, 111, 134,
    155, 163, 189,
    197-0, 215, 217-8,
    253, 255-6, 353,
    374, 381-3; γ,
    21-2, 26, 85, 96-7,
    120, 125, 130, 155,
    157-8, 169, 189,
    192, 194, 218-9,
    228, 260, 271, 278,
    308, 350, 354, 362,
    375, 401-2, 411,
    489, 500, 556,
    580-1, 584; A,
    42, 338, 662; B,
    416-0; M, 20, 75,
    88, 97, 216, 270.
xliv. 1– 5. P, 70.
 6– 9. β, 147, 232; A, 402;
    M, 204, 221.
 10. A, 374; P, 70.
 11–21. α, 26; γ, 423, 609;
    A, 390-8, 410, 658;
    B, 152; P, 221;
    M, 58, 105, 159,
    206, 219, 221.

THE DIATESSARON—continued.
xliv. 22–33. γ, 354; A, 410-4,
    428; M, 159.
 34–40. A, 374-6, 380-4.
 41–43. β, 355; A, 380,
    386-8; P, 70; M,
    230.
 44–50. γ, 128; A, 610; M,
    105, 112, 159,
    219-0, 224, 229-0.
xlv. 1– 9. III. 63; β, 44, 49,
    126, 133; γ, 475;
    A, 422, 602-4, 624,
    662-4; M, 105,
    108, 159, 206, 221.
 10–18. I. 493; II. 61; γ,
    423, 609; A, 416,
    423-6, 436; P, 70;
    M, 153, 222.
 19–22. α, 4, 201; β, 145,
    219, 256; γ, 15,
    597; M, 224-5.
 23–28. II. 308; A, 434, 522;
    M, 229.
 29–xlvi. 4. I. 168, 463; II. 404;
    α, 26, 30, 192; β,
    200, 203, 258, 384,
    387; γ, 25, 112,
    170, 195, 208, 206,
    528, 586; A, 122,
    156; P, 59, 174;
    M, 137, 173, 222-3,
    235, 271.
xlvi. 5–15. II. 343; β, 231; γ,
    44; A, 664; P,
    51; M, 223-4, 263.
 16. A, 430.
 17–43. I. 466; III. 28, 31;
    α, 20, 45, 133, 201,
    208, 235, 297; β,
    83, 122, 204, 207,
    210, 219, 256, 276,
    388; γ, 16, 156,
    208-9, 283, 294,
    307, 442, 586;
    [B, 354]; P, 258;
    M, 50, 58, 95, 106,
    209, 224-5.
 44–xlvii. 9. I. 37; III. 379; α,
    153, 229, 235, 266,
    335; β, 125, 128,
    148, 184, 369; γ,
    22, 44, 107, 127,
    260, 415, 482, 557;
    [B, 354]; P, 80;
    M, 179, 225, 227.

SCRIPTURAL INDEX.

THE DIATESSARON—*continued*.
xlvii. 10-18. α, *56, 266*; γ, *278, 285, 415*; M, *3, 223, 271*.
19-44. III. *122*, 171, 677; β, *43, 427*; P, *80-1*; M, *50, 137, 179, 227-8, 271*.

xlviii. 1-21. α, *37*, 248; β, 43; γ, *213, 225, 244*; A, *234, 666*, 670; B, 746; C, *xxvii.*; M, *228-9, 231-5*.
22-23. II. 129, 486; α, 281; β, 126, 147, 232; γ, 150, 600; B, 468; M, 159, 235.
24-33. II. 434, 487; III. 622, 681; α, 139, 281; β, 47-8, 126, 147, 283; γ, 150, *450*, 600; A, 574, 596, 612, 616; B, 468, 784; M, *154*, 159, 186, *234-6*.
34-43. II. 433; β, 48; A, 24, 438, 664; B, *150*; M, *186*, 223, *232, 236*.
44-48. β, 47-8; γ, 244; A, *430-2*, 596; M, 186, *237*.
49-55. A, *432-4*; B, 150; M, 51, 231, 237.

xlix. 1- 6. III. 246; α, 49; β, 48; γ, 245; A, *440-2, 446-8*, 610, 674; B, 352; P, 161; M, 187.
7-18. II. 474; III. 371, 434-6, 459; γ, 203, *368*, 589; A, *434*; M, 51, 231, 237.
19-42. I. 400, *511*, 558; α, 49, 115; β, 48, 232; γ, 245, *411*; A, 682; B, 352, 762; P, 161; M, 187, 199, *237*, 256.
43-49. I. *511*; β, 48; γ, 473; A, 356, 452, *456*, 590; M, *238-9*.
50-55ª. β, 48; A, *458-0*.

THE DIATESSARON—*continued*.
l. 5- 9. I. 406; A, 596; M, 165.
10-18. III. 164, 216; A, 460; M, *238*.
19. β, 48.
20-37. II. *122*, 468; III. 216, 223, *498*; β, 232; γ, *473*; A, 460-2, 468, 476, 644; B, 138; M, 239.
38-51. I. 400; III. *498*; α, 49; γ, 244, 473; A, 472, *480-4, 488-0*, 644, 666, *676*, 708; B, 138, 436; M, 199, *239*.

li. 1- 6. I. *348, 469*; II. *302*; III. *498*; γ, 473; A, *498-0*, 598, *628*, 642, 678; M, *238-9*, 243.
7-14. I. 418; II. 304; III. 149; α, 138; β, 47, 243, 404; γ, 284, 449-0, 495; A, 400, 616; M, 109, 113, 159, 206, 229, *239-1*, 256, 267.
15-16. A, 154; B, 308; C, 868; M, 239, *241*.
17-18. M, *241*.
19-23. γ, *596, 599*; M, *207, 242*.
24-27. II. 24; III. 681; β, 45, 48, 284; γ, 574; A, 500, 598, 688-0; B, 308; M, 55, 71, *243, 245*.
28-43. II. *3*, 526; β, *44, 48*; A, *504-8*, 668, 686-8; C, *292*; M, *116*, 202, *243*, 245, *249-0*.
44-48. II. 469, 486; III. 16, 103, 155, 261, 370, 539, 572, 586, 677; α, 70; β, *48*, 160, 208, 376, 392; γ, 166, 200, *256*, *474-5*; A, 502, 668, 688; M, 176, *242-5*.

THE DIATESSARON—*continued*.
li. 49–51. γ, *574*; M, 26, *54*,
245, *270*.
52–54. II. *309*, *558*; α, 41;
β, *48*, *232*; γ, *246*;
A, 100, 508, 608,
614, 682, 700, 710;
M, 30–1, 71, *245*,
247, 254, *257*, 268.

lii. 1– 7. I. 524; II. *232*; III.
122; β, *45*, *321*,
428; γ, 247, 574;
A, *230*, 282, *510–2*,
598, 690; M, *117*,
247, *254*, *256*, *265*.
8–13. I. 524; II. 412; III.
122; α, 41; β, 48;
γ, 246; A, 598,
682; B, 724; M,
54, 158, 186, 204,
208, *245–6*, 249–0,
254, *256–7*, 268.
14–20. I. 213; II. 308; β,
48, 253; A, 478,
512; P, *66*; M,
115, 245, *259–0*.
21–23. M, *258*.
24–39. III. 37; A, 516–8,
616, 672, 684; M,
47, 249, *266*.
40–44. A, 174, 524; M, *204*,
266.
45–liii. 17. I. 178; β, 247; γ,
128, *307*, *423*, 467;
A, 528–0, *534–6*,
684; B, 470; M,
254, *266–8*.
liii. 18–25. II. 408; A, *536–8*,
684; C, 646; M,
29, '54, 120, 123,
268–1.
26–30. γ, 467; M, 254,
267–8.
31. A, 544.
39–61. III. 57; γ, 320; A,
554; B, *226*; M,
270.

liv. 1– 7. β, 48; A, *544–6*; M,
24, 270.
8–16. II. 440; β, 48; γ,
467; A, 546, *550*;
M, 105, 239.
17–18. I. 213; γ, *466*, *468*;
A, 552–4; M, 269.

THE DIATESSARON—*continued*.
liv. 19–22. II. 307, 543; III.
16; α, *234*; β, *48*;
γ, *467–8*; A, 546,
558–4; B, 468;
M, 261, 269–0.
23–24. A, 564–6.
25–38. III. 158; β, 48; A,
74, 610; C, 126.
39–47. II. 559; α, 139; β,
49, 133; γ, 178,
449; C, 784; M,
101, 237, *271–2*.

lv. 3–11. I. 113, *505*; II. *215*,
[*294*], 440; III.
75; β, *6*, *207*, *389*;
γ, *56*; B, *186*; P,
195; M, *106*, *158*,
226, *274*, 287.
12–15. A, 674; M, 251.
17. A, 566.

PASSAGES NOT FOUND IN THE
DIATESSARON:—

S. MATTHEW.
i. 1–17. I. 172, 451, 552; III. 601;
γ, 476.

S. LUKE.
iii. 23b–38. I. 144, 172, 309; β, *324*.

ACTS OF THE APOSTLES.
i. 6–11. III. 101, 580; β, 48;
C, 882; M, *109*, *158*,
179, *215*, *274*.
15–26. I. 397; II. 129; III.
390; β, 127, 349; γ,
14, *158*; A, 616;
M, 105, 109, 112,
159, 240.
ii. 1– 4. III. 51, 139, 597; M,
273–4.
5–13. II. 435; P, 77.
14–36. I. 261, 333, 431, 478;
β, *213*, *251*; M, 16,
119, 254, *274*.
37–42. I. *557*.
iii. 1–10. C, 10; M, *51*.
11–26. γ, *556*; P, *51*.
iv. 5–12. B, 482.

SCRIPTURAL INDEX.

ACTS OF THE APOSTLES—*continued.*
iv. 13-22. II. 404; III. 86; γ, 44.
23-31. I. *406-7.*
32-35. β, *175.*
v. 1- 6. α, 139; β, 236, 399; γ, 8, 284, 449, 495; M, 109, 112, *226.*
7-11. α, 139; β, *236*; γ, 8, 284, 449, 495; M, 109, 112, *226.*
12-16. I. 519; C, 962.
33-42. I. *371*; β, *136*; M, *64*, 209-0.
vi. 1- 6. I. 434; γ, *354.*
vii. 2ᵇ-50. I. 197; II. *114*; III. 86, 358; α, *233*; β, *95*, 406; A, *636.*
51-53. I. *406.*
54-viii. 1ᵃ. β, *210*; γ, *17*; C, xix.; M, 94.
viii. 1ᵇ- 3. I. 382; β, 310.
9-13. P, 267.
14-24. III. 687; β, 289.
26-40. III. 154; P, 33; M, *262.*
ix. 1- 9. I. 288, 360, 535; II. 474; β, 100, 208, 270, *310*, *349*, 392; γ, 3, *130*, 170, 320, *596*; A, *202-4*, *218-0*, *224*, *228-2*, *238*; P, 3, 112, 164-5, 239.
10-19ᵃ. I. 193, *288*, 535; III. *xxiv.*; β, 100, 208, 310, 349, 392; γ, 3; B, *6*; P, *246*; M, 50.
19ᵇ-22. β, 208, 311, 392.
23-25. β, 208, 311, 392.
36-43. γ, 590.
x. 1- 8. β, *112.*
9-16. β, 291.
34ᵇ-43. β, *74*; M, *222.*
xi. 1-18. β, *291.*
xii. 1-19. α, 185, *326.*
20-24. α, 234.
xiii. 4-12. α, 139; β, *185*; γ, 449; P, *247*; M, *34.*
13-16ᵃ. P, 264.
16ᵇ-41. I. 158; α, *111.*
44-52. II. *303*; P, 264; M, *91.*
xiv. 1- 7. P, 264.
8-18. III. 118; P, 113.
19-28. β, *128*; γ, *279*, *296*, *470*; P, 265.

ACTS OF THE APOSTLES—*continued.*
xv. 7ᵇ-11. III. 187.
14-21. β, 196; γ, 215, *351*; P, 243.
22-29. β, 196; γ, 215; P, 202, 243.
xvi. 16-18. III. 680; β, 283.
19-34. P, 118-9.
xvii. 16-22ᵃ. III. 87, 146; γ, 464; P, 65.
22ᵇ-31. III. 87; α, *329*; β, 58, 263; γ, *189*, 464; C, *228*; P, 65.
xviii. 12-17. γ, *241.*
xix. 1- 7. A, 106.
8-20. β, 392.
xx. 18ᵇ-35. III. 18, 189; β, 235, *244*, 398; γ, *110*; P, *118*, 263.
xxi. 7-14. γ, *110*; P, 150.
17-26. β, 196; γ, 215; P, 65 202.
xxii. 3-21. I. 193; α, 194; β, 100, 270, 310, 349; A, *204.*
xxiv. 24-27. II. 96; B, 210.
xxvi. 2-23. I. 193, 344; β, 270, 349; A, *206.*
xxvii. 9-26. α, *303*; P, 111.
27-44. P, 111.
xxviii. 30-31. P, 256.

ROMANS.
i. 1- 7. III. 122; P, *3-4*; M, 16.
8-17. P, *4.*
18-23. III. 64, 141; γ, *101*, *233*; P, *4-5.*
24-25. γ, *59-0*; P, *4-5.*
26-27. III. 178; α, 130, 211; β, *151*, *190*; γ, *60*, *444*, *505*; P, 5.
28-32. α, *134*, *206*; γ, *57*, *60*, *430*, *434*, *444*; P, *6.*
ii. 1-16. III. 430; α, 29, *33*, *132*, *171*, *304*; β, 68, *131*, *163*, *203*, *214*, *221*, *252*, *333*, *370*, 375, *378*, *387*; γ, 59, *63*, *67*, *95*, *111*, *123*, *133*, *157-8*, *226*, *236*, *260*, 278, *374*, *442*, *554*, *559*, 580, *596*; C, 136; P, *6*; M, *106.*
17-29. α, 43; γ, *52*, *104-5*; A, 164; P, *2*, *6-7*, *10.*

ROMANS—*continued.*
iii. 1– 8. α, 10, *207*; γ, *98, 195*;
P, *7–8.*
9-18. γ, 52, *283*; P, *8.*
19-31. β, *238, 400*; P, 2, *8–0.*
iv. 1-25. III. 187; P. *10–3.*
v. 1-11. III. *522*; α, 4, *6, 62*; β, *328*; γ, *39, 93, 348, 560*; P, *13–4*; M, 279.
12-21. I. *271, 562*; III. 440, *506, 544*, 607, *615*; P, 8, *14–6*; M, 46, 231, 249.
vi. 1-11. I. 327, 479, *492*; II. *199*; γ, *183*, 196, *202, 416*; P, *8, 16–7*; M, *245.*
12-14. β, *364*; γ, *318*; P, *17.*
15-23. α, 232, 245; γ, *598*; P, *17–8*; M, *45.*
vii. 1– 6. [II. 199]; III. 102; P, *18–9.*
7-25. II. *356*; α, 136, 232; β, *196, 379*; γ, 102, *216, 234, 324*, 446, *509*, 578; C, 222; P, *19–4.*
viii. 1-11. α, *95*; γ, *286, 324, 340,* 593, *596*; P, *24–6.*
12-17. α, *25*; β, 308; γ, *xxxv. 42*, 318, *355, 596*; P, *26–7*; M, *63, 120, 179.*
18-25. II. *250*; III. 62; α, *231*, 266; β, *331*; γ, 189, *416, 555*; P, *27–8*; M, *227.*
26-30. I. *413*; II. 399; γ, *xxxiv. 162, 225, 322, 340*, 4*35,* *588*; P, *28–9*; M, *227.*
31-39. II. *303*; III. 548; α, *323*; β, *52–3, 137, 311*; γ, *xxxiv. 39, 83, 580–1*; P, *29.*
ix. 1-13. I. *174*; α, *201*; γ, *592*; P, *29–0*, 84.
14-18. β, *116*; P, *30–1.*
19-29. I. 460; II. *225*; III. 53, 67, 78, 174, 608; α, 130; β, *116*; γ, 505; P, *31–2.*
30-33. I. 404; P, *32*; M, *28.*
x. 1-15. β, *310*; B, *196*; P, *32–3.*
16-21. III. 135; α, 35; B, *196*; P, *34*; M, *127.*
xi. 1-12. P, *34–5.*
13-24. α, 133; β, 355; γ, *443*; P, *35–7*; M, 241.
25-32. I. *384*; β, *154*; γ, 107, 201, *433*; P, *37–8.*

ROMANS—*continued.*
xi. 33-36. I. *466*; III. 13; β, 167; γ, *2*; P, *38.*
xii. 1– 2. α, 283; β, 89, 318; γ, *169, 318, 325–6*, 328; P, *39.*
3-21. α, *279, 304, 308*; β, 101, *120–1, 128, 139*, 172, 187; γ, *11*, 107, *109, 353*, 589; P, *39–0*; M, 71, *217.*
xiii. 1– 7. β, *136*; γ, *130*; P, *40.*
8-10. III. 229, 643; α, *109*; β, *210*; γ, *15, 17, 220, 338*; P, *40–1*; M, 224.
11-14. III. 489, 539; α, *170*, 226; β, *211, 415*; γ, *184, 206, 371, 400, 554, 596.*
xiv. 1-12. α, 17, *29, 31, 102, 204, 304, 318*; β, 50, *97, 127*, 139, *195, 197, 253, 380–1*; γ, *133, 154, 217–8, 277, 375, 407*; B, 704; P, *41–2.*
13-23. α, *100*, 306; P, *42–3.*
xv. 1-13. II. *158*; α, *100, 318*; β, *172*; γ, *590, 594*; P, *43–4*; M, *27, 121.*
14-21. P, *44.*
22-29. P, *44–5.*
30-33. P, *45.*
xvi. 17-20. α, 207; β, *153*; γ, *65, 317*; P, *45–6.*

1 CORINTHIANS.
i. 1– 3. P, *47–8.*
4– 9. α, *194*; P, *48.*
10-17. II. *491*, 493-4, *559–0*; P, *48–9.*
18-25. β, *6*; γ, *96, 227, 402*; P, *49–0*; M, *87, 198, 243.*
26-31. I. *177, 268*; α, *82, 248, 280, 311*; β, *77, 171*; γ, 52, *121*; P, *50*; M, *50.*
ii. 1– 5. II. *129*; β, 73; P, *50–1.*
6-16. I. 440; II. 332; III. 97; α, *35, 38, 54, 155, 234, 335*; β, 73, *179, 184, 208, 308, 369, 392*; γ, *21*, 34, *44, 96, 149*, 188, *220*, 228, *369, 384, 402, 409, 555*, 582, 593; C, *708*; P, *51–2*; M, 117, *217, 226*, 258.

SCRIPTURAL INDEX. 163

1 CORINTHIANS—*continued.*
iii. 1- 9. II. 518; III. 43; α, 133;
β, 205, 221, 389, 410;
γ, 28, 209, 293, 442;
P, 52-3; M, 106.
10-15. α, 27, 141; β, 63, 310;
γ, 28, 178, 451, 496;
B, 422; P, 53.
16-17. I. 459; II. 334; III.
101; α, 103, 265, 277;
β, 157; γ, 207, 331,
596; P, 53; M, 226.
18-23. β, 86, 90, 139, 393; γ,
48; P, 53-4.
iv. 1- 5. III. 489; α, 33, 132; β,
170, 366, 378; γ, 70,
442, 456; P, 54-5; M,
109, 179.
6-13. III. 175, 642; α, 94,
323; β, 413; γ, 94,
156; P, 55.
14-21. α, 304; β, 165, 171; γ,
8, 90, 107-0, 183, 329,
336, 507; P, 55-6.
v. 1- 8. II. 242; α, 167; β, 240,
247; γ, 8, 335, 589,
594, 611; P, 56-7; M,
160.
9-13. P. 57.
vi. 1-11. III. 123, 643, 682-3; α,
15, 279; β, 140, 151,
284, 286; γ, 259, 369,
590, 596; P, 57-8; M,
223.
12-20. III. 473; α, 78, 202,
246; β, 130, 172; γ,
88, 225, 596; C, 878;
P, 58-9; M, 47, 226.
vii. 1- 7. β, 164; γ, 598; P, 59-0.
8-24. α, 11, 114, 253; β, 82,
164-5; γ, 594; P,
60-1.
25-40. I. 375; II. 338; III.
309; α, 36; β, 156-7,
165; γ, 74, 328, 383,
554, 570, 594, 596; P,
61-2.
viii. 1-13. P, 62-3.
ix. 1-27. III. 376; α, 87, 192, 206,
230; β, 92, 94, 164-5,
415, 419; γ, 110-1,
210, 327, 334, 556, 589;
P, 64-6; M, 109.
x. 1-13. I. 263; II. 112; III.
574; α, 89, 246, 261;
β, 44, 117, 328; γ, 51,
108, 132, 213, 239; Δ,

1 CORINTHIANS—*continued.*
52; P, 66-7; M, 12,
121.
x. 14-22. II. 409; γ, 169; P, 67-8.
23-xi. 1. α, 98, 202, 304; β, 165,
172, 187; γ, 51, 54,
107-0, 132, 225, 239,
329-0, 336; P, 68-9.
xi. 2-16. β, 165, 172, 246, 410;
γ, 132, 596; P, 69-0.
17-34. β, 331; γ, 12, 434, 609;
Δ, 416, 426; P, 70-2.
xii. 1- 3. P. 72.
4-11. I. 324, 527; II. 9, [289],
300; P, 72.
12-31. I. 78; II. 268; III. 23,
30; α, 114; β, 112,
169; γ, 315, 333, 352;
P, 72-3.
xiii. 1-13. I. 462; III. 25, 66; α,
3-5, 274; β, 112, 169,
210; γ, 14, 17, 220,
284, 333; P, 73-5; M,
100, 109-0.
xiv. 1-19. α, 88, 102; β, 73, 172;
γ, 200, 333; P, 28,
75-6.
20-25. P, 76-7.
26-33. α, 275; γ, 353, 467; P,
77.
34-36. P, 78.
37-38. P, 78.
39-40. γ, 187; P, 78.
xv. 1-11. α, 301; P, 78; M, 106.
12-19. γ, 128-9; P, 78-9.
20-28. I. 189, 237, 561; β, 162,
197, 216-7, 247, 254-5,
273, 378, 381; γ, 128,
192, 195-6, 218, 316;
Δ, 166; P, 79-1; M,
268.
29-34. III. 376; α, 224, 240,
309; β, 153, 239, 363,
401; γ, 116, 129, 153,
278; P, 81, 84; M,
217.
35-49. I. 365; III. 333; β, 240;
γ, 214, 318; B, 606,
610; P, 82.
50-58. I. 438; II. 248; III. 15,
144, 249, 335-7, 544,
636; α, 39, 52, 168;
β, 192, 230, 233, 251;
γ, 123, 125, 129, 143,
183, 192, 195-6; P,
83-4; M, 20, 261.
xvi. 1- 9. P, 84; M, 111.

1 CORINTHIANS—continued.
xvi. 15-18. P, 84.
19-20. β, 292.

2 CORINTHIANS.

i. 1- 2. P, 85-6.
3-11. III. 482; α, 214; β, 175; γ, 114, 344, 555; P, 86-7.
12-14. P, 87.
15-22. B, 200; P, 87-8.
23-ii. 4. γ, 589; P, 88.
ii. 5-11. β, 112, 135, 292; γ, 589; P, 88-9.
12-17. II. 199; α, 2; P, 89-0.
iii. 1-11. I. 27; II. 142; III. 118, 316; β, 46, 73; P, 90-1.
12-18. III. 17; α, 43; P, 92-3.
iv. 1- 6. III. 31; γ, 339; P, 93-4; M, 208.
7-15. α, 240; β, 273; γ, 598; P, 94-5.
16-18. α, 24, 103; β, 93; γ, 298; P, 95.
v. 1-10. I. 462; α, 17, 318; β, 50, 139, 152, 193, 197, 252, 378, 380; γ, 28, 96, 123, 154, 217, 402, 554; P, 95-6.
11-19. III. 23, 532; β, 248; γ, 112, 334; P, 96-7; M, 65.
20-vi. 10. I. 359; α, 37, 226, 246; β, 175, 328, 339; γ, 110, 279, 306, 337, 349, 501; P, 97-8.
vi. 11-13. P, 98-9.
14-vii. 1. α, 27, 265; β, 78, 151, 211, 234; γ, 360, 371, 400, 550; P, 99.
vii. 2- 4. I. 354; P, 99-0.
5-16. α, 83; β, 125; γ, 560; P, 100-1.
viii. 1-15. II. 435, 522; III. 175; α, 178; β, 79, 102, 206, 390; γ, 21, 288, 292, 352, 553, 560; A, 24; P, 102-3.
16-24. P, 103-4.
ix. 1- 5. P, 104.
6-15. α, 31, 96, 309; β, 101; γ, 555; P, 104-5.
x. 1-18. III. 9; α, 23, 82, 89, 280, 311, 317; β, 77, 92, 164, 171; γ, 21, 36,

2 CORINTHIANS—continued.
87, 91, 121, 341; A, 200; P, 105-8.
xi. 1-15. α, 78, 190, 194, 219, 222; β, 59, 87; γ, 482, 594; P, 108-0.
16-33. I. 294; α, 25; β, 414; γ, 110, 220, 279, 477, 590; A, 222; P, 110-1.
xii. 1-10. α, 235, 315; β, 118, 424; γ, 220, 224, 349, 464; P, 37, 112-3.
11-13. P, 113-4.
14-18. P, 114.
19-21. γ, 590; P, 114.
xiii. 1-10. I. 183; γ, 12, 597; P, 115-6.
11-12. γ, 103, 235; P, 116.
14. γ, 335; P, 116.

GALATIANS.

i. 1- 5. I. 189; P, 125.
6-10. III. 80; α, 250; γ, 54; P, 126.
11-17. β, 100; P, 126-7.
18-24. β, 100; P, 127.
ii. 1-10. III. 15; γ, 590; P, 127-8; M, 155, 274.
11-21. α, 335; β, 165, 184, 369; γ, 297; P, 128-0, 202.
iii. 1-14. I. 36, 237, 299, 359; II. 290; γ, 112, 203; P, 130-1.
15-22. I. 158; γ, 203; P, 131-2.
23-29. β, 205, 207, 221, 239, 389, 391; γ, 27, 54, 132; P, 132-3.
iv. 1- 7. I. 189; II. 18; III. 548; P, 133; M, 184.
8-11. P, 134.
12-20. γ, 202, 596-7; P, 134-5.
21-v. 1. I. 76, 384, 454; III. 474; α, 292; P, 135-6; M, 34, 246.
v. 2-12. III. 186; α, 247; β, 196, 240, 380; γ, 112, 203, 216; P, 136-7.
13-15. α, 115; β, 141; γ, 338; P, 137.
16-24. I. 434; α, 80, 229; β, 204, 388, 432; γ, 208, 283-4, 398, 429, 596; P, 137-8.
25-26. P, 138.
vi. 1- 5. α, 23, 29, 31, 100, 243, 249, 306; β, 103, 122,

SCRIPTURAL INDEX.   165

GALATIANS—*continued.*
 136, 211; γ, *132*, 352, *354*; P, *138.*
vi. 6-10. II. 351; α, 29, 31, *35-6, 83, 219, 221, 246, 251*; β, 132, 140, 177, 216; γ, *28, 63, 67, 93, 133-4, 158, 383, 482*; B, 714; P, *138-9.*
11-16. α, 179; β, *211, 248, 312*; γ, *334, 372, 400, 408*; P, *139*; M, *97.*
17. P, *139.*
18. P, *139.*

EPHESIANS.

i. 1- 2. P, *141.*
3-14. I. *344*; γ, *114*; B, 108; P, *141-3*; M, 266.
15-23. β, 145, 171; γ, 139, *333*; A, *220*; P, *142-3*; M, 48-9.
ii. 1-10. I. *520, 561*; III. 532; α, *207, 291*; γ, *352*; P, *144-5.*
11-22. I. *178, 313*; II. 343, *445*; α, 334; β, 184, 369; γ, *295*; P, *145-6*; M, *97.*
iii. 1-13. P, *146-8.*
14-19. I. *466*; α, 232; γ, *333*; P, *148-9.*
20-21. P, *149.*
iv. 1-16. I. *452, 527, 534*; III. 539; α, 114; β, 198; γ, *202, 295, 297, 326, 483*; C, 772; P, *112, 149-1, 243.*
17-24. I. *527*; α, *32*; β, *79,* 86, 196; γ, *109,* 216, *318, 371, 400*; P, *151.*
25-32. II. 334, *500*; α, 93, *240,* 254; β, *80,* 130, 157, *172, 358*; γ, *13-5, 51, 63, 109,* 148, *556, 593*; P, *151*; M, *164.*
v. 1-14. I. *557*; α, *105, 207*; β, 78, *146,* 388; γ, *51,* 104, 109, *236, 470*; P, *152-3.*
15-21. α, *36, 325*; β, 77, *128, 156, 203, 221, 248,* 387; γ, *18, 109, 295,* 340, *366,* 400; P, *153.*
22-33. I. *373*; II. 420; III. 50; α, 311; β, *156*; γ, *334, 485, 594, 596*; P, *153.*

EPHESIANS—*continued.*
vi. 1- 4. β, *196-7*; γ, *7,* 216; P, 154.
5- 9. α, *107, 312*; γ, *338*; P, 154.
10-20. I. 430; II. *200*; α, *167, 230*; β, 84, *137, 148,* 171, 241, 334, 347, 412, *415*; γ, *36, 38,* 44, 54, 64, 80, *87, 94,* 317, *335, 344, 556*; P, *154-6*; M, *208.*
21-22. P, *156.*
23-24. P, *156.*

PHILIPPIANS.

i. 1- 2. P, *157.*
3-11. P, *157-8.*
12-30. α, *204,* 320; β, *108*; γ, *119, 555*; P, *158-0.*
ii. 1-11. I. 266, *310*; II. *90, 196, 215,* 392; α, *11,* 115, 218, *316*; β, *85, 112, 122,* 197, *215, 253, 362*; γ, *147,* 218, *292, 294,* 297, *306, 352, 410, 560*; P, *160-1, 204*; M, *108, 179.*
12-18. β, *87, 157*; γ, 3, *11,* 56, *69, 114*; P, *161-2.*
19-30. P, *162-3.*
iii. 1-16. I. 193, 288; α, *25, 188, 232, 277,* 334; β, *85,* 126, *132,* 182, *184, 312, 361, 369*; γ, *34,* 110, *336, 353,* 555; C, 778; P, *163-5*; M, 34, 73, 169.
17-21. I. *493*; α, *266*; β, *113,* 248; γ, *12, 107, 408,* 554; P, *165-6*; M, *209.*
iv. 2- 3. β, 353; C, 746; P, *166.*
4- 7. α, *236*; γ, *94, 559*; P, *166-7.*
8- 9. β, *191*; P, *167.*
10-20. P, *167-8.*
21-22. P, *168.*

COLOSSIANS.

i. 1- 2. P, *169.*
3- 8. P, *169-0.*
9-23. I. *18*; III. *213,* 508, 610; α, 4; γ, *130, 162, 184, 294*; P, *170-2*; M, *5, 27,* 48, *63, 97,* 113, *223,* 270.

COLOSSIANS—*continued*.
i. 24-29. I. *324*; γ, *332*, *596*; P, *172-3*; M, 48.
ii. 1- 5. III. 28; β, *207*, 211, *392*; γ, *27*; P, *173*; M, *3*, 217.
6- 7. P, *173-4*.
8-15. II. 415; III. 186, 460; β, 45, *342*, *367*; γ, 109, *204*, 529; P, *174-5*; M, 113, 263.
16-19. III. 186; P, *175*; M, 272.
20-23. III. 186; P, *176*.
iii. 1- 4. α, 244, *265-6*; β, *93*, 122, *307*, 364; P, *176*.
5-11. I. *137*; β, 196, *379*, *388*; γ, *112*, *209-0*, 214, 216, 593, *598*; P, *176-7*; M, 67.
12-17. α, *36*, *299*; β, *162*, *248*; γ, *8*, *366*, 400; P, *177*.
iv. 2- 6. α, 312; P, *177-8*.
7- 9. P, *178*.
10-17. P, *178*.

1 THESSALONIANS.
i. 1. P, *179*.
2-10. γ, *326*; P, *179-1*.
ii. 1-12. P, *181-2*.
13-16. P, *183*.
17-20. P, *183-4*.
iii. 1-10. β, *166*; P, *184-5*.
11-13. P, *185*.
iv. 1- 8. α, *329*; β, *87*, 388; γ, 60, *66*; P, *185-6*.
9-12. γ, 210; P, *186*.
13-18. I. *493*; II. *498*; III. *258*, 335, 337, 352; α, 27, 39, 52-3, 153, *168*; β, *355*; γ, *24*, 127, *129-0*, 149, *192-4*, 556, 559; B, 404; P, *186*; M, 20, *202*.
v. 1-11. III. 544; α, *168-9*, 230; β, 137; γ, *17*, 94, *114*; P, *187-8*, *190*.
12-22. α, *37*, 221, *255*, *322*; β, *106*, *112*, *146*; γ, *19*, 54, *109*, *170*; P, *188-9*.
23-24. γ, *326*, *335*; P, *189*.
26-27. P, *189*.

2 THESSALONIANS.
i. 1- 2. P, *191*.
3-12. γ, *416*, *553*; P, *191-2*.

2 THESSALONIANS—*continued*.
ii. 1-12. I. *191*; β, 222; γ, *191*, *317*; C, *204-6*; P, *193-7*.
13-15. P, *197*.
16-17. P, *197*.
iii. 1- 5. β, *102*; P, *198*.
6-15. α, 222, *325*; β, *172*, 334; γ, *351*; P, *198-9*.
16. P, *199*.
17-18. P, 199.

1 TIMOTHY.
i. 1- 2. P, *243-4*.
3-11. γ, *598*; P, *244-5*; M, *224*.
12-17. III. *371*; α, *53*, 137; γ, 3, 448, *456*, 510; P, *245-6*; M, 111, *113*.
18-20. P, 113, *246-7*.
ii. 1- 7. III. 161; α, *30*, *274*; β, 131, *149*, 181, *206*, 390; γ, *xxvi*. 112, *142*, 494; P, *247-8*.
8-15. I. 35; P, *248*.
iii. 1-13. α, *218*; β, 362; P, *249*.
14-16. II. *433*; III. 6; P, *243*, *249-0*, *256*.
iv. 1- 5. α, *81*; β, 199, 379, 383; γ, *407*; P, *250-1*.
6-16. I. *393*; α, *304*; β, 79, *88*, *94*, *165*; γ, *100*; P, *251-2*.
v. 1-16. β, *168*; γ, *28*, *101*, *195*, *210*, *232*, *365*; P, *252-3*.
17-25. α, 98, *225*, *306*; P, *253*.
vi. 1- 2. P, *253*.
3-10. I. *318*; α, *77*, *248*, 311; β, *74*, 101, *177*, *362-3*; γ, *119*, 283, *285*, *358*, *432*; P, *253-4*.
11-16. I. 7; III. *132*, 538, *640*; α, *109*, *243*, *245*; β, 207, 391; γ, *27*, *297*, *325*, 556; P, *254-5*.
17-19. γ, *107*; P, *245*.
20-21. P, *245*.

2 TIMOTHY.
i. 1- 2. P, *257*.
3-14. β, *84*; P, *257-8*.
15-18. α, 108; P, *258-9*.
ii. 1-13. α, 33, 59, *192*; β, 79, *85*, *92*, *166*, 197, 381; γ,

2 TIMOTHY—*continued.*

15.3, 217, 416, 555; P, 259-1; M, 16.
ii. 14-26. I. 460-1; III. 96; α, 96, 103, 106, 244-5, 312, 329; β, 132, 176; γ, 372, 598; P, 261-1; M, 266.
iii. 1-17. α, 89, 215, 235; β, 89, 342, 345, 356; γ, 49, 57, 148, 178, 324, 336, 416; B, 412; P, 263-5; M, 63.
iv. 1- 8. α, 231, 233, 315; β, 79, 97, 108, 157, 165, 414; γ, 51, 94, 106, 220, 417; C, 746; P, 266-7; M, 231.
9-18. α, 22, 258; γ, 127; P, 113, 256, 267-8.

TITUS.

i. 1- 4. P, 269-0.
5- 9. P, 270.
10-16. III. 190; α, 234, 280; β, 127; γ, 370; P, 270-2.
ii. 1-14. I. 345; II. 235; III. 41, 538; β, 77, 131, 172, 193, 196, 211, 214, 252, 379; γ, 109, 146, 216, 374, 417; P, 272-3.
15. P, 273.
iii. 1-11. I. 490; γ, 130; C, 902; P, 274-5.

HEBREWS.

i. 1-14. I. 456; III. 14, 49, 114, 516, 529; α, 69, 114, 171; β, 6, 308, 333, 376; γ, 130, 487, 506; A, 130; P, 112, 203-5; M, 5.
ii. 1- 4. P, 205.
5-18. I. 529; α, 280; A, 166; P, 203, 205-7.
iii. 1-19. III. 18; α, 102; β, 45; γ, 209; P, 207-9.
iv. 1-13. II. 398; III. 544; α, 133, 242, 299; β, 95, 139; γ, 277, 417, 442, 573; P, 209-1; M, 215.
14-16. III. 31; P, 211.

HEBREWS—*continued.*

v. 1-10. α, 114; β, 17, 141; P, 211-3.
11-14. γ, 341; P, 213-4.
vi. 1- 8. II. 428; β, 162; γ, 202, 506; P, 214-5.
9-12. α, 234, 245, 290; β, 82; P, 215-6.
13-20. III. 51; C, 656; P, 216-7.
vii. 1- 3. I. 159-0; P, 217.
4-10. I. 62; γ, 590; P, 218; M, 17.
11-25. I. 160; P, 218-0.
26-28. P, 220.
viii. 1-13. γ, 190; P, 221-2; M, 286.
ix. 1-10. I. 223, 458; III. 187, 571; γ, 529, 575; B, 536; P, 223-4.
11-22. III. 555, 681; β, 283; P, 224-5.
23-28. I. 322; γ, 116, 196; P, 225-6.
x. 1-18. I. 529; P, 25, 226-7; M, 273, 286.
19-25. III. 15; α, 234, 256; γ, 555; P, 227-8.
26-31. III. 50; α, 30, 128, 219, 235, 313; β, 170, 203, 221, 387; γ, 128, 416, 482, 596; C, 156; P, 228-9.
32-39. α, 109, 115, 256, 272; β, 365; γ, 154; P, 201, 229-0.
xi. 1-12. I. 460; II. 345; III. 179; β, 108; γ, 45, 408, 557, 605; P, 230-2.
13-16. α, 45; β, 237, 400; P, 232.
17-40. I. 77; II. 5, 400, 435, 465; α, 38, 140, 231, 236, 248, 266, 273, 301, 310; β, 44, 164, 205, 211-2, 218, 221, 250, 255, 389; γ, 22, 28, 156, 199, 220, 281, 294, 302, 304, 364, 371, 451, 553-5, 605; P, 232-6.
xii. 1-13. III. 669; α, 7, 301, 307; β, 90, 136, 327, 329; γ, 66, 327, 336; P, 236-8.
14-17. I. 81; α, 40, 128, 130, 138, 234; β, 121, 130;

HEBREWS—*continued.*
γ, 197-8, *297*, *448*,
495, *554*; P, *238*.
xii. 18-29. III. 49-0, 475; γ, *189*;
P, *238-0.*
xiii. 1- 6. III. 395; α, 310; β,
164, *240*, *402*; γ, *109*;
P, *240*; M, *26.*
7-17. I. *328*, *511*; III. *489*;
α, *248*; β, *90*; γ, *21*,
553-4; P, *240-1.*
18-19. P, *241.*
20-21. P, *241.*
22-23. P, *201*, *242.*

S. JAMES.

i. 2- 4. α, 2; γ, *99*, *231.*
5- 8. III. 97; β, *108*; γ, *460.*
12-18. III. *626*; α, *231-3*; β, *77*,
86, *147*, *154*, 353; γ,
594, *596.*
19-27. α, *8*, *80*; β, *121*; γ, *272*;
A, 250.
i. 1-13. α, 43, *108*; β, *131*, *200*,
384; γ, 5, *521.*
14-26. III. 149; α, *77*, *280*; γ,
219, *364*, *571*, *608*; M,
111.
iii. 1-12. III. 152; α, *114*, *280*; β,
209; γ, *66*, *89*, *433.*
13-18. α, *252*, *328.*
iv. 1-10. α, 42, *81*, *90*, *254-5*, *304*;
β, *87*, *93*, *120*, *127*, *147*,
186; γ, *16*, *51*, *296.*
11-12. α, *275.*
13-17. II. *338*; α, *134*, *230*, 275;
γ, *82*, *204*, *244.*
v. 1- 6. β, *143*, *218*, *256*; γ, *99.*
7-11. γ, *154.*
12. III. 643; γ, 570.
13-18. II. 467; III. 459; α, *18*,
254; β, *174*, 358, *364*;
γ, *20*, 240, 242, 287.
19-20. α, 87; β, *88*, *209*; γ,
594.

1 S. PETER.

i. 3-12. I. *331*; II. 399; III. 6;
β, *207*, *308*, *391*; γ, *24*,
27, 127, *149*, *220*, *555.*
13-25. α, *207*, *215*; β, *77*, *93*; γ,
66, *82*, 126, *282*; B,
314.
ii. 1-10. II. 330; III. 539; β,
196; γ, 216; M, 79.

1 S. PETER—*continued.*
ii. 11-12. α, *45*; γ, 119.
13-17. α, 105.
18-25. II. *298*; β, *88*; γ, *571-2.*
iii. 8-12. α, *208*; β, *142*, *210*, *322*,
429; γ, *14*, 17.
13-22. I. 549; III. 538.
iv. 1- 6. α, 247; β, *162*, *172.*
7-11. α, *310*; β, *209*; γ, *14*,
113.
12-19. β, *150*; γ, *92*, *360*, *519*,
578.
v. 1-11. α, 58, 77, 97, 146, *236-7*,
255, *266*, *304*, *314*; β,
87, *93*, *101*, 115, *120*,
127, 130, *176*, 196, 307,
371, 380; γ, *19*, *122*,
152, *226.*

2 S. PETER.

i. 1-11. γ, *104*, *235.*
12-21. III. 83.
ii. 1-22. α, 19, 103, *210*; β, *81*,
101, 106, *130*, *153*, *157*,
161-2, *181*, 198; γ, *40*,
59-1, *104*, 174, 187,
236, 547.
iii. 1- 7. I. 136; γ, 59, 189.
8-13. I. 167, 415; II. *342*; III.
544; β, *193*, *203*, 213,
251, *387*; γ, 59, *75*, *94*,
133, 145, *154*, *157*,
189-1, *226*, *554*, *596*,
599; P, 239-0.

1 S. JOHN.

i. 5-10. α, *31*; β, 196; γ, 216.
ii. 1- 6. II. *286*; β, *199*, *382*; γ,
204-5.
7-11. α, *4*, *116*; γ, *14*, *113.*
12-17. III. *511*; α, *31*, *37*, *73*,
291, *334*; β, *92*, *143*,
184, 214, *218*, *252*, *255*,
369; γ, *23*, 110, *132*,
153, *374.*
18-29. α, *69*, 332; γ, 44, *113*,
154.
iii. 1-12. α, *10*; γ, *329.*
13-24. III. *607*, *617*; α, *4*, *132*,
250; β, 122, *150*, *364*,
432; γ, *13*, 15, *113*,
195, *330*, *360*, *366-7*,
442, 502.
iv. 1- 6. γ, *108.*

SCRIPTURAL INDEX.

1 S. JOHN—*continued.*
iv. 7–21. III. 48, 53; α, *3–4, 116, 162, 242*; β, *169, 209–0*; γ, *13, 15–7, 81, 170, 306, 586.*
v. 1–12. III. 128; α, 70.
13–17. α, *281*; γ, *113*, 198, 590.
18–21. III. *511*; α, *94, 97.*

2 S. JOHN.
i. 4–11. III. *511*; γ, *52*, 113.

3 S. JOHN.
i. 2–4. α, *76.*

S. JUDE.
i. 1–2. γ, *61.*
3–4. II. 487; γ, *61.*
5–16. I. 37; β, *153, 161*, 325; γ, *62*; C, 232.
17–23. γ, *62.*
24–25. γ, *62.*

REVELATION.
i. 4–7. β, *194, 214, 253*; γ, *146, 375*; M, 270.
9–20. B, 794.
ii. 1–7. γ, 190, *597.*
12–17. γ, 190.
18–29. γ, 67.
iii. 1–6. III. *529.*
7–13. γ, 575.
14–22. II. 428; γ, 190.
iv. 1–11. III. *498, 576*; β, *194,*

REVELATION—*continued.*
214, 229–0, *252*; γ, 143, *146, 374*, 591.
v. 1–14. I. 229; II. 332, 417, 436; III. 93, *452*; γ, 190, 530.
vi. 7–8. γ, 190.
12–17. α, 39; β, 193, 213, 251; γ, 145, *157*, 373, 553, 556.
vii. 1–17. I. 283; γ, 576; M, 266.
viii. 3–5. γ, 575.
10–11. γ, 190.
xi. 1–13. II. 414; III. 189; β, 228; γ, 142.
xii. 1–6. γ, 190.
xiii. 11–18. I. 192; γ, 191.
xiv. 9–12. γ, 136.
13. III. 258.
14–16. β, 161.
17–20. β, 161.
xv. 5–8. γ, 190.
xvi. 1. γ, 190.
xvii. 1–18. I. *192*; β, 353; γ, 190–1.
xviii. 4–20. γ, 191.
xix. 19–21. β, 198, 256.
xx. 1–3. γ, 190–1, 547.
4–6. γ, 189–0, 192.
7–10. γ, 190.
11–15. β, *194, 214, 253*; γ, *147, 375.*
xxi. 1–8. III. 607; β, 193, 213, 248, 251; γ, 145, 576.
9–xxii. 5. γ, 190, 374, 530; M, 12.
xxii. 10–15. γ, *67.*

APPENDIX.

CONTAINING AN ANALYSIS OF THE PASSAGES IN WHICH ZAHN'S RECONSTRUCTION GAVE A DIFFERENT ORDER FROM THAT OF THE ARABIC DIATESSARON.

IN this Appendix no attempt is made to enter into all the reasons which Dr. Zahn assigns for the conclusions he arrived at as to the order occupied by different passages in Ephraem's copy of the *Diatessaron*. The sole object is to ascertain whether there is in the result of his labours anything calculated to throw discredit upon the order of the Arabic version. Passages which Zahn, before the recovery of the Arabic, placed in the same order as they occupy in the Arabic—even though he so placed them with some degree of doubt or hesitation—are here presumed to throw no serious doubt upon the accuracy of the Arabic order. The question considered here is whether those passages which he placed in a different order from that which has since been found in the Arabic, were *necessarily* in a different order in Ephraem's *Diatessaron*, or whether the new light now obtained may not serve to explain away the discrepancies. Many of the passages were necessarily placed by Zahn in his reconstruction more or less by inference, conjecture, and probability; and if the Borgian and Vatican MSS. serve to modify in a few of these doubtful cases the conclusions at which he arrived, there is nothing in that to cast any reflection upon the excellence of his work, of which no one is more convinced than the writer. In this Appendix *all* the passages in which his order disagrees with the Arabic are considered, and no others.

I. *Diat.* iii. 46-iv. 11; John i. 7-28; Mœs. pp. 37-40; Zahn, § 6.

Ephraem has commented upon the mission and testimony of S. John the Baptist before the scene between the child Jesus and the doctors in the temple. This arrangement is historically impossible; and we cannot therefore suppose that it was so arranged in Ephraem's copy of the *Diatessaron*, nor is it in the Arabic or the *Codex Fuldensis*. There can be no doubt that Ephraem's Commentary in its present form departs at this point from the order of the work upon which he was commenting. There are, in fact, signs of confusion in Ephraem's remarks, since he puts the temple scene after the preaching of S. John, and yet before the account of S. John's dress.

II. *Diat.* v. 33-41; Luke iv. 14b-22ª; Moes. pp. 128-131; Zahn, § 32.

This passage forms in S. Luke a portion only of a longer passage giving an account of what took place at Nazareth on *one* occasion. But in the Arabic this is divided, and represented as taking place on two different occasions, the latter of these coinciding with a visit to Nazareth described at Matt. xiii. 54-58 and Mark vi. 1-6. This mode of dividing the passage enabled the harmonist to escape a serious difficulty; for in S. Luke the visit to Nazareth is put at the very beginning of our Lord's ministry. Immediately after His temptation He is represented as proceeding to Galilee, where He goes about preaching in the synagogues of towns and villages, arriving at Nazareth in the course of His journey. There He makes a public claim to be fulfilling a prophecy of Isaiah at a time when He has not yet called any of the twelve disciples nor wrought any *recorded* miracle, though it is implied that He had wrought miracles at Capernaum. Yet this reference to Capernaum seems to apply better to a later stage of His ministry; and the remarks of the Nazarenes and His reply to them bear marks of close resemblance to those recorded in the first two Gospels at the places already mentioned, which are represented there as made at a much later period, and long after the calling of the disciples. In fact, one part of S. Luke's narrative postulates a date at the very beginning of Christ's ministry; and the other part appears to belong to a much later date; and yet the evangelist treats the two parts as referring to the same occasion. It would seem as if S. Luke's informant had unconsciously blended together incidents belonging to two different visits of Jesus to Nazareth; and if we suppose the division found in the Arabic to be due to Tatian, the thought arises, whether he may have been aware of some tradition existing in the time of Justin to the effect that the facts warranted this separation.

As the phrase, "as his custom was," which is given by Moesinger (p. 129) in spaced type, certainly belongs to Luke iv. 16, near the beginning of these verses, and is followed by part of ver. 24, and a little later by ver. 25-27, Zahn had no alternative in the absence of the Arabic but to suppose that the whole block occurred at the later position in Ephraem's *Diatessaron*.

In order to understand the situation, now that we have the Arabic to help us, we must go somewhat into detail. Ephraem opens this subject by quoting Matt. xiii. 54 (*Diat*. xvii. 37). Upon this verse, which speaks of "his own city," he remarks that it was written to convict the Marcionites of falsehood—*i.e.*, as Moesinger rightly suggests, the falsehood that Jesus had no human birth or parentage. Then, according to Codex B, which Moesinger follows at this point, he goes on thus: "After these things, it saith, he entered, as his custom was, into their synagogues on the sabbath day." "After these things" is not found in any Gospel in this connection; and Professor Robinson prefers the reading of Codex A, which makes this part a remark of Ephraem and not a quotation, the meaning being, "After this it saith, 'He entered,'" etc. If this be the better reading, the words of Ephraem would imply that this citation came next after Matt. xiii. 54 in his copy. Turning now to the Arabic, we find in the corresponding place (*Diat.* xvii. 38) the similar words from S. Mark, "And when the sabbath was come, Jesus began to teach in the synagogue." The probability therefore is that Ephraem's *Diatessaron* contained this verse more in the form of Luke iv. 16 than of Mark vi. 2, and including in particular the clause, "as his custom was."

But how does this affect the following verses, Luke iv. 17-22^a, which describe the actual teaching in the synagogue? The reasoning of Ephraem seems to prove decisively that these were not in his copy at this point. For he is dealing with an argument of the Marcionites, which may be thus stated : It was in the synagogue that Jesus taught the Nazarenes ; therefore His teaching was necessarily of a religious character, and had reference to their God—the God of the Old Testament, or Demiurge. *Something* which He said so enraged them that they brought Him out to cast Him down headlong from the precipice. What was that something? Presumably He told them that He came from the superior God of the universe, and in opposition to their God—nothing short of this could have inflamed them so. To this argument Ephraem gives a double reply: (1) that it was the "custom" of Jesus, as shown by this verse, to teach in the synagogue wherever He went ; and His teaching did not usually enrage His hearers, as it certainly would have done, if He had been in the habit of preaching such a doctrine as the Marcionites attributed to Him ; and (2) that our Lord Himself stated the reason for their rejection of Him, and it was not anything of that kind, nor founded on what He had *said*, but it was the fact of His having been born there that caused Him to receive such different treatment there. Now in Luke iv. 17-21 we have some particulars of what Christ said in the synagogue at Nazareth ; and if these verses followed immediately in Ephraem's copy, and were applied to the same occasion, he would not have failed to draw attention to them, and to reply to the Marcionites that, so far from setting up a new God in opposition to the God of the Old Testament, Jesus declared in that synagogue that He was fulfilling the words of Isaiah, the prophet of the Old Testament God. Moreover, in *Marcion's Gospel*, ver. 17-19 of Luke iv. are omitted, and ver. 20, 21 modified so as to contain no allusion to this teaching of Jesus ; and Ephraem would not have failed to charge the Marcionites, as other Fathers did, with deliberate excision of the passage to suit their own views. His silence on these points seems to us conclusive evidence that these verses did not occur here in Ephraem's *Diatessaron*. If so, there is no reason to doubt that it was Tatian who divided S. Luke's narrative ; and that he placed the two portions where we find them in the Arabic— excepting part of Luke iv. 16, which he may have inserted at both places, for we find other connective verses used more than once. This view is confirmed by the fact that they are similarly divided in the *Codex Fuldensis*, where the two parts of S. Luke's narrative occur at cap. 18 and cap. 79 respectively.

III. *Diat.* v. 49-vi. 4; Luke v. 1-11; Moes. p. 59; Zahn, § 14.

A few lines only are devoted by Ephraem to the miraculous draught of fishes, which accompanied the final calling of S. Peter; and Zahn, following the order of the Commentary, places this occurrence later than it is found in the Arabic. Here then is a real difference between the two, and it only remains to consider which is more likely to be the true order of Tatian. One fact seems to us decisive in favour of the Arabic order, and that is the relative position of the remarks upon the baptism by the disciples at Aennon. According to S. John, who alone records it, Jesus after His baptism and temptation, and calling some disciples, visited Galilee, and it was not until He had been to Jerusalem for a Passover, and had received the visit of Nicodemus, that His disciples baptized in Jordan. Is it to be supposed that Tatian—who puts the visit of Nicodemus at a later period than S. John does—would put this baptism before the final calling of the chief of the disciples, thus either excluding him from all share in that work, or representing our Lord as delegating the important office of baptism to men who had not yet finally abandoned their worldly calling? We cannot doubt, therefore, that the Arabic preserves in this case the original order of Tatian; nor does it seem improbable that this order existed also in Ephraem's copy of it; for (1) there are evidences in other places that some passages of the Commentary have become displaced from their true position, perhaps by accidental confusion of the leaves; and (2) though we find Ephraem adhering with remarkable consistency to the order of the Arabic, we cannot be certain that he never once departed from the order of his copy. The *Codex Fuldensis* supports the Arabic order.

IV. *Diat.* vii. 46; Mark iii. 21; Zahn, § 27.

The attempt of Christ's relations to take Him is not mentioned in the Commentary, and therefore no difference between Ephraem's copy and the Arabic can be traced here. The position of this verse in the Arabic is peculiar. Cf. *Diat.* vii. 46, note.

V. *Diat.* xiii. 36-37; Mark vi. 12-13; Zahn, § 24.

This passage also is not in Ephraem; and it is therefore only the inference of Zahn, which differs from the Arabic. He naturally supposed that the subject of these verses followed immediately after that of ver. 11 was concluded, and could not have guessed that the account of our Lord's visit to the home of Martha and Mary came between His address to the Twelve before sending them away, and the account of their doings when they were away.

VI. *Diat.* xiv. 9 ; Luke xvi. 17 ; Moes. p. 65 ; Zahn, § 26.

Part of the preceding verse, "The law and the prophets *were* until John," is quoted by Ephraem, evidently parenthetically (Moes. p. 42), in connection with the baptism of Jesus, and a second time (Moes. p. 104) in a very appropriate place among the comments passed by Jesus upon John the Baptist on the occasion of the visit of two of John's disciples. It is at this point that the whole verse occurs in the Arabic, followed almost immediately, and in a very natural sequence, by the succeeding verse now under consideration, viz.: "It is easier for heaven and earth to pass away than for one jot to perish from the law." But in Ephraem's Commentary this latter is found only at p. 65, between the two citations, "I am not come to destroy the law or the prophets, but to fulfil ;" and, "Whosoever shall break one of the commandments." These passages come from Matt. v. 17 and 19, and between them occurs in S. Matthew a very similar verse to that which we are considering, viz.: "Verily I say unto you, Till heaven and earth pass away, one jot or one tittle shall not pass from the law till all be fulfilled." Now it is, of course, possible that Tatian exchanged these verses ; but it seems highly improbable that he entirely separated Luke xvi. 17 from Luke xvi. 16 in order to substitute it for the similar verse of S. Matthew ; and we may more reasonably conclude either that Ephraem, trusting to memory, quoted the wrong verse owing to their similarity, or that he intentionally quoted a parallel passage from elsewhere. In any case, there is not sufficient evidence to show decisively that Ephraem's copy differed here from the Arabic versions. Here also the *Codex Fuldensis* agrees with the Arabic.

VII. *Diat.* xiv. 43, 44 ; Mark vi. 30, 31 ; Zahn, § 34.

This account of the return of the twelve disciples is not mentioned in the Commentary ; and there is therefore no evidence here of any difference of order. It is Zahn's inference alone which disagrees with the Arabic.

VIII. *Diat.* xv. 17–26 ; Luke x. 3–12 ; Moes. pp. 90–98 ; Zahn, § 24.

These verses, which contain the instructions of Jesus to the seventy (or seventy-two) disciples before sending them forth on their mission, are placed by Zahn along with the similar instructions to the Twelve, and consequently in a different order from the Arabic. This is due to the fact that Ephraem, who mentions both the sending of the Twelve and the sending of the Seventy apparently just at the places where they occur in the Arabic, says nothing about any instructions to the latter, but proceeds at once to comment on what took place at their return ; whereas he discusses at great length the instructions to the former, and in citing them he introduces several readings peculiar to the verses we are considering, thus suggesting that he found these blended with the very similar verses of Matt. x. Of course it might have been the case that Ephraem was quoting from memory, and owing to his familiarity with S. Luke's Gospel, inadvertently adopted his phraseology in quoting verses so much like his ;

or it might have been that Ephraem, in arranging the order of his Commentary, found it more convenient to consider the two sets of instructions at one time because of their similarity, and therefore deliberately discussed these verses out of the order of his *Diatessaron*. But we are satisfied that the true explanation is, that Tatian, whilst preserving a separate mention of the mission of the Seventy, did not preserve a separate account of the directions they received from our Lord, but harmonised the two sets of directions into one more complete set, and placed this in connection with the earlier mission—the sending of the Twelve. The chief evidence of this is to be found in the *Codex Fuldensis*, in which the instructions to the Twelve (cap. 45) contain several clauses borrowed from Luke x., thus showing evident signs of harmonisation. But where we should have expected (cap. 68) to find the injunctions to the Seventy, we find instead that the narrative passes at once from Luke x. 2ᵃ to Luke x. 16, skipping the verses now in question, and also three others denouncing Chorazin and other cities; and Ranke informs us that the MS. of the Codex shows no signs of discontinuity at the place. This independent testimony renders it practically certain that in the version represented by the Arabic these verses have been removed from participating in the earlier passage where Tatian harmonised them, and have been restored in full to their true place in relation to the mission of the Seventy, by persons who found the statement that the Seventy were sent forth, and naturally missed the directions for their journey. With them they probably moved also the denunciation of the cities. In making this restoration, however, they did not altogether obliterate the traces of harmonisation from the earlier passage, the expressions "two and two" (*Diat.* xii. 43) and "lambs" (*Diat.* xiii. 1) being apparently derived from Luke x. 1 and 3.

According to the *Codex Fuldensis*, it would appear that, while Tatian removed the instructions given to the Seventy, he left as applying to them the comforting assurance which follows at ver. 16, "He that heareth you heareth me; and he that rejecteth you rejecteth me: but he that rejecteth me rejecteth Him that sent me." This might very naturally be the case; but Ephraem quotes part of this (Moes. p. 94) when commenting on the charge given to the Twelve. The question therefore arises, whether this also stood at the earlier place in his copy. On the whole, the evidence seems against this view. Had it been there, it could not well have stood in the exact order in which it is quoted; and the drift of the passage in which it stands, seems rather to point to it as an illustration taken from a distance.

IX. *Diat.* xx. 12–16; Luke xi. 37–41; Zahn, § 77.

These verses are not mentioned by Ephraem; and we have therefore no evidence that they occupied in his harmony a different position from that which they have in the Arabic. Zahn very naturally assumed that they were placed in connection with the discourse which follows them in their Gospel; but in reality Tatian removed them from their setting in St. Luke to combine them with other remarks of our Lord upon clean and unclean things.

X. *Diat.* xxv.-xxvii. ; Matt. xviii. ; Moes. pp. 162-165 ;
Zahn, §§ 45-50.

This chapter of S. Matthew is very curiously subdivided and arrranged in the Arabic ; and if Ephraem's copy followed the same order, it was impossible for Zahn to discover that order from the brief fragments which Ephraem has cited. He has therefore constructed a different arrangement; but now that we have access to the Arabic, we find that Ephraem's citations occupy exactly the same relative order in his Commentary as they do in the Arabic. There is thus no evidence here of disagreement between the respective copies ; but their agreement, as far as they go together, in so singular a sequence, furnishes a strong ground for supposing that they agreed throughout in the treatment of this chapter.

XI. *Diat.* xxvii. 24-25 ; Luke xii. 47-48 ; Zahn, § 79.

There is no allusion to these verses in the Commentary, and therefore no apparent difference from the Arabic. Zahn naturally assumed that they went with the preceding verses, but the Arabic shows that they did not.

XII. *Diat.* xxviii. 33-41 ; Luke xii. 13-21 ; Zahn, § 54.

The parable of the Rich Fool. This also is not in the Commentary. Zahn was very nearly right in his inference ; but he put it after instead of before the incident of the Rich Young Ruler.

XIII. *Diat.* xxxi. 36-52 ; Luke xix. 11-27 ; Zahn, § 80.

The parable of the Minas (Pounds) is not alluded to in the Commentary. Zahn supposed it to have been harmonised with the parable of the Talents, and placed it accordingly. His reasons for the supposition were not derived from anything Ephraem said, but from Aphraates. This passage therefore furnishes no ascertainable difference of order between Ephraem's copy and the Arabic.

XIV. *Diat.* xxxiii. 1-17 ; Mark xi. 19-26 ; Moes. pp. 182-189 ;
Zahn, § 61.

The visit of Nicodemus is placed between the Cursing of the Fig-tree and the discovery by the disciples, on the following day, that it had withered. Ephraem comments upon both the cursing and the withering before he speaks of Nicodemus. There is in this nothing to suggest that his order differed from the Arabic ; for any one commenting on the Gospel narrative in the order of the Arabic, and consequently beginning to refer to the Fig-tree before he spoke of Nicodemus, would naturally prefer to close the incident of the Fig-tree before proceeding further.

In demy 8vo, price **10s. 6d.**,

THE EARLIEST LIFE OF CHRIST
EVER COMPILED FROM THE FOUR GOSPELS;

BEING

'The Diatessaron of Tatian' (Circ. A.D. 160).

Literally Translated from the Arabic Version, and containing the Four Gospels woven into One Story.

With an Historical and Critical Introduction, Notes, and Appendix.

BY

Rev. J. HAMLYN HILL, D.D.

THE BISHOP OF GLOUCESTER AND BRISTOL writes: 'This is a work of very great importance, and of unique interest. It has been given to the world in an admirable form, and reflects the greatest credit on the able and conscientious Editor. The history of the work, as told in a clear and well-written Introduction, will enable the reader to appreciate the vast care and pains that have been bestowed on this singular recovery of the first Harmony of the Gospels. The Notes are short, clear, and helpful; and the eleven Appendices of a practical value, which the general reader will as fully recognise as the scholar and critic. Mr. Hamlyn Hill has performed the difficult duty of Editor with conspicuous success.'

'Truly an excellent piece of work, which we commend most warmly to the student and to the general reader. The problems raised by the Diatessaron are by no means yet exhausted, and every one who takes an interest in the question of the Gospels ought to make himself acquainted at first hand with the material on which we have to work. Such could not be more easily or safely studied than in Mr. Hamlyn Hill's fascinating volume.'—*Church Bells.*

'Tatian's book is worthy of study for itself, as it is a reverent piecing together of the Gospels so that the marvellous story runs on unbrokenly in the familiar words. . . . The Church of to-day may find in his book, as the Church of his day did, a true spiritual possession.'—*Christian Leader.*

'A solid and scholarly piece of work. We very cordially recommend it to all serious students of Holy Scripture and of early Christian literature.'—*Tablet.*

'Let us hope that every student of the New Testament and of historical Christianity will speedily make its acquaintance.'—*Expository Times.*

EDINBURGH: T. & T. CLARK, 38 GEORGE STREET.
LONDON: SIMPKIN, MARSHALL, HAMILTON, KENT, & CO. LIMITED.

T. & T. CLARK'S PUBLICATIONS.

THE ANTE-NICENE CHRISTIAN LIBRARY.

The Ante-Nicene Christian Library. A Collection of all the Works of the Fathers of the Christian Church prior to the Council of Nicæa. Edited by the Rev. Professor ROBERTS, D.D., and Principal JAMES DONALDSON, LL.D., St. Andrews. In Twenty-four handsome 8vo Volumes, Subscription Price £6, 6s. net; or a selection of Twelve Volumes for £3, 3s. net.

Any Volume may be had separately, price 10s. 6d.

This Series has been received with marked approval by all sections of the Christian Church in this country and in the United States, as supplying what has long been felt to be a want, and also on account of the impartiality, learning, and care with which Editors and Translators have executed a very difficult task.

The following Works are included in the Series :—

Apostolic Fathers, comprising Clement's Epistle to the Corinthians; Polycarp to the Ephesians; Martyrdom of Polycarp; Epistle of Barnabas; Epistles of Ignatius (longer and shorter, and also the Syriac Version); Martyrdom of Ignatius; Epistle to Diognetus; Pastor of Hermas; Papias; Spurious Epistles of Ignatius. One Volume. **Justin Martyr; Athenagoras.** One Volume. **Tatian; Theophilus; The Clementine Recognitions.** One Volume. **Clement of Alexandria,** comprising Exhortation to Heathen; The Instructor; and the Miscellanies. Two Volumes. **Hippolytus,** Volume First; Refutation of all Heresies, and Fragments from his Commentaries. **Irenæus,** Volume First. **Irenæus** (completion) and **Hippolytus** (completion); Fragments of Third Century. One Volume. **Tertullian against Marcion.** One Volume. **Cyprian;** The Epistles and Treatises; **Novatian; Minucius Felix.** Two Volumes. **Origen:** De Principiis; Letters; and portion of Treatise against Celsus. Two Volumes. **Tertullian:** To the Martyrs; Apology; To the Nations, etc. Three Volumes. **Methodius; Alexander of Lycopolis; Peter of Alexandria Anatolius; Clement on Virginity;** and Fragments. One Volume. **Apocryphal Gospels, Acts, and Revelations;** comprising all the very curious Apocryphal Writings of the first three Centuries. One Volume. **Clementine Homilies; Apostolical Constitutions.** One Volume. **Arnobius.** One Volume. **Gregory Thaumaturgus; Dionysius; Archelaus; Syrian Fragments.** One Volume. **Lactantius;** together with the Testaments of the Twelve Patriarchs, and Fragments of the Second and Third Centuries. Two Volumes. **Early Liturgies and Remaining Fragments.** One Volume.

ST. AUGUSTINE'S WORKS.

The Works of Aurelius Augustine, Bishop of Hippo. Edited by MARCUS DODS, D.D. In Fifteen Volumes, demy 8vo, Subscription Price £3, 19s. net.

Any Volume may be had separately, price 10s. 6d.

The 'City of God.' Two Volumes.	The Harmony of the Evangelists, and the Sermon on the Mount. One Volume.
Writings in connection with the Donatist Controversy. One Volume.	
The Anti-Pelagian Works. Three Volumes.	'Letters.' Two Volumes.
Treatises against Faustus the Manichæan. One Volume.	On Christian Doctrine, Enchiridion, on Catechising, and on Faith and the Creed. One Volume.
On the Trinity. One Volume.	
Commentary on John. Two Volumes.	'Confessions.' With Copious Notes by Rev. J. G. PILKINGTON.

'For the reproduction of the "City of God" in an admirable English garb we are greatly indebted to the well-directed enterprise and energy of Messrs. Clark, and to the accuracy and scholarship of those who have undertaken the laborious task of translation.'—*Christian Observer.*

N.B.—Messrs. CLARK offer a Selection of Twelve Volumes from either or both of those Series at the Subscription Price of Three Guineas net (or a larger number at same proportion).

www.ingramcontent.com/pod-product-compliance
Lightning Source LLC
Chambersburg PA
CBHW032149160426
43197CB00008B/829